EARLY EDUCATION: THE PARENTS' ROLE

A Sourcebook for Teachers

edited by
ALAN COHEN
University of Durham

Alan Cohen lectures in Education at Durham University. He taught in primary and secondary schools in Britain and the USA and in colleges of higher education before taking up his appointment in the School of Education at Durham. His publications include: *Readings in the History of Educational Thought* (with N. Garner), *A Student's Guide to Teaching Practice* (with N. Garner), *Primary Education: A Sourcebook for Teachers* (with L. Cohen), *Special Educational Needs in the Ordinary School: A Sourcebook for Teachers* (with L. Cohen), *Multicultural Education: A Sourcebook for Teachers* (with L. Cohen), *Disruptive Behaviour: A Sourcebook for Teachers* (with L. Cohen), *Early Education: The Pre-School Years: A Sourcebook for Teachers* (with L. Cohen), *Early Education: The School Years: A Sourcebook for Teachers* (with L. Cohen).

First published 1988

Paul Chapman Publishing Ltd
London

British Library Cataloguing in Publication Data

Early education, the parents' role: a source book for teachers.
1. Great Britain, Education Role of parents
I. Cohen, Alan *1928*

370.19′31

ISBN 1-85396-037-3

Typeset by Burns and Smith, Derby
Printed and bound by St. Edmundsbury Press, Bury St. Edmunds, Suffolk.

CONTENTS

Section Three
PARENTS, TEACHERS AND SPECIAL EDUCATIONAL NEEDS

INTRODUCTION

RECENT DEVELOPMENTS IN HOME AND SCHOOL RELATIONS

The involvement and participation of parents in school life are a comparatively recent phenomenon, which emerged in the late 1960s largely as a result of government attempts to increase the participation of citizens in decision-making. Viewed in this sense, Beattie (1985) suggests that parental participation was but one small part of much wider changes which 'affected government, places of work and tertiary educational institutions as well as schools. These changes centred on the idea that democracy should be extended beyond the formal periodic elections of political assemblies' (p. 3), and with respect to the issue of parental participation in the running of schools, it was 'an attempt to actualize a more idealistic and dynamic notion of democracy' (p. 4).[1]

Long (1986) sees the Plowden Report (CACE, 1967) as the starting-point in the process of involving parents since it espoused a perspective which was effectively 'school supporting' and gave official recognition to the problem of 'good relations' between teachers and parents by advocating positive action and thought from schools on parental involvement, home visiting and increased community involvement (p. 1).[2] It is certainly the case that the Plowden Report recommendations for parental involvement in schools were profoundly influenced by recent sociological research which suggested the importance of the relationship between the educational process and parent participation through the formal structures of the school. Beattie (1985) affirms that the Plowden exhortations were 'basically an exposition of the newly popular sociological perspective on the family':

> A strengthening of parental encouragement may produce better performance in school, and thus stimulate the parents to encourage more; or discouragement in

> the home may initiate a vicious downward circle. Schools exist to foster virtuous circles. They do this most obviously through their direct influence upon children . . . Some schools are already working at the same time from the other end, by influencing parents directly, and the children indirectly through the parents. (Quoted in Beattie, 1985, p. 180)

In the last two decades there have been increasing demands for more meaningful, closer and effective links between the home and the school,[3] with the result that far-reaching changes and innovations have been brought about in the field of home–school relations, changes which Bastiani (1987) suggests, 'at different times, appear to be characterized by widespread and deeply held *beliefs and values*, rather than differences of form and approach' (p. 89). Bastiani argues that the dominant beliefs and values that characterize the nature of home–school relationships have influenced policy and practice over the years; that sometimes the dominant ideology and related forms seem to have emerged as a gradual adaptation to slow changes in social contexts and attitudes, whilst at other times the dominant ideology appears to have resulted from more radical departures from cherished beliefs and practices. Thus, beliefs about home–school relationships appear to be sometimes characterized by general consensus and at other times by disagreement and conflict (p. 89). Halsey (1987) captures this sense of 'fluctuating' ideologies in his comments on the 'lesson' of Plowden twenty years on:

> We learnt painfully that educational reform had not in the past and was unlikely in the future ever to bring an egalitarian society unaided. Plowden policies in effect assumed fundamental reforms in the economic and social institutions of the country at large. Given these reforms, which include the devolution of power to localities, democratic control by community members over national and professional purveyors of expertise in planning, health, employment and education, income and capital equalization, co-ordinated employment policies and well planned housing and civic amenities, realistic demands can be put on the education system. The schools can be asked, in partnership with the families they serve, to bring up children capable of exercising their political, economic and social rights and duties in such a society. They can be so constituted as to socialize children in anticipation of such a society: but to do so without the wider reforms is to court frustration for individuals if not disaster for the social order. (p. 7)[4]

Bastiani (1987) discusses four 'home and school ideologies' which he suggests encapsulate the main beliefs and values that have characterized the field of home–school relations over the past two or three decades and which have greatly influenced policy and practice. The four ideologies, together with their salient central values, political ethos and pragmatic translation into key policies and strategies are shown in Table I.1. Bastiani argues that *compensatory ideologies* have not only dominated theory, research, policy and practice in the field of home–school relationships for many years in post-war Britain, but continue to this day as a powerful and important influence, especially when the relationships between school and working-class communities are being considered. Thus, large-scale surveys and researches in the 1960s, such as Plowden, 'in their concern to chart educational access and performance, became increasingly concerned to unravel something of the differential effects of home, school and neighbourhood in ways that were to influence both policy and practice. Within such a perspective a powerful "environmental correlates" tradition developed' (p. 91).[5]

Table I.1 Home and school ideologies

	Central values/political ethos	*Key policies and strategies*
Compensation	Environmentalism and social engineering Ideology of equal opportunity	Compensatory and positive discriminatory measures Family intervention
Communication	Consensus politics Rationality as the basis of social behaviour	Enhanced professionalism (through improved communication and relationships) The 'good practice' model of educational change
Accountability	Consumerism: interests rights and responsibilities Monetarist economic and social policies	Identifying and meeting customer needs and wishes Working with external audiences, e.g. parents, employers, etc.
Participation	Participatory democracy and the 'Open Society' - devolved power and shared responsibility - partnership between equals - pluralism and diversity	Parental involvement at home and at school Parents as educators Community education and development

Adapted from Bastiani (1987), p. 90. Reproduced by permission of the publishers: NFER-NELSON, Windsor, England.

The view, espoused by Plowden (and widely accepted and embraced by the teaching profession), that 'the major forces associated with educational attainment are to be found within the home circumstances of the children' (Wiseman, 1964), in short, that parental attitudes and interests in their children's educational development are of significantly more importance than home circumstances, such as family size, income, material conditions of the home, etc. led to the logical conclusion that one of the major tasks facing schools and teachers was that of 'making the least "successful" families more like the most "successful", opening the door for the extensive application of deficit models of family life and the implementation of the interventionist, compensatory and positive discriminating strategies of the late 1960s and early 1970s' (Bastiani, 1987, pp. 92–3).[6] By the mid-1970s, however, politicians had become increasingly disillusioned with the proposition that economic growth could be stimulated by educational investment. Furthermore, many educationists were coming to realize the limitations of their influence on individual and social development and to appreciate that their belief that the extension of educational provision would produce socially equalizing effects and fulfil democratic ideals had not happened on anything like the scale they had originally envisaged. The Plowden Report had also strongly emphasized the importance of contact and communication with parents – 'the school should explain to them so that parents can take an informed interest in what their children are doing. Parents will not understand unless they are told.' Bastiani (1987) comments that 'from such a viewpoint, problems of relationships between families and schools can be largely attributable to failures of communication. If parents do not know, it is because they are not adequately informed. If they do not understand it is because they lack appropriate opportunities to see, to discuss and to become involved' (p. 95). Thus, the increasingly important policy of rational and open *communications* attempted to overcome any sense of alienation parents might feel by directing their attention to the extent and quality of practical facilities and arrangements available for contact and communication between teachers, parents and children (p. 97). This ideology (see Table I.1) was but part of important changes taking place in the primary education scene as a whole, for until the mid-1970s, when criticism and controversy over primary pedagogy and curriculum had reached a peak, no detailed investigation of either teaching methods (*formal* or *progressive*) or curriculum (*range, structure, appropriateness, consistency, continuity*) had been attempted. It was not until 1976 that a number of attempts were under way to examine aspects of pedagogical and curriculum dissension more rigorously. Increasing government concern about the cost-effectiveness of schools, the coherence and relevance of the school curriculum, the worries about 'standards' and the need for schools to be more responsive to public needs (Munn, Reading 6), represent an ideological shift of emphasis away from liberal egalitarianism towards *accountability*[7] – a market forces or 'consumerism' ideology. Thus, within the context of accountability policies, parents are seen 'as a major external audience with whom schools, to be effective, need to create and sustain a dynamic and constructive relationship, based upon mutual respect and the full exchange of information' (Bastiani, 1987, p. 100).[8]

The last home and school ideology suggested by Bastiani is that of *participation*. In a sense, participatory ideologies (by definition) have always been of crucial importance to the furthering of home–school relations, but in recent years ideological shifts of emphasis have significantly changed and extended the notion of 'participation' as a model of interpersonal and institutional behaviour. The most important characteristic of a participatory ideology, according to Bastiani, is that 'it recognizes the existence of both shared goals *and* complementary roles for teachers and parents. The only way in which such divergent elements can be reconciled, however, is through the devolution of power and shared responsibility, where teachers and parents work together, despite their differences, through non-hierarchical relationships, in a partnership of equals' (p. 100).

A participatory perspective then, in emphasizing the role of parents and teachers as a 'partnership of equals', would stress the importance of co-operative rather than joint activity. Wolfendale (1983) distinguishes between the characteristics of parents viewed as 'clients' and those of parents perceived as 'partners' – these latter include:

- parents are active and central in decision-making;
- parents have equal strengths and 'equivalent expertise';
- parents contribute to, as well as receive services;
- parents share responsibility, so they and professionals are mutually accountable.

In recent years, for example, more and more parents of children with special educational needs have become directly involved in processes of assessment and diagnosis, taking on the role of teachers of their own handicapped children.[9] In such cases, their involvement is based on the premises:

- that parents are experts on their own children;
- their skills complement professional skills;
- parents can impart vital information and make informed observations;

- parents have the right to be involved;
- parents should contribute to decision-making;
- parents can be highly effective teachers of their own children. (Wolfendale, 1986, p. 33)

As valuable as ideological analysis is as a means of teasing out and examining the attitudes, beliefs and central values which underpin and fashion educational policy and practice, it would be a mistake to assume that attitudinal change is a linear, one-dimensional process. Pathological and compensatory ideologies (the deficit family model) continue to be widespread and influential to this day and participatory ideologies, theoretically attractive as they are, tend to be highly elusive in practice (Bastiani, 1987, p. 103).

PARENTS AS EDUCATORS

Perhaps the most important influence on the nature of home and school relationships which has gained momentum in recent years is the recognition of the *complementary* status of parent and teacher roles. Of the many and varied forms of parental involvement, parents' involvement in their children's reading progress and parental involvement with children who have special educational needs provide the fullest expression of this complementary relationship between parents and professionals. In Topping and Wolfendale (1985), Topping poses the question: 'If home factors are so powerful an influence, why has the education world been so slow to attempt to mobilize this power? In the hurry to put together "compensatory" programmes (which served only to give disadvantaged children more of the same and knock them deeper into the hole they were already in), parents tended to get overlooked - at least until recently' (p.22).[10] Topping illustrates the importance and effectiveness of parental involvement on children's reading behaviour in the following way:

Main factors in effectiveness of parental involvement

Compared to teacher input, parental:
M Modelling - is more powerful
P Practice - is more regular
F Feedback - is more immediate
R Reinforcement - is more valuable

(Topping and Wolfendale, 1985, p. 25)

Figure I.1 illustrates the various ways in which parents are involved in their children's reading.

We have seen earlier how the idea of enjoining the efforts of parents to assist children's educational progress and development is largely rooted in

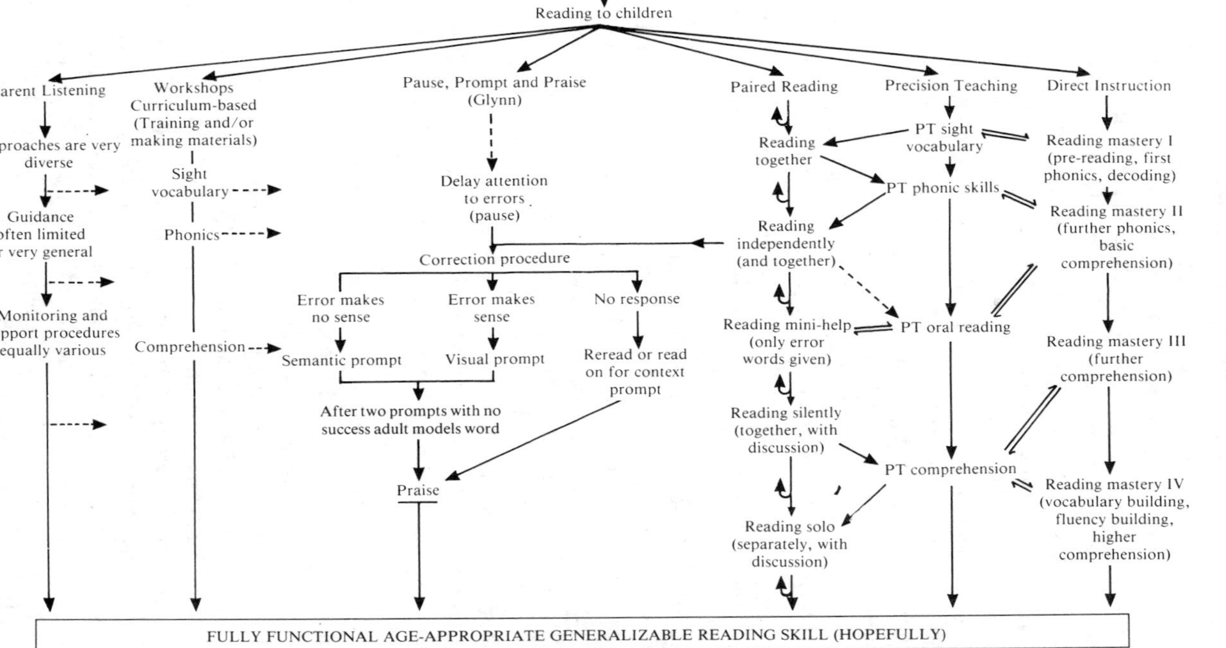

Figure I.1 Parental involvement in reading: the options and their interaction (Topping and Wolfendale, 1985, p. 30)

For a discussion of 'pause, prompt and praise' (Glynn) see Reading 4.
For a discussion of 'paired reading' see Reading 2. Source: Glynn (1981).

a compensatory ideology. Goode (1987) suggests that 'from Plowden onwards, a central focus has been the family's contribution to the outcomes of schooling. Studies have been dominated by a problem-oriented approach - the decline of the extended family network, the disintegration of the nuclear family, family dynamics requiring therapeutic intervention, the life-cycle of the family in terms of crises. Writings on the family are doom-laden' (p. 109). She argues that when the family is looked at *in its own terms* rather than from the viewpoint of its contribution to external systems, a quite different picture emerges for, seen from this perspective, the school context and outcomes are but one part of an environment which is infinitely rich in opportunities for children's intellectual, social, developmental, affective and experiential learning to take place in ways which may or may not be compatible with school-based learning. This is precisely the point which is examined in a number of readings in the sourcebook (see particularly Atkin and Bastiani, Reading 1, Tizard and Hughes, Reading 3 and Hughes and Watt, Reading 8).

Goode (1987) refers to the concept of 'educative style'[11] (Leichter, 1974) when examining (over the whole range of the outcomes of familial education) what parents *do* as opposed to who and what they are. 'Educative style', then, is an approach which concentrates on processes of interaction, 'What might be called the "hidden curriculum" of the home - the processes within the home which lead to the development of educative styles - are also significant for what has been called "deutero-learning" or learning to learn: learning how to ask questions, how to organize activities, how to appraise external valuations. They are all important for an understanding of education, even if they are not explicitly seen by participants as educational, and even if they do not necessarily involve "teaching" and "learning" (pp. 109-110).

It follows that examining what parents *do* and how families evolve 'educative styles' suggests the need for a different theoretical framework - one based upon an ecological approach (Hobbs, 1978; Bronfenbrenner, 1979; Apter, 1982). Such an approach would involve the idea of mapping each child's particular ecosystem in order to study the juxtaposition of that child to his or her parents, siblings, relations, locality, friends, the school network with relation to teachers and peer groups, thus enabling one to analyse the systems of which each child is a part so that the information could be used as a basis for problem-definition and problem-resolution (Wolfendale, in Topping and Wolfendale, 1985, p. 7). In similar vein, Dowling (1985) considers how the two most influential systems in an individual's development (the family and the school) may be brought together as part of a therapeutic strategy to deal with problems in children. She examines the concepts of general systems theory as they apply to family and school functioning, specifying particularly the interaction between them when difficulties and problems of an educational nature occur in this dual context. Dowling discusses a systems way of thinking as referring to 'a view of individual behaviour which takes account of the context in which it occurs. Accordingly, the behaviour of one component of the system is seen as affecting, and being affected by, the behaviour of others' (p.6).

What parents *do* about their children's 'education', then, would appear to be of immeasurably more importance than educators have hitherto suspected. The same is true of what parents learn from their children.[12] In short, as Newson (1976) has argued, *parents are experts on their own children*. The overarching influences on parents' educative roles are illustrated diagrammatically in Figure I.2.

Until comparatively recently, there has been little evidence about *how* parents develop understandings of educational processes in general, how they make sense of their children's schooling and how they behave as educators in their own right. In Reading 1 Atkin and Bastiani add to the discussion of Goode (1987) by providing a clear picture about *what* parents experience and do in relation to their children's education and *how* they think about it. The authors suggest that their data demonstrate that parents' concepts about teaching consist of a loosely knit collection of ideas and beliefs which can be described in relation to three dimensions:

1. *Teaching as ideology*: which draws attention to the different values and beliefs that are held about education (particularly in relation to how children learn and to the nature of the adult role with regard to learning).
2. *Teaching as pedagogy*: which relates to the range of strategies, techniques and materials which parents use to promote learning.
3. *Teaching as context*: which ranges on a continuum from 'teaching happens in any environment' to teaching which reproduces the essential features of classroom life.

Figure 1.1 (see p. 30) illustrates the range and variety of parental viewpoints about 'teaching'.

The research suggests that parents' ideas about teaching and learning are by no means obvious or straightforward, and that like teachers, parents have widely differing educational philosophies, which lead them to interpret educational roles and tasks in a variety of ways. In fact, rather than parents and teachers having *different* understandings, there is as much variety amongst parents in relation to concepts of teaching as there

The active role of the child in the process

Confirmatory
Actively encouraging, supporting and confirming the work undertaken by the school.

(a) *Home-based*
'Bringing the school into the home', i.e. school-based learning shared.

Homework - attitude to
- help with

Exams - attitude to
- help with

(b) *School-based*
- Parents in the school
- Parents in the classroom

(c) *Linking* (a) and (b) are teacher–parent contacts and communications
- how they affect the parent-as-educator roles.

Complementary
Attitudes, relationships and activities, initiated by parents which by their nature are likely to promote learning.

Socialization, pre-school experience, preparation for school.

Modelling specific skills, attitudes and behaviour.

Developing traits conducive to learning, growth development etc. 'moulding'. Regulating the child's handling of materials in space, or activities in time.

Outings and activities - providing experiences, resources, mediating the world to the child.

Having aspirations and expectations.

Careers guidance.

Compensatory
Parent-initiated action to encourage the school to meet a requirement in which it is perceived to be failing, undertaking the task oneself, or supplying alternative personnel to do so.

Supplying the school with information about the child, alerting the school.

Undertaking home 'teaching'.

Hiring a tutor.

Removing child to another school.

The developmental aspect of how parental roles change over time

Figure I.2 Parents as educators - a typology (adapted from Goode, 1987, p. 118) Reproduced by permission of the publishers, NFER-NELSON, Windsor, England.

is amongst the teaching profession.[13] This perspective, which stresses the range and diversity of parental viewpoints, offers evidence which is of potential value in the development of more effective communication, contact and involvement between families and schools, particularly in relation to children's learning.

The readings in this sourcebook have been selected with the aim of providing a comprehensive account of current issues and emphases in the field of home–school relations. Two major themes of paramount importance have influenced the editor's choice. The first theme echoes a sentiment expressed in the Court Report (1976): 'we have found no better way to raise a child than to reinforce the ability of his parents to do so'. The second theme is concerned with a fundamental principle which underpins the 'participatory' ideological perspective – the idea of partnership:

> (Partnership is) [...] a relationship in which the professional serves the parents, by making appropriate expertise available to them for their consideration. The relationship is, therefore, one of *complementary expertise,* since the expert knowledge of the parents, on themselves, their aims, their situation generally, and their children, complements what the profession has to offer including professional knowledge and skills to communicate it. [...] Using this framework of partnership therefore, the professional accepts his/her expertise and limitations; perceives parents as knowledgeable; acknowledges that many of the problems are not easily resolved; and believes that the best approach is to pool their expertise and to experiment together in mutually agreed ways. Although the parents are seen as having ultimate executive control, the professional's role is to offer for discussion alternative ways of viewing the situation and intervening. Decisions, therefore, are made on the basis of negotiation[...][14] (Davis, 1985).

NOTES

1. Beattie (1985) lists four main reasons for the introduction and extension of participatory democracy (suggested by Pennock, 1979):

   Institutional and conservative aims
   (i) *Responsiveness*: participation should improve governmental output by increasing flows of information and enabling a more flexible response to needs.
   (ii) *Legitimacy*: participation should make governmental output more acceptable to the governed.

   Reformist and revolutionary aims
   (iii) *Personal development*: individuals may achieve their full moral and intellectual development *only* if they have some responsibility for matters which affect them.
   (iv) *Overcoming alienation*: participation should bring individuals together and thus enable them to understand more clearly the collective purposes of society. (Adapted from Beattie, 1985, p. 5)

It is equally important to note, however, that until the mid-1960s what interaction there was between parents and schools usually took place on 'assumptions delimiting traditional spheres of influence'. Thus, in matters concerned with curriculum, methods, resources and the like, decisions were totally in the control of professionals (teachers and administrators) who were themselves ultimately, though distantly, answerable to the political system of the day. The specific responsibilities of parents were confined to the health and care (physical, moral and religious) of their children (Beattie, 1985, p. 2). Darling (1986) observes 'that the *full* educational potential of the parent–child relationship has been inhibited as a result of a loss of parental confidence induced to a part by the school system, the consequence of which is that parents have tended to see teachers as the "experts" who possess specialized skills and knowledge which they, as lay persons, do not possess. Thus, where parents are convinced of the teachers' "mysterious knowledge" they become inhibited from doing their best to teach their own children and are effectively persuaded to hand over control of their children's education' (p. 22). The author wryly comments, 'Making people feel inadequate has become a growth industry' (p. 23), yet the reality is that 'what parents are usually unaware of is that teachers themselves are confused and anxious about their own role and how to execute it' (p. 24).

For a succinct historical account of parental involvement in schools see Hurt, J. (1985) 'Parental involvement in schools: a historical perspective', in Cullingford, C. (ed.) *Parents, Teachers and Schools*, London, Robert Royce, pp. 17–39.

2. For an interesting account of the notion of 'community involvement', see Reading 8.
3. For example, in government reports over the last two decades:

The Plowden Report (CACE, 1967): 'By involving the parents, the children may be helped' (para. 114). The Report devotes a whole chapter to 'participation by parents' (pp. 37–49).

DES (1975) Green Paper: *Education in Schools. A Consultative Document,* London, HMSO: 'Until recently many parents have played only a minor part in the educational system. The Government are of the view that parents should be given much more information about the schools and should be consulted more widely' (p. 5).

DHSS (1976) *Fit for the Future* (Court Report) London, HMSO: 'Families could be better at bringing up their children if they were given the right information, support and relationships with the caring professions when it was needed and in a more acceptable way' (p. 25).

DES (1977) *A New Partnership for our Schools* (Taylor Report) London, HMSO. The Report called for increased numbers of parents as school governors, a recommendation which was subsequently adopted in the 1980 Education Act. 'Both individually and collectively the parents constitute a major source of support for the school. It is not a source which has been tapped fully in the past. We believe that governing bodies should encourage the widest and deepest parental commitment to their schools' (p. 87).

DES (1978) *Special Educational Needs* (The Warnock Report) London, HMSO: 'We have insisted throughout this report that the importance of the role of parents in the education of their children with special educational needs is dependent upon the full involvement of their parents: indeed, unless the parents are seen as equal partners in the educational process the purpose of our report will be frustrated' (p. 150).

'The relationship between parents and the school which their child is attending has a crucial bearing on the child's educational progress. On the one hand, if parents are to support the efforts of teachers they need information and advice from the school about its objectives and the provision being made for their child: on the other, a child's special needs cannot be adequately assessed and met in school without the insights that his parents, from their more intimate experiences of him, are able to provide. Close links between school and parents must therefore be established and maintained as we have stressed throughout this report' (p. 155).

The legal framework for facilitating the widely advocated participation of parents in the education process was provided by the 1981 Education Act, which amended the law relating to special education, providing for the considerable extension of parents' rights in relation to referral, assessment, placement and reviewing procedures, and by the 1986 Education Act (*Education (No. 2) Act,* 1986, London, HMSO) which, via the statutory governors' annual report to parents and the annual parents' meeting, gave the whole parent body the opportunity to become more closely involved in the life of the school.

The Education (No. 2) Act 1986 will be in full operation in 1989 and will give parents important new rights of access to information about what their children are being taught. The Act also establishes more links between governors and parents as a whole, and has been widely seen as an attempt to limit the power of LEAs and teachers by placing more in the hands of governors and parents. It prescribes in considerable detail the composition of school governing bodies with increased representation of parents, and lists the responsibilities of the new boards in relation to curriculum, discipline, financing and staffing of schools.

See Sallis, J. (1987) 'The 1986 Education Act', *Parents and Schools*, London, CASE, for a comprehensive summary of the 1986 Education Act.

4. See also Galton, M. (1987) 'Change and continuity in the primary school: the research evidence', *Oxford Review of Education,* **13**, 1, 81–93; Kogan, M. (1987) 'The Plowden Report twenty years on', *Oxford Review of Education,* **13**, 1, 13–21.

5. For a discussion of the relationship between 'disadvantage' and compensatory education within the British context, see Woodhead, M. (1976) *Intervening in Disadvantage,* Windsor, NFER: Mortimore, J. and Blackstone, T. (1982) *Disadvantage in Education,* London, Heinemann; Topping, K. (1985) 'Parental involvement in reading: theoretical and empirical background', in Topping, K. and Wolfendale, S. (eds) *Parental Involvement in Children's Reading,* London, Croom Helm, chap. 2, pp. 17–31.

During the period after 1950 educational growth in Britain increased at a pace hitherto unknown since the Education Act 1870. One of the most pervasive demands from millions of parents in the immediate post-war years was to have more and better education for their children than they themselves had received. Describing the first twenty-five years of post-war education, MacLure (1984) writes: 'The period was one of unparalleled expansion in England and Wales. For a quarter of a century after the end of the Second World War, the social, economic and demographic conditions were uniquely favourable for educational development. It began with a strong political consensus behind the new Education Act which raised expectations and promised wider opportunities for everyone. On this basis, the education system was reconstructed and modernized . . . the consensus did not last: it crumbled in the 1960s, about the time the demographic trend turned down. The optimism and the expectations faded with the onset of a recession which ended the longest period of sustained prosperity the modern world has known' (p. ix).

The period following the publication of the Plowden Report was marked by a gathering force of virulent criticism of child-centred ideology and progressive approaches to teaching and learning. Inevitably the primary curriculum itself became an area of controversy as demands increased for the investigation of its range, structure, appropriateness, consistency and continuity. Richards (1982, p. 12; 1979, pp. 39–55) has identified four major ideologies as areas of conflict:

1. *Liberal romanticism* ('developmental', 'progressive') – which celebrates the supremacy of the child in the teaching–learning situation and regards the curriculum as the sum total of learning experiences both offered to them and created by them as they interact with their surroundings.
2. *Educational conservatism* – which stresses the importance of continuity with the past and the curriculum as the repository of worthwhile cultural elements which need transmitting from one generation to another.
3. *Liberal pragmatism* – which views the curriculum as a set of learning experiences largely but not entirely structured by the teacher, but respecting to some degree both the individuality of the child and the importance of cultural transmission.
4. *Social democracy* – which views the curriculum as a means of realizing social justice and focuses around the social experiences of pupils.

Richards (1987) suggests that since the mid- or late 1970s liberal pragmatism has become more and more prominent in the professional debates on primary education, and that as an ideology, liberal pragmatism 'is characterized by a concern for planning and policy-making at school and local authority levels, for systematic progression and continuity between and within schools and for evaluation and assessment of children's learning at each level from the class to the education system nationally' (p. 8).

Bastiani's model of home and school ideologies (Table I.1) can be regarded as a subset of the larger debate about how primary education is being scrutinized and conceptualized. A larger perspective would suggest that the increasing importance accorded to 'participation' ideology in home–school relations, with its emphases on devolved power and shared responsibility, partnership between equals and pluralism and diversity (Bastiani, 1987) is an articulation of the current and pervading ideology of liberal pragmatism in primary education (Richards, 1987), itself an element in the wider 'reformist' aims for the extension of participatory democracy in society at large (Pennock, 1979).

6. For a comprehensive review of 'interventionist' (compensatory) projects,

particularly concerning pre-school programmes designed as an 'inoculation against failure', see Woodhead, M. (1985) 'Pre-school education has long-term effects: but can they be generalized?', *Oxford Review of Education*, **11**, 2, 133–55.

7. For a discussion of 'accountability', see Reading 6 and Elliott, J., Bridges, D., Ebbutt, D., Gibson, R. and Nias, J. (1981) *School Accountability,* London, Grant McIntyre; Gray, J. (1981) 'Towards effective schools', *British Educational Research Journal*, 7, 59–69; MacDonald, B. (1979) 'Hard times: educational accountability in England', *Educational Analysis, 1,* Summer; Becher, T., Eraut, M. and Knight, J. (1981) *Policies for Educational Accountability*, London, Heinemann.
8. In Reading 6 Munn questions whether the information which schools must now statutorily provide about themselves is of interest and value to parents, and indeed whether this information promotes effective home-school communication. She suggests that parents are predominantly interested in different kinds of information about schools from that now on offer, and that by placing schools in competition with each other the government is more likely to constrain than to promote effective home-school communication. Bastiani (1987) writes that 'Despite an increasing sense of obligation to explain and justify both policy and action, home-school relations are still conceived as being professionally led and organized to achieve school goals and purposes' (p. 100).
9. See Daly, B., Addington, J., Kerfoot, S. and Sigston, A. (eds) (1985) *Portage: The importance of parents,* Windsor, NFER-Nelson; Dessent, T. (ed.) (1984) *What is important about Portage?*, Windsor, NFER-Nelson; Cunningham, C. and Davis, H. (1985) *Working with Parents: Frameworks for Collaboration,* Milton Keynes, Open University Press; Pugh, G. and De'Ath, E. (1984) *The Needs of Parents: Practice and Policy in Parent Education*, Basingstoke, Macmillan Educational; Topping, K. (1986) *Parents as Educators: Training Parents to Teach their children*, London, Croom Helm; Bishop, M., Copley, M. and Porter, J. (1986) *Portage: More than a Teaching Programme?*, Windsor, NFER-Nelson; Hedderly, R. and Jennings, K. (eds) (1987) *Extending and Developing Portage*, Windsor, NFER-Nelson.

   In Topping and Wolfendale (1985) Wolfendale asserts that the term 'parental involvement' is often used synonymously with 'participation' and even with 'partnership'. Yet, she claims, each term differs in semantic and in executive senses, for recent developments show that 'not only has the frequency of parent–teacher contact increased dramatically over the last decade but the type of contact has and is still changing. That is, from the minimal contact that characterized pre-1970 – parental attendance at school concerts, plays, annual open evenings – we can chart, on a chronological continuum, the continuation of these traditional activities alongside the introduction of a qualitatively different form of parent–teacher, home–school linkage. "Involvement" is an active noun and is rightly used to denote the range of activities' (p. 13).

   For an attempt to define the notion of 'partnership' between parents and professionals in education, see Pugh (1987) Reading 10, Wolfendale (1987) Reading 9, Widlake (1987) Reading 11, and Mittler, P. and McConachie, H.

(eds) (1983) *Parents, Professionals and Mentally Handicapped People*, London, Croom Helm; McConachie, H. (1986) *Parents and Young Mentally Handicapped Children: A Review of Research Issues,* London, Croom Helm, 'Involving parents in teaching', chap. 10, pp. 140–61.

10. In Topping and Wolfendale (1985) Wolfendale comments that 'children from allegedly "depriving" backgrounds have been the recipients of "compensatory" intervention approaches. These have been characterized by: extra input in the way of resources, including staff, equipment and in-service, special curricula, language programmes, cognitively oriented approaches, fostering of home-school-community links. In recent years, the inherently negative approach of directing intervention mainly to those children who are deemed "at risk", who apparently need the inoculation of special programmes, has been transformed. Intervention can be defined as an intentional match between carefully articulated education and curricular aims and the necessary objectives towards realization of these. In recent years this has broadened to encompass all children' (p. 4).
11. Goode (1987) describes 'educative style' as including 'such components as the manner of criticizing and appraising the mode of integrating experiences over time, the level and rate of activity, the ways of combining and segregating particular tasks, the character of response to cues from others, the mode of scanning and searching for information, and approaches to embarrassment in learning situations. These components of educative style interact in different ways as the individual engages in, moves through and combines diverse educational experiences over a lifetime' (p. 109).
12. Describing the 'shared learning' which takes place within the family, Goode (1987) writes, "Parents perhaps find it more acceptable than teachers that they can learn from their children, and that it is not a one-way process. Studies of mother–child interaction have demonstrated that the care-taker's behaviour is shaped by the child, and the concept of lifelong education suggests by implication that parents, although older and more experienced than their children, continue to learn from them as they enter new parental roles. Parents learn about children, about child development and its trends, about teaching and learning, about strategies of schooling, about the variety of behaviour and experience to which their children's associates will expose them. In this sense contact with the life of a child opens up a new vision of the world, and the full range of the child's activities becomes a potential source of education for the parent. The experience of adjustment and readjustment to changes in the child, given the child's comparatively rapid rate of maturation, is another potential source of education for the parent. The fact that interaction with the child inevitably requires continuous shifts on the part of the parent serves as a pressure for continuous learning' (p. 110).
13. For example, see Sandow, S., Stafford, D. and Stafford, P. (1987) *An Agreed Understanding? Parent–Professional Communication and the 1981 Education Act*, Windsor, NFER–Nelson.

    Sandow et al. examine the assumptions which underlie the assessment procedures laid down by the 1981 Education Act, by looking at parents' perceptions of the process by which their children are considered for special educational provision. The authors suggest that 'much has been published on parent-professional relations in special education, almost all of which assumes certain shared priorities: that children with special educational needs should be educated in an integrated setting, and that parents and professionals expect and wish to operate a system of joint support for the children and mutual understanding called "partnership" ' (preface). The study questions the reality and applicability of these assumptions by reporting discrepancies between parental views and perceptions and the expressed views of professionals concerned with assessment. The authors suggest that their results demonstrate a considerable mismatch between parental and professional priorities, and that, in some respects, the experience of the parents and professionals and the organizational constraints of the 1981 Education Act may combine to defeat the intentions of the Act. Sandow et al. report that 'integration is theoretically a prority, but the practice has been to segregate 70 per cent of the sample. A worrying trend is towards separate provision for many children with emotional and behavioural difficulties, often referred by schools who find their present facilities, skills and the pressures generated by the needs of other pupils make it impossible to cope with difficult children. Had the appropriate financial support for training been made available concurrently with the legislation, the pressure for segregation might have been minimized. Instead, the pressure for examination success leads schools to exclude children who are likely to fail, or who are seen as likely to interfere with the success of others' (p.158).

14. Atkin and Bastiani with Goode (1988) develop this concept of 'partnership' and 'complementary expertise' by examining the *developmental nature* of the 'dynamic' element of home-school relations. They show how the family and the school move and change through time: 'they each have a "life-cycle" and the point in this cycle at which each participant has arrived, will influence what each is looking for, expecting from, and is able to contribute to the relationship with the other' (p. 25). The authors emphasize the role of the child as an active mediator of the relationship and offer the diagram in Figure I.3 as an analytic tool to illuminate the design, engineering and operation of a particular 'model' of home-school relationships.

REFERENCES

Apter, S. (1982) *Troubled Children, Troubled Systems.* Oxford, Pergamon.

Atkin, J. and Bastiani, J. with Goode, J. (1988) *Listening to Parents: An Approach to the Improvement of Home-School Relations.* London, Croom Helm.

Bastiani, J. (ed.) (1987) *Parents and Teachers (1): Perspectives on Home-School Relations.* Windsor, NFER-Nelson.

Beattie, N. (1985) *Professional Parents: Parent Participation in Four Western European Countries.* Lewes, Falmer.

Bronfenbrenner, V. (1979) *The Ecology of Human Development.* Harvard University Press.

Cameron, R. J. (1984) *Working Together: Portage in the UK.* Windsor, NFER-Nelson.

Central Advisory Council for Education (CACE) (1967) *Children and Their Primary Schools* (the Plowden Report). London, HMSO.

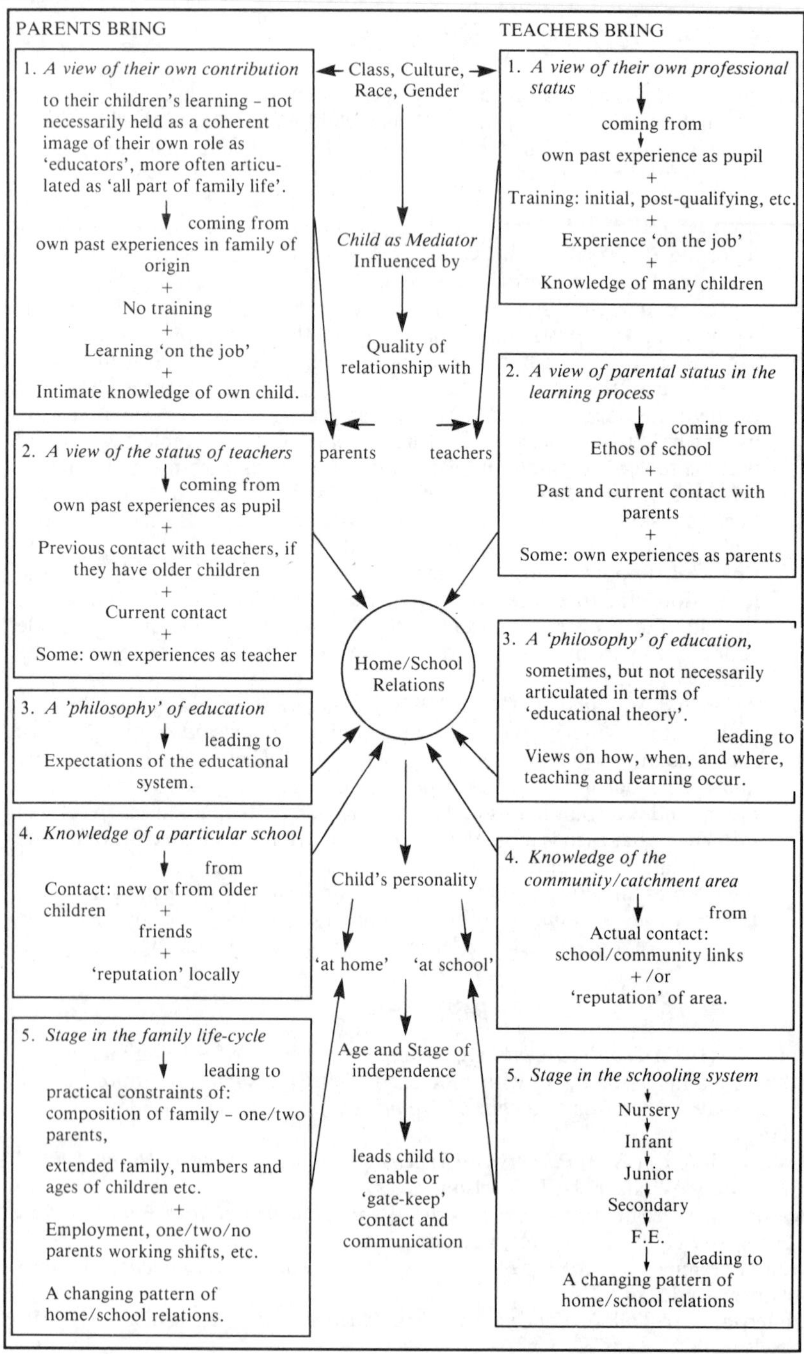

Figure I.3 A model of home–school relationships (Atkin and Bastiani with Goode, 1988, p.24) Reprinted by permission of Croom Helm, publishers.

Darling, J. (1986) 'Parents, teachers, and the messages of experts'. *Culture, Education and Society, Universities Quarterly*, **40**, 1, 21-30.
Davis, H. (1985) 'Developing the role of parent advisor in the child health services', in De'Ath, E. and Pugh, G. (eds) *Partnership Paper 3*. London, National Children's Bureau.
Dowling, E. (1985) 'Theoretical framework - a joint systems approach to educational problems with children', in Dowling, E. and Osborne, E. *The Family and the School: A Joint Systems approach to Problems with Children*. London, Routledge & Kegan Paul.
Goode, J. (1987) 'Parents as educators', in Bastiani, J. (ed.) op. cit., pp. 108-24.
Halsey, A.H. (1987) 'Plowden: history and prospects'. *Oxford Review of Education*, **13**, 1, 1-8.
Hobbs, N. (1978) 'Families, schools and communications: an ecosystem for children'. *Teachers' College Record*, **79**, 4, 172-209.
Leichter, H. J. (1974) 'The family as educator'. *Teachers' College Record*, **76**, 3, 88-114.
Long, R. (1986) *Developing Parental Involvement in Primary Schools*. London, Macmillan.
MacLure, S. (1984) *Educational Development and School Building: Aspects of Public Policy 1945-1973*. London, Longman.
Mittler, P. (1978) 'Choices in partnership'. *The World Congress of the ILSMH on Mental Handicap*.
Newson, E. (1976) 'Parents as a resource in diagnosis and assessment', in Oppe, T. and Woodford, F. (eds) (1976) *The Early Management of Handicapping Disorders*. IRMMH, Amsterdam/Oxford, Elsevier.
Pennock, J. R. (1979) *Democratic Political Theory*. Princeton University Press.
Richards, C. (1979) 'Primary education: myth, belief and practice', in Bloomer, M. and Shaw, K. (eds) (1979) *The Challenge of Educational Change*. Oxford, Pergamon.
Richards, C. (ed.) (1982) *New Directions in Primary Education*. Lewes, Falmer.
Richards, C. (1987) 'Primary education in England: an analysis of some recent issues and developments'. *Curriculum*, **8**, 1, 6-12.
Topping, K. and Wolfendale, S. (eds) (1985) *Parental Involvement in Children's Reading*. London, Croom Helm.
Wiseman, S. (1964) *Education and Environment*. Manchester University Press.
Wolfendale, S. (1983) *Parental Participation in Children's Development and Education*. New York, Gordon and Breach.
Wolfendale, S. (1986) 'Involving parents in behaviour management: a whole school approach'. *Support for Learning*, **1**, 4, 32-8.

SECTION ONE

PARENTS AS EDUCATORS

INTRODUCTION

Section One of the sourcebook consists of five readings, the first of which criticizes much of the research to do with parental involvement in teaching, claiming that it 'perpetuates a simplified and somewhat crude notion of "teaching", which does not do justice to its complexity, nor to the multi-dimensional views of teaching which are held by parents' (p. 24). The article examines how parents *think* about teaching and discusses how a wider understanding of the concepts, beliefs and behaviour which parents hold has profound implications for the relationship between home and school.

Reading 2 contrasts two methods of encouraging reading development - *shared* reading and *paired* reading. The authors describe 'shared' reading as a modelling technique which consists of partner and child reading aloud together from a book of the child's own choice, where the partner pays no attention to the child's mistakes and continues reading even when the child can manage only a few words of the text. Shared reading differs substantially from paired reading since it is a modelling technique and is not based on behavioural reinforcement schedules. The article presents a critique of the paired reading technique in order to compare it as a method with that of shared reading. A later section describes a pilot study of the shared reading approach and discusses the advantages of using this method for home reading.

In Reading 3 Tizard and Hughes offer compelling evidence to dispel the widely held assumption that working-class children, for example, receive a very much restricted linguistic input from their parents. Indeed, the 'myth' of linguistic deficit contrasts sharply with the authors' findings that the homes of most (if not all) young children provide a stimulating environment where the communication which takes place between mothers and young children is often far richer than that which occurs between young children and their teachers. Tizard and Hughes comment: 'One of our strongest impressions from this study was of the amount which children learnt from simply being around with their mothers: discussing what each was doing, or had done, what they would do next, arguing with each other and, above all, endlessly asking and answering questions' (p. 49).

In Reading 4 the authors argue that the disadvantage experienced by children with limited reading skills invariably continues throughout their school life unless some intervention is applied which will allow them to improve, and to improve quickly, and that unless they make dramatic progress in their reading ability, the secondary curriculum in particular, will be largely unavailable to them. The article describes a relatively new, powerful tutoring method, which the authors assert can be employed by either parents or peers with low progress readers. The procedure known as 'pause, prompt and praise', it is claimed, is at least as powerful a technique as paired reading.

The last reading in this section examines how sexual inequalities, which are inherent in our education system, are introduced at a very early age, in fact, during the pre-school years. France's account adds weight to Thomas's argument (suggested further reading 3) that sex-typed roles restrict personal fulfilment for *both* males and females by severely limiting the options each is allowed to pursue, and that sexual equality is dependent on the elimination of sex bias in the earliest years of education.

In describing how sex role and behaviour differences are established in the daily lives of very young children, the author presents an overview of the various influential theories that tend to describe and explain sex differences, and goes on to suggest a number of strategies which may help young children to grow up with an approach to life that does not rely on sex and race stereotypes.

Reading 1

ARE THEY TEACHING? AN ALTERNATIVE PERSPECTIVE ON PARENTS AS EDUCATORS

J. Atkin and J. Bastiani

INTRODUCTION

A recent issue of this journal [*Education 3–13*] contained an account by the Thomas Coram research team into the views of parents and reception

Atkin, J. and Bastiani, J. (1986) 'Are they teaching? An alternative perspective on parents as educators'. *Education 3–13*, **14**, 2, 18–22. Reprinted by permission of the publishers.

class teachers on ways of preparing children for school (Farquhar et al., 1986). The team presented data which suggested marked differences between them particularly in relation to the question of parents teaching their children academic skills. Seventy-three per cent of the parents are reported as stating they *taught* reading, writing or number skills while the teachers preferred parents to encourage language and reading to children. A previous article by the same team (Blatchford et al., 1985) also drew the conclusion that 'it appears that skills on entry, which Wells and Raban found to be closely related to achievement at seven years (knowledge of literacy), are themselves closely related to *direct parental* teaching at home' (our emphasis).

The implications that we believe teachers are intended to draw from this research are that many parents act like teachers and that in the interests of educational achievement, schools should actively encourage them to do so. However, unless we have some understanding of parental concepts of teaching and the kind of behaviour associated with it, it is questionable whether the phrase 'direct parental teaching' is a legitimate description of what parents actually do or think they are doing. Indeed, from the way the research is reported, it is impossible to tell whether it was the parents who labelled their behaviour 'teaching' or whether the researchers themselves categorized responses that in some ways referred to activities with books, number games, etc. as 'teaching'.

As a result of our own work in the area of home–school relationships, we believe this research perpetuates a simplified and somewhat crude notion of 'teaching', which does not do justice to its complexity, nor to the multi-dimensional views of teaching which are held by parents. In this article we intend to take a closer look at how parents think about teaching and discuss how a wider understanding of their concepts, beliefs and behaviour has implications for the relationship between home and school, that extends beyond the encouragement of 'teacher-like' behaviour on the part of parents.

OUR RESEARCH

Our study of parental perspectives arose from the work we had been doing for over a decade in in-service education in the home, school and community field.[1] We had become increasingly aware that there was a lack of real evidence about how parents develop understandings of educational processes in general, how they make sense of their children's schooling, and how they act as educators of their own children. In order to investigate this, a number of separate but linked studies were set up in which a broad range of parents from all social classes and with very different kinds of experience of schools were interviewed. The studies shared a common approach which we call 'listening to parents'. We placed the emphasis on enabling parents to give accounts in which they could develop their own concerns and points of view, set within a loosely structured framework. The interview was therefore treated as an opportunity for extended description, reflective analysis and comment rather than definite answers to pre-specified and codifiable questions. We believe it is through a methodology such as this, derived from symbolic interactionism and phenomenology, that a clearer picture is gained not only about *what* parents experience and do in relation to their children's education but *how* they think about it.

WHAT IS TEACHING?

What emerges from our data is that the concepts of teaching held by parents consist of a loosely knit collection of ideas and beliefs which can be described in relation to three dimensions. We have called these dimensions *teaching as ideology*, *teaching as pedagogy* and *teaching as context*. These dimensions are not simply a matter of polar opposites (an act of behaviour is either 'teaching' or it is not), but rather each exists in the form of a continuum, with subtle shadings of distinctions along it. When these dimensions are put together, the result is a highly complex and dynamic concept of teaching which reflects different models of learning, pedagogical strategies and appropriate settings. In analysing our data with these dimensions in mind we have concluded that, rather than parents and teachers having *different* understandings there is as much variety amongst parents in relation to concepts of teaching as there is amongst the teaching profession. Mismatches between parents and teachers of the kind claimed by the Thomas Coram team are then more likely to be mismatches between particular parents and individual teachers, with different notions of teaching.

TEACHING AS IDEOLOGY

This dimension draws attention to the different values and beliefs that are held about education particularly in relation to how children learn and to the nature of the adult's role in relation to learning. The continuum can be seen as moving from a *reactive* role for the adult, characterized by phrases like 'being a pair of ears', 'showing an interest', 'being available', to a *proactive* role described as 'deliberate', 'coaching', 'having a lesson', 'teaching them X, Y and Z'. Here is a 'reactive' mother reflecting on how she helps her child:

Mother: I think a lot of parents do it without realizing that you're doing it. Just the fact that you show interest in what they're doing, and erm, you know, sort of become involved. Not to take over. I think it's important that you don't take over . . . But I think by being interested, you make them want to find out even more. Not necessarily saying, 'Right, get your books out, we'll have so and so done', you know I think you've got to be available . . . I think you can help in education, for your particular child, just by knowing what they're interested in, and by stimulating it, and just, as I say, just being a pair of ears, really . . . We do a lot of things together as well . . . things that aren't a bit educational in one way, erm, we went to fetch the Christmas tree from the woods. We all went . . . and I think even things like that, it's just an opening to, er, you get things back, erm, even ordinary things, it's just an opportunity . . . but I think that children learn, you know . . . they learn without realizing they're learning . . . but I don't think you ever think, it, it must be educational to a degree . . . I don't think you ever set a time of day aside and think, 'Right, we'll do some clever stuff!' you know.

Many of our parents characterized teaching as a conscious, deliberate act which took place at a set time of day, in a set place with a particular aim and noticeably marked by the child 'sitting still' and used this construct to deny that they taught their children.

Father: In terms of actually *teaching* her anything, no, we avoided that really, I mean, we used any opportunities that were available, er, if she looked at a word and wanted to know what it was we'd tell her, she did pick up some words like that, but we didn't make any kind of formal attempt to teach her anything, it was all just incidental, the way it should be [laughs].

Mother: We didn't try to sit down and coach them in anything. We tried to encourage them by taking an interest in what they were doing. We didn't get them extra lessons or teaching elsewhere, or anything like that.

Other parents with a different set of values and beliefs did see themselves as teaching in deliberate, formal ways.

Father: Children from the day they're born really have to be guided by somebody. I'm not saying, you know, shoved, I'm just saying, being guided . . . and if that sort of thing's going off at school, where they can *choose* what they do, from that age, they're going to, you know, pick the easiest and pick what they consider fun . . . They didn't start teaching her her tables until she was about eight or nine.

Mother: Oh no. I taught her her tables. I mean no one there taught her her tables . . . I'd taught him the alphabet before, you know, from these 'A' is for Apple, and just sat and taught him from there.

This dimension then reflects the theories about teaching and learning that underpin how parents see their own role in the educative process, and we suggest the differences between them relate to beliefs and values that can also differentiate the teaching profession.

TEACHING AS PEDAGOGY

This dimension relates to the particular kinds of strategies, techniques and materials that are used by the parent to promote learning, in other words the 'how' of teaching. Here the continuum is seen to range from the indirect 'doing the things a mother would normally do' to the direct 'sitting them down with the blackboard'.

For many parents the circumstances of everyday living provide the opportunities to use the strategies they consider appropriate:

Mother: I like to think I prepared them as well as I could, it wasn't something I did consciously, I certainly didn't say 'Well you've got to be able to read, and you've got to be able to write your name, you've got to be able to do X, Y and Z.' No, we didn't do that at all, it was a matter of being interested in the children, letting them take an interest in everything that was going on at home, they used to help me cook, they used to help me do the shopping, we used to go out as a family a lot, and still do incidentally, and, erm, we talked to them all the time, tried to answer questions and just tried to bring them up as children, as normal children.

Others are slightly less indirect.

Father: We didn't go overboard at all, we did what we normally think most parents would do and just as they developed and came through, we read books to them, normal things, encourage them, play number games, and the other little games they play. But it wasn't consciously with school in mind.

Here is one parent, himself a teacher, making a clear distinction between his idea of indirect, but nevertheless conscious, teaching with a methodology characterized by testing and formality.

Father: Both my wife and I read to him a great deal, apart from the nightly spot, we generally tried to build up an interest . . . so if he happened to be looking, I'd show him the book I was reading, not that I very often got the opportunity to sit down and read in his presence [laughs] . . . um or such things as records, if there was a record on, then we'd show him the record sleeve, in other words, what we were mainly concerned about doing was showing or trying to show a connection between the written word and actual happenings - at no time did I actually make a *formal* attempt to teach him to read. That is not to say, however, that he didn't look at it . . . to the extent that I would trace the lines when I was reading to him, so that again he would begin to make the connection. If he asked what a word was, then I would tell him - but there was no question of feedback, in as much as 'come on, I told you that word ten minutes ago, what is it now?' so there was, as I said, no question of testing or formal work in that sense.

It is, perhaps,the different kinds of behaviour this dimension indicates that lead us to question the phrase 'direct parental teaching' used in the Thomas Coram research. For teachers the words may conjure up images of children being directed into drill-like alphabet work, counting activities or copy writing, with parents taking a didactic, instructional role. We found hardly any parents describing what they did in this way (the mother who taught the alphabet and tables was almost the only exception). Far more common were parents who capitalized on the stuff of family life, the 'going places, seeing things, looking at books', as their educative strategy. Moreover, many parents were often very alert to their children's reactions to what they saw as direct teaching.

Mother: There were various things about Paul which showed that he could make use of books, he was always very interested in books, you could read to him for hours and hours. I had no success with trying to teach him to read at all because he *sensed* any kind of teaching and then stopped. But he loved being read to.

TEACHING AS CONTEXT

We have already referred to parents who saw teaching as happening anywhere and everywhere and others who conceived of it being located in a particular kind of setting, usually sitting down at a table. This dimension of the concept of teaching not only distinguished these kinds of differences but also highlighted the way parents compared home-based learning with learning in school. The continuum could be characterized as ranging from 'teaching happens in any environment' to 'teaching happens in a classroom, sitting still at a desk'. Parents who hold the latter concept of teaching can be particularly anxious about their children's behaviour in school.

Mother: He does know that it'll be *different* [from the nursery] because I've told him it's going to be different . . . I'd say 'Well it's going to be different when you go into Mrs C's class. You've got to sit down and she's going to actually *teach* you how to read and how to write', and I said 'You've got to sit still while she actually teaches you all this.' You see, trying to instil in him that he's got to learn how to sit still.

Mother: I think if somebody sort of said to Jenny, 'Right', you know, 'You've got to sort of sit and learn' then I think she would, but I think she lacks the discipline to learn at the moment because she thinks that, you know, you can sort of get up and have a little skip and then come back.

This dimension, then, also reveals the way context is seen as exercising various degrees of control over the child. The freedom to follow an activity for as long as one wishes, which is seen by most parents to characterize the home (and the nursery) setting, is contrasted with school where the child is directed by the teacher. Similarly, parents themselves exercise different forms of control in their teaching. They determine whether they will be in a particular place (for example always sitting at the kitchen table), or use the setting where the child happens to be (for example the floor, the bath, the garden); they decide whether to set aside a particular time of day, on a regular basis, or to use incidental opportunities, as they arise.

PARENTS AS EDUCATORS: A WIDER VIEW

So parental notions of teaching and learning are by no means obvious or straightforward to explain. Parents, like teachers, have widely differing educational philosophies. As a result, their images of teaching range from behaviour which is intended to achieve particular outcomes, using specific materials, in a formal setting, where strict attention is required, through a continuum to incidental, supportive approaches in which motivation, the development of attitudes, interests and skills, together with the personal characteristics of the child, are all given as much, if not more, attention than teaching content. In a similar way the notion of 'teaching' can also be used to make, or to avoid making, distinctions between school-based learning, directed by professionally trained teachers, and home-based learning with its own salient characteristics, located in the family setting.

The range and variety of parental viewpoints can be summarized as in Figure 1.1.

		Reactive (Teaching) ←→	Proactive (Teaching)
Ideology	*Beliefs* and *Intentions*	• Child-centred model of learning • Incidental activities • 'Teacher' support for child's activities	• Conscious planning • Systematic implementation • 'Teacher' direction and control
Pedagogy	*Tasks* and *Approaches*	• Spontaneous approaches • Improvisation of task • 'Home-made' techniques	• Structured tasks and materials • Regular, planned activity • Formal techniques
Context	*Settings* and *Circumstances*	• Exploiting the educative potential of home settings and family experience	• Reproducing the essential features of classroom life and work

Figure 1.1 Parental viewpoints about teaching

The alternative perspective, which stresses the range and diversity of parental viewpoints, offers information which is of potential value in the development of more effective communication, contact and involvement between families and schools, particularly where the learning of pupils is a central concern. Against this background, the present practice of most schools appears to be rather crude, limited and one-sided, assuming, as it does, that parents are a homogeneous group.

Whilst we have given considerable emphasis to the uncovering of a fuller picture of parental beliefs about teaching and the behaviour thought to be appropriate to these views, this should not be seen as the basis of a *static* portrayal of the relationship between families and schools, along the lines of a classic demarcation dispute. For parental attitudes and behaviour will be responsive to, and influenced by, their actual *experience* of schools and teachers, particularly in the early stages.

So in summary, parental belief and experience lead to a variety of interpretations of educational roles and tasks, in which the capacity and willingness of parents to see themselves as educators are complex, dynamic and, above all, problematic.

Such a perspective is important, not so much for its own sake, as for its capacity to inform practice and to identify important areas of growth and development. For there are many important and relatively unexplored areas in the field of home-school relations. In our view, it is not enough to examine these as a series of ready-made issues. What is required is a searching examination of how such issues come to be regarded as important together with a critical analysis of the assumptions incorporated in the key concepts, methods of inquiry and forms of evidence.

Against such a background, this account can be seen as direct challenge to the assumptions and methods used by the Thomas Coram research. As an alternative, we have tried to pinpoint the views of parents concerning the nature of 'teaching' and their roles in it, *as they see it themselves*. For we have found such an approach to be an important means of bringing research, policy and the development of practice together in a productive way.

NOTE

1. The Development of Effective Home-School Programmes Project - a continuing programme of research, study and professional development. A list of publications is available from the authors of the reading.

TOPICS FOR DISCUSSION

1. Discuss the evidence which leads the authors to assert that 'rather than parents and teachers having *different* understandings there is as much variety amongst parents in relation to concepts of teaching as there is amongst the teaching profession'.
2. In what ways do 'teaching as ideology ', 'teaching as pedagogy' and 'teaching as context' reflect *different* models of learning, pedagogical strategies and appropriate settings?
3. 'Parental attitudes and behaviour will be responsive to, and influenced by, their actual *experience* of schools and teachers, particularly in the early stages.' Discuss.

SUGGESTIONS FOR FURTHER READING

1. Widlake, P. and Macleod, F. (1985) 'Parental involvement programmes and the literacy performance of children', in Topping, K. and Wolfendale, S. (eds)

Parental Involvement in Children's Reading. London, Croom Helm, chap. 9, pp. 92–8.
Knapman, D. (1985) 'The Elmwood Project, Somerset', in Topping, K. and Wolfendale, S. op. cit., chap. 7, pp. 75–81.

Widlake and Macleod describe developments in Coventry's Community Education Project (CEP). In its infancy, in the early 1970s, the project provided additonal support and innovative services to teachers, pupils and parents in the area by: (a) developing a programme in schools designed to encourage home-school-community links; (b) initiating in-service training and support programmes for teachers; (c) developing an adult programme seeking to respond to community needs; (d) establishing a home-tutoring scheme for immigrant mothers; and (e) assisting with the extension of pre-school provision. In the 1980s strategies and supporting materials have been developed which have widened, deepened and informalized parental involvement in many of the schools (p. 92). The authors write that 'some schools are now beginning to evolve a parents' syllabus from their home-school programmes. Each school's syllabus is structured to ensure that during their time with the school, parents will be *given a share* in most aspects of the curriculum side by side with their child's progress through the school' (p. 93).

Knapman discusses a project in which a group of parents of slow-learning children were invited to a series of discussion meetings where specific advice and tips were given, and actual 'modelling' work with children was carried out. The specific aim of the project was to advise parents how best to manage and support their children's reading work, to involve staff in practical tutorial sessions with parents and their children and to provide a good and suitable range of reading material which would be freely available. The author comments on some of the more faulty reading support methods and approaches commonly observed in homes. These include reading sessions occurring too late in the evening, reading sessions which last too long or are spaced too far apart, reading work taking place in inappropriate settings, parents exerting too much pressure on reading, work that is spoilt by anxiety or loss of temper, the use of inappropriate material, parents giving too much time to mistakes or difficulties and too little attention to praise and encouragement, incorrect or inadequate cues given when the child becomes stuck, and imprudent use of siblings, relations, friends, etc. for reading work (p. 75). Knapman shows how the project not only produced gains in the young children's reading ability (p. 81) but also significantly affected school-parent relationships and basic attitudes.

2. Hannon, P., Jackson, A. and Weinberger, J. (1986) 'Parents' and teachers' strategies in hearing young children read'. *Research Papers in Education*, **1**, 16–25.

Hannon and his colleagues studied how fifty-two children, aged five to seven, were heard to read in school by their class teachers and at home by their parents. Tape recordings were made of children reading in both settings, and the recordings were analysed in terms of moves made by adults. The researchers found considerable similarities between the parents' and teachers' strategies in terms of the relative frequencies with which they made different kinds of moves. The most frequent moves for each group were providing words or giving directions about reading. The authors found that a greater proportion of parents' moves were in response to children's miscues, but that the responses to miscues made by parents and teachers were fairly similar. Both occasionally used phonic techniques, which for parents invariably meant 'sounding out' words, whereas the teachers, as might be expected, demonstrated a wider range of techniques. The authors conclude that 'no justification exists for considering parents incompetent in hearing their children read' (p. 6).

3. Kemp, M. (1985) 'Parents as teachers of literacy', in Clark, M.M. (ed.) (1985) *New Directions in the Study of Reading*. Lewes, Falmer, pp. 153-67.

Kemp writes that 'the assumption that "teachers know best" has become increasingly under challenge and literacy must soon take its place with, for example, health as a topic for more public (as distinct from professional) investigations of when and how it may be acquired, what the literacy curriculum shall contain in its various levels and how its components might be taught, particularly in early schooling' (p. 157). Kemp argues that because the learning and teaching of literacy are age-related and based on teachers' collective knowledge about children's developmental characteristics, arbitrary decisions are made about the timing and techniques of literacy teaching, which fortunately turn out to be favourable to most children's styles and rates of learning. However, if we were to think of literacy learning as being more developmental in nature, we would need to consider also, the author claims, 'how and whether some aspects of it might be unlocked and moved from school to pre-school and home. As well, we would need to consider whether all or only some homes could assume and manage the same sort of role in literacy as happens in their children's development of talking' (p. 158).

In discussing bringing home and school together in literacy teaching, Kemp considers that an effective literacy teaching support system must cater for three groups of children: the advanced, the amorphous 'average' group, and the slow developers. An effective support system then must fulfil three roles - a preventive, a surveillance and a corrective role. Thus, the author argues, the preventive role entails schools helping parents to recognize 'and act upon those conditions which will enable reading and writing to evolve naturally and in harmony with their children's growing awareness of detail, and enjoyment of language and stories' (p.159). It also means that schools must participate in community education so that parents are shown how to apply to literacy learning the same skills and principles they naturally and effectively apply to their child's learning of oral language. The surveillance role necessitates the schools's constant, continued contact, and knowing every child and parent before and during the early years of schooling. The corrective role, Kemp asserts, emphasizes 'the school's capacity to plan, execute and sustain action which will smooth the way for any child who has difficulties in learning to read and write' (p. 159). In a later section of the reading Kemp describes a pilot programme developed in Australia, which attempted to bring teachers, counsellors, children and parents together in a corrective function in literacy.

REFERENCES

Farquhar, C., Blatchford, P., Burke, J., Plewis, I. and Tizard, B. (1986) 'A comparison of the views of parents and reception teachers'. *Education 3-13*, **13**, 2, 17-22.

Blatchford, P., Burke, J., Farquhar, C., Plewis, I. and Tizard, B. (1985) 'Educational achievement in the infant school: the influence of ethnic origin, gender and home on entry skills'. *Educational Research*, **27**, 1.

Reading 2

SHARED READING: SUPPORT FOR INEXPERIENCED READERS

M. Greening and J. Spenceley

Shared reading is a simple and flexible way of encouraging reading development. It is essentially a modelling technique which consists of partner and child reading aloud together from a book of the child's own choice. The partner pays no attention to the child's mistakes and continues reading even when the child can manage only a few words of the text. Shared reading enables parents and voluntary helpers to support children's reading development and improve their attitude to books. It is a flexible technique, which can be used at different stages of reading development even with beginning readers. The method is easy to demonstrate to parents and projects are simple to organize as intensive monitoring is unnecessary. The method is being used extensively throughout the primary age range in Cleveland county schools.

The shared reading method was devised in 1983 by L. Mottram (teacher with Cleveland Learning Support Service) and D. Guy (Senior Educational Psychologist, Cleveland County Psychological Service). It was essentially a simplification of the simultaneous reading mode devised by Morgan (1976). This adaptation was necessary in order to make the method suitable for very inexperienced readers. Shared reading has, however, been found to differ substantially from paired reading, as it is a modelling technique and is not based on behavioural reinforcement schedules. A critique of Morgan's paired reading technique is presented in this article in order to compare that method with shared reading. A description and evaluation of the Shared Reading Project is also included in this comparison of the two methods.

Greening, M. and Spenceley, J. (1987) 'Shared reading: support for inexperienced readers'. *Educational Psychology in Practice*, **3**, 1, 31–7. Reprinted by permission of the publishers.

A DESCRIPTION OF PAIRED READING

There have been many articles describing the use of the paired reading method (Heath, 1981; Bushell et al., 1982; Bush, 1983; Robson et al., 1984). They have given an account of the involvement of parents in aiding their children's reading development. The technique was devised by Morgan (1976) and was based on the use of two separate components. Firstly the simultaneous mode when parent and child read in synchrony. The child is required to attempt every word of the text, and the parent corrects all errors, the child repeating the corrections before continuing. The second component is the independent reading mode when the child reads alone receiving instruction and reinforcement from the parent when necessary. Paired reading requires parent and child to change over from the simultaneous mode to the independent mode by the child giving a signal such as knocking. When the child makes an error during the independent reading the correction is supplied after four seconds have elapsed. Then the simultaneous reading mode is resumed until the child signals to recommence independent reading. The complicated system of signalling and of providing positive reinforcement has been described in detail by Morgan (1976) and Morgan and Lyon (1979) and the reader is referred to these articles.

The advantages of paired reading

Paired reading has proved to be an effective method of involving some parents in helping their child's reading development. The method was specifically designed to overcome some of the difficulties parents may have when hearing their child read at home.

Morgan (1976) described the benefits of paired reading in some detail.

1. Paired reading was considered 'sufficiently simple to be used effectively by the child's own parents at home' (Morgan and Lyon, 1979). Parents could use the method effectively provided that they were given a number of training sessions and were also closely supervised throughout the project.
2. Paired reading provided the framework for a specific structured technique for parents to use. This had the advantage of reducing parental uncertainty and boosting confidence.
3. The use of positive reinforcement schedules to encourage correct responses helped prevent parents from making criticisms and giving other forms of negative feedback.

4. The termination of unsuccessful attempts after four seconds meant that the child was not allowed to experience failure.

A critique of the paired reading method

There are, however, several disadvantages inherent in the paired reading method.

1. Paired reading theory regards the independent reading mode as the main component of the technique. The aim is to use the simultaneous mode only for a brief time and to encourage child and parent to use the independent reading mode as soon as possible. This in practice has meant that the method is only 'suitable for those children who have a basic phonetic knowledge' (Carrick-Smith, 1982). When using the paired reading method it is not feasible to include inexperienced readers who have virtually non-existent skills. Yet it is these children who cause most concern because of their lack of progress.
2. Morgan argues that during independent reading 'no attention is made to the child's mistakes'. This conclusion is based on the argument that the correct use of the paired reading method prevents the parent from making negative comments. However, the parent stops the child, indicates the error, waits four seconds for self-correction, and then if necessary supplies the correction. The child then has to repeat the word. Parent and child then resume the simultaneous reading mode. Can this method really be described as paying no attention to mistakes? The child is still allowed to experience failure and the parent's role is still that of correcting mistakes. Certainly failure is minimized when using paired reading but it is not eliminated.
3. One of the important principles of paired reading is that children are free to choose their own books. However, in practice the use of the independent mode may have a limiting effect on the child's choice of book. It is more difficult for parents to listen to children reading from books that are at frustration level. Indeed, Morgan (1979), Carrick-Smith (1982) and Bushell et al. (1982) all found that many pairs had difficulty in using the independent mode appropriately.
4. In order to overcome difficulties in using the technique paired reading projects require frequent monitoring sessions. Morgan and Lyon (1979) concluded that three to four half-hour training sessions were needed for parents to learn the basics of the technique, 'although a longer training period would probably have been necessary were the parents not subsequently closely supervised at weekly intervals'.
5. The fact that paired reading requires a great deal of time to be spent on

project organization has limited the number of schools willing to run projects. Even in schools where paired reading has proved to be a successful technique, 'the reason most frequently quoted for not having adopted the paired reading technique as a general school policy was the time required for staff to make the scheme a success' (Robson et al., 1984). Griffiths and Hamilton (1984) thought that paired reading, although a valuable technique for children with persistent reading difficulties, could not have a wide application because of the intensive work involved when running projects. Dyson and Swinson (1982) took a similar view when deciding against using the paired reading method for their project.

6. Indeed, the majority of the projects reported in the literature have been organized and run by psychologists (Morgan, 1976; Heath, 1981; Bushell et al., 1982; Robson et al., 1984). Even when schools expressed a willingness to continue with paired reading, 'the transfer of responsibility for running such a project, from outside personnel to the school staff was seen to be a complicated procedure' (Robson et al., 1984). When projects have been organized by teachers there has been considerable input and advice from support services (Jungnitz et al., 1983). This has serious implications for hard-pressed support agencies.
7. The paired reading technique is consistently seen as a remedy for reading failure. This is valuable, but it ignores the fact that what is most needed is parental involvement with reading from the earliest years of schooling, so helping to prevent failure in the first place.

Although these difficulties inherent in using the paired reading method are related to the complexity of using the independent mode, the effectiveness of the simultaneous mode had been disregarded. Heath (1981), Morgan (1976) and Bushell et al. (1982) all agree that the simultaneous reading mode is an easy skill to acquire. However, they regard simultaneous reading purely as a stepping stone to the independent mode. It is our contention that they have consistently undervalued the significance of the simultaneous reading mode as a valid and powerful technique for aiding children's reading development. To clarify these issues it is helpful to compare shared reading with paired reading.

SHARED READING AND PAIRED READING: A COMPARISON OF THE METHODS

Morgan (1976) in his rationale of the paired reading method draws heavily upon behavioural learning theory and he hypothesized that the technique worked at two levels.

1. The first level was to provide a means for the child to acquire the correct responses when reading. This would occur during the simultaneous reading mode when the parent provided the appropriate model.
2. The second level was to provide a means of reinforcing the probable recurrence of those responses by the use of behavioural reinforcement procedures. The independent reading mode with the systematic use of positive verbal reinforcement was designed to provide this.

Bushell et al. (1982) concluded that the above description was an impoverished model which denied psycho-linguistic accounts of the nature of reading. They argued that the paired reading method enhanced the use of contextual cues and promoted semantic and syntactic prediction. But does this statement really apply to the independent reading mode, which is a rather disjointed procedure with the child frequently stopping because of errors and omissions? Heath (1981) proposed a different explanation as he thought that the effects of the use of positive reinforcement could not account for all the benefits of paired reading. He suspected that the child reading with the parent using the simultaneous reading mode 'was one of the most potent components of paired reading'. Morgan (1976) was unsure as to the relative importance of the simultaneous mode and the independent mode in the acquisition of reading skills. He concluded that 'the question of which components of the tuition package are effective remains open'.

Recent research by Scott (1983) found that paired reading produced some of its effects by improving children's usage of syntactic and semantic cues. Participating in simultaneous reading encouraged children to use textual cues and that this, coupled with the model pronunciation, intonation and rhythm provided by the parent, were important factors in improving reading. There is some tentative evidence to support the view that simultaneous reading is the effective component. Bushell et al. (1982) in their study found that children's reading improved after using simultaneous reading even when they had not progressed to using the independent mode.

Morgan's method of simultaneous reading is a rather disjointed procedure as the child has to attempt every word and parent and child stop to correct all errors. This procedure impedes the flow of reading and lessens the effectiveness of context-cueing strategies. The child is still allowed to experience failure when reading and the onus is put on the parent to correct all errors. Shared reading is, however, a continuous process that maximizes the advantages of modelling and enables the child to concentrate on the story. The method overcomes the disadvantages inherent in Morgan's simultaneous reading mode.

This simplified version of simultaneous reading was used by our colleagues in Stockton for their parental involvement project (Mottram, 1985). Their project had, however, been organized with regular home visits as an integral part of the project organization. Given the difficulties that this entails for class teachers, it was felt that an important feature of our pilot project would be to evaluate the effectiveness of the method when no home visits were made.

THE SHARED READING PROJECT

Stage 1. The pilot project

The aim of the pilot project was to investigate the effectiveness of using the shared reading method as a valid way of involving parents in their children's reading development. It was hypothesized that:

1. The use of the shared reading method would maximize the utilization of 'modelling', so aiding children's reading development.
2. The simplicity of the method meant that it was easy to acquire, therefore there would be no need for home visits to be made. Supervision and monitoring of the project could be kept to a minimum.
3. If provided with a suitable tuition package, class teachers would be able to run their own projects with parents.

The pilot project to investigate the effectiveness of shared reading was undertaken in a primary school during the autumn term in 1983. The project was confined to children who were in the second form of the junior department. Eight children took part in the project, and all were receiving regular tuition from the peripatetic remedial teacher who visited the school each week. The children were selected for the project because of their poor reading levels. In view of the fact that this was a pilot project only those children whose parents were supportive were included (Spenceley, 1985).

The parents were invited to the initial meeting where they were shown a video film demonstrating shared reading. They were asked to read with their child for at least ten minutes a night, six nights a week for eight weeks. The parents were told that their children would bring books of their own choice to read at home. They were also told that their child had practised shared reading with the teacher and knew how to use the method. Parents were told that if they had any problems they should visit the school to discuss them. Because this was a pilot project the parents were asked to attend an interim meeting, which was held two weeks after the initial meeting. This was held to see how the project was progressing and to deal with any difficulties that may have arisen. The parents reported that they and their children enjoyed reading this way and that there were no problems (Greening and Spenceley, 1984a).

Results of the pilot project

The eight children in the project were tested at the beginning and at the end of the project on the Holborn Reading Test. The results are given in Table 2.1.

Table 2.1 Results of the pilot project

N=8	*CA (years) at start of project*	*Pre-project RA (years)*	*Post-project RA (years)*	*RA gains (in months)*
S1	8.10	6.00	7.06	18
S2	8.03	6.00	6.06	6
S3	8.04	6.09	7.06	9
S4	8.05	6.06	7.06	12
S5	8.04	6.09	7.06	9
S6	8.08	6.06	7.09	15
S7	8.05	6.09	7.06	9
S8	8.08	6.03	7.06	15
Mean	8.48 (yrs)	6.43 (yrs)	7.40 (yrs)	11.62 (mths)
				SD = 4.06

All the children made gains in their reading ages. The Holborn Test was used at the beginning and end of the project to test the children and there may have been a practice effect. This would not, however, fully account for the reading age gains that the children made. The teachers reported that the children read much more fluently, used contextual cues and had more regard for punctuation. Parents and teachers reported that the children's attitude to reading and to books was much more positive.[1]

The results of the pilot project were encouraging and demonstrated that shared reading was an effective technique for aiding children's reading development. Seven parents were interviewed at the end of the project in order to obtain their views on shared reading. The parents were enthusiastic saying that they and their children had enjoyed reading the books and that they thought that shared reading was an effective way of helping their children.

One interesting development that resulted from this feedback was the realization that the parents did not view shared reading as a remedial technique but thought it a good way of helping younger children. Most of the parents commented that they wished they had been shown the method when their child started school as subsequent reading difficulties may then have been avoided. This caused us to reconsider our assumption that shared reading was a remedial technique and to view it as a valid method for helping many children including beginning readers. It was decided to run a shared reading project in an infant school to assess the effectiveness of the method with young children.

Stage 2. The infant project

This project was undertaken in the spring term 1984 and ten children were included in the sample (Greening and Spenceley, 1984b). The project lasted five weeks and the parents were asked to read with their child for ten minutes a day, six days a week. The parents had the shared reading method demonstrated to them at the initial meeting. There were no home visits and there was no interim meeting. At the end of the project the parents were invited into the school to give their views.

Results of the infant project

The children were tested at the beginning and end of the project on different forms of the Salford Reading Test. Only five children scored on the pre-project test so only these gains could be effectively measured. The results appear in Table 2.2.

Table 2.2 Results of the infant project

S	*CA at start of project (years)*	*Pre-project RA (years)*	*Post-project RA (years)*	*RA gains (months)*
1	6.04	no score	no score	–
2	6.03	no score	7.02	–
3	5.03	no score	6.04	–
4	5.08	no score	no score	–
5	6.04	no score	6.02	–
6	5.10	6.02	7.00	10
7	7.00	6.00	6.11	11
8	6.05	6.02	7.00	10
9	6.08	6.01	7.00	11
10	6.07	6.02	6.07	5
Mean	6.51(yrs) (N = 5)	6.11(yrs) (N = 5)	6.90(yrs) (N = 5)	9.4(mths) (N = 5)
				SD = 2.50

These results have to be viewed with caution as this was a very small sample. The children included in the sample were selected because it was thought that their parents would be supportive to the project.

Changes in the reading strategies of the children

The main difference noted was that by the end of the five-week project all the children were using context and picture cues. An example of this was provided by the children's reading behaviour when assessed on the Salford Reading Test. When the pre-project test was carried out, all ten children read word for word. After the project was completed, they read expecting a sentence to make sense and used context-cueing strategies.

Response of the parents

At the end of the project parents were invited into school to discuss their views. Eight mothers were able to attend the meeting and all reported that they found shared reading from books of the child's choice to be an interesting and enjoyable way for them to help their child's reading development. Some commented that it had enabled them to form a closer relationship with their child.

All the mothers and children wished to continue to read together using the shared reading method. In the school where the infant project was piloted shared reading has now become an integral part of its language development policy.

Stage 3. Extending shared reading in Cleveland county

Other schools within Cleveland county became interested in organizing their own shared reading project. A new video tape and teachers' manual was produced in August 1984 and many schools in the area began to organize their own projects.

Results of the project stage 3

Data were obtained from nine primary schools in the area. The sample consisted of 107 children throughout the primary age range. These included some beginning readers, children with poor reading attainment and some who had severe and long-standing reading difficulties. All the projects ran for eight weeks and parents were asked to read for at least ten minutes a night for six nights a week whilst the project lasted. Parents were introduced to the method by viewing the video tape in school at an initial meeting. Home visits were not undertaken. Parents were asked to contact the school if they had problems; however, schools reported few difficulties. In one school children whose parents did not take part in the project were helped in school by adult volunteers. All the children in the sample were tested before and after the project on different forms of the Salford Reading Test. Table 2.3 shows the results.

Table 2.3 Results of stage 3

N= *107*	*CA at start of project (years)*	*Pre-project RA (years)*	*Post-project RA (years)*	*RA gains (months)*
Mean	8.27	7.48	7.98	6.00
				SD = 4.12

The range of reading age gains varied from no observable gain in six cases to a maximum reading age gain of twenty-four months. Of the sample 20.5 per cent made reading age gains of nine months or more. Feedback from the schools emphasized that many children showed an improved attitude to reading and this often generalized to increased motivation in school. The children were more enthusiastic and discriminating in their choice of books. They were also more confident and fluent readers. Improvements in attitude and fluency were observed even in children who made minimal reading age gains during the project. A high degree of satisfaction with the shared reading method was reported by children, parents and teachers. Class teachers were pleased with the shared reading package and found project organization economical in terms of time.

Shared reading has proved to be an effective method of aiding children's reading development. The results obtained during the three stages of the Cleveland Project compare favourably with the results reported in the research literature on paired reading; Morgan (1976); Heath (1981); Bushell et al. (1982); Robson et al. (1984). If the results in terms of reading age gains are similar, what then are the advantages of using the shared reading technique?

ADVANTAGES OF USING SHARED READING

1. Shared reading has been found to be a successful technique for home reading because it is supportive to the child and easy for the parent to operate. It eliminates stress because neither child nor parent experiences failure and both can derive interest and pleasure from the activity.
2. Children learn practical and social skills through their participation in

family life. Shared reading should be viewed as one of many activities which parents and children enjoy together. Parents have found that shared reading provides an emotionally rewarding experience which fosters closer relationships.

3. Shared reading must not be seen as a substitute for parents reading *to* their children. Rather, it is a transitional stage between hearing a story read and becoming a fluent independent reader. Shared reading is a technique which can be used whenever children find the text too difficult to manage on their own, whether this is at the beginning stages of reading or later.
4. When taking part in shared reading, the parent provides the child with an instant and effective model. The child's attention is focused on the printed word by active participation in the reading activity. The significance of phonic cues and punctuation marks is learnt in a natural way. Also, the child acquires the habit of reading for meaning, becoming familiar with the stresses and rhythms of the written word and using context cues effectively.
5. Shared reading provides children with the opportunity to read any books they choose, even those which they might otherwise find too hard. This freedom of choice is in itself highly motivating and enriches children's reading experience by enabling them to tackle reading material centred on their own interests rather than that which is dictated by their own independent reading level.
6. Children's reading levels have been raised as a result of involvement in shared reading projects. More important, attitudes to books have improved and motivation to read has increased. This positive response to reading has, with many children, generalized to an improved attitude to school, and to the work expected of them in class.
7. Class teachers are finding that shared reading projects are simple to organize as they require little professional time spent in initial training sessions, and subsequent monitoring is kept to a minimum (Greening and Spenceley, 1985).
8. The responsibility for organizing and running shared reading projects is placed firmly with the school. Teachers can, provided they have the necessary enthusiasm and commitment to follow the guidelines outlined in the Teachers' Manual, run their own successful projects on shared reading.

NOTE

1. It was felt that comparison between shared reading and other methods of parental involvement with reading should take account of factors other than

improved reading attainment. These would include attitudes to books, fluency, reading comprehension and motivation to read. Rigorous evaluation of these factors was outside the scope of the present investigation.

TOPICS FOR DISCUSSION

1. In what ways does 'shared reading' differ substantially from 'paired reading'? Critically evaluate the evidence the authors offer to suggest the superiority of one method over the other.
2. Discuss the specific difficulties which *parents* might have in using the 'paired reading' method with their children.
3. 'Shared reading must not be seen as a substitute for parents reading *to* their children. Rather, it is a transitional stage between hearing a story read and becoming a fluent independent reader.' Discuss.

SUGGESTIONS FOR FURTHER READING

1. Swinson, J.M. (1986) 'Paired reading: a critique'. *Support for Learning*, **1**, 2, 29-32.

After reviewing various approaches which have been adopted to involve parents in their children's reading (from encouraging parents to listen to their children read in a traditional fashion, that is, by helping the child to analyse unknown words and correcting mistakes, to the adoption of precision teaching approaches such as 'paired reading') the author concerns himself not so much with making comparisons of the efficacy of these alternative approaches, but rather with more fundamental questions. Specifically, Swinson considers whether or not the success of the various projects is a reflection not necessarily of the differing approaches employed, but of the common denominator involved, namely the involvement of parents. He makes the point that at the moment there is no *conclusive* evidence as to the superiority of one method of listening to children read as opposed to another. Thus, he claims, three recent studies which have attempted to compare the effectiveness of paired reading with a traditional listening approach have failed to find any significant difference between the two methods.

Summarizing recent research evidence, Swinson concludes that in general it would appear that the gains made by individual children vary with:

(a) the degree of the child's reading delay - thus, children with greater delay make the least progress;

(b) the age at which the parental involvement is encouraged - thus, one research programme found children in their top infant and first two years of junior school made substantially larger gains than those in their last two years of junior education;

(c) the length of any project, longer projects showing greater gains in terms of total reading age improvement (p. 29).

In a later section of the paper the author summarizes the arguments for 'paired reading' and discusses some of the criticisms levelled against this approach, noting that his criticisms of the paired reading approach 'are not criticisms of the technique itself, but rather of its blanket application in all settings' (p. 31). Swinson examines the numerous advantages which he claims there are for encouraging parents to listen to their children read using conventional approaches. For example, he argues, the 'conventional' approach is one in which primary school teachers are already experts and which they would find easy to train parents to do, and that if a traditional approach is adopted the school is not dependent on the availability of an expert. Furthermore, the traditional approach is probably the method of which most parents are already aware and the one which they may have used in the past. Swinson writes that the traditional approach can be used over a long period of time without loss of enthusiasm or support and that it has the value of consistency, so that if the same method is used at both school and home there is not only a greater sense of common purpose but also less possibility for confusion or misunderstanding on the child's part (p. 31). In short, the author suggests 'there would appear to be no unequivocal evidence that any one approach to encouraging children to read, paired reading or traditional listening, is more effective', and that the benefits of using the traditional form of intervention 'have been shown to be every bit as effective as any alternative approach, including paired reading. For these reasons, the traditional approach appears to be the one that teachers should encourage parents to adopt' (p. 32).

2. Hannon, P. and Tizard, B. (1987) 'Parent involvement - a no-score draw?'. *The Times Educational Supplement*, 3 April, p.21.

In the first section of the article Hannon argues that the debate on parental involvement in reading is strong on conviction but weak on evidence. Earlier misgivings on the value of parental involvement have been overlaid 'by a new orthodoxy which holds that to involve parents is a sure way to boost children's reading. By "reading" is usually meant their scores on certain kinds of tests.' The most extravagant claims, Hannon suggests, have been made in the case of 'paired reading' techniques, but even more traditional and straightforward approaches in which parents simply listen to their children reading a school book at home have often been over-sold. As a result, the author claims, no matter how cautiously researchers express their conclusions and findings 'they are [often] quickly seized upon, simplified, distorted and somehow absorbed into the orthodoxy'. As an example, Hannon cites his examination of reading-test scores in one part of the Belfield Reading Project where he found that more than seventy children who had completed the project obtained scores hardly any better than the reading-test scores of comparable children who had passed through the school before parents had been involved. This finding, he suggests, demonstrates the misconception that parental involvement invariably 'raises' test scores. In the Belfield project the results of testing suggested that there might have been slight gains for children in the project, but that the gains were too small to be statistically significant. Hannon discusses this finding with reference to the research of Tizard, Schofield and Hewison (1982) in the Haringey project where, in a very carefully designed experiment, the authors reported susbstantial test gains for the children who took part in the project. Their research, Hannon claims, is almost the only evidence we have that large test gains can be produced by involving parents, again demonstrating that the research base for parental involvement is not anything like as extensive as is popularly believed. Hannon attempts an explanation for the different findings which have emerged, suggesting that three 'explanations' are particularly plausible. The first is concerned with the effects of home visiting, which figured in both projects but was better resourced and probably more intensive in the Haringey project. Second, the author suggests, 'the effects of parental involvement depend upon what it is being compared to, and it is at least conceivable that there was less scope for improvement in control groups at Belfield (where there was certainly some pre-existing parental involvement) than at Haringey where there might have been less'. A third possibility is that improved school practice towards parents in the form of close collaboration and the supply of reading books for children may be particularly valuable for ethnic minority families who constituted a larger proportion at Haringey than at Belfield. Hannon writes that reading tests measure something more than reading ability and that this 'extra' something may be cultural understanding. It follows, therefore, that even if children's reading improves, their test scores might not, and that we need to be critical about the way in which reading is to be assessed and to be readier than we have been to develop more appropriate forms of assessment. Thus, aspects of involvement such as home–school communications and how parents hear their children read can be examined against our expectations of good practice. In a later section of the article Barbara Tizard discusses the Haringey project and findings as well as a recent study in thirty-two infant schools, where the researchers found that it was rarely possible to speak of a *school's* parental involvement policy since practices varied so much from year to year. Furthermore, the team found that irrespective of the school or teachers' policies, parents gave their children similar amounts of help. The frequency of help given by parents did not depend on the teachers' parental involvement policy. Tizard suggests that parental help with reading succeeds only if it is part of a carefully planned approach. Thus, sending reading books home with all children at frequent intervals and establishing regular and productive communication systems with parents demand a high level of organizational efficiency on the part of the teacher. Similarly, progress and improvement cannot be expected unless the parents are involved in helping the child to move to more advanced reading, and unless extra staff are available to support the teacher and the parent. Without this extra support, the author suggests, some teachers may in fact devote less time than before to reading, believing that the task can be largely left to parents. Tizard reports that her team found evidence that little time in school was spent on reading – in top infant classes only 2 to 3 per cent of the school day was spent by the children in *any* form of reading.

3. Russell, P. (1985) 'Portage – partnership with parents', in Daly, B., Addington, J., Kerfoot, S. and Sigston, A. (eds) *Portage: The Importance to Parents*. Windsor, NFER-Nelson, pp. 17–27.

In this reading Russell describes the evolution of home visiting services, discusses questions to do with parent motivation and the advantages of parental involvement on infant development and gives consideration to the place of Portage in this important area of parental participation, particularly in the light of recent changes and developments in the field of special educational needs. The author affirms that recent developments in home visiting in this country have seen a twofold thrust.

1. Educational home visiting, which is aimed at linking the parent and the child to a *school-based* service, that is, preparation for the child's formal education.
2. Voluntary schemes, which are often linked with education services but frequently are more involved in *self-help* and general support and counselling.

Russell discusses factors involved in the successful development and maintenance of parental motivation and considers the effect of parent support on the developing child. In addressing herself to the question 'Why Portage?' (as opposed to other models of intervention) Russell argues that the strengths of Portage are that:

1. It *must* utilize what the parents already know.
2. It *must* involve a caring and trained home visitor who is able to link back to a wider network of professionals.
3. It is a *private* service in that it can proceed in a venue chosen by the parents.
4. The parents can select priorities for the children, which are compatible with their own life-styles. Thus, for example, parents with a child who presents difficulties in terms of *behaviour* problems may rightly see the resolution of these problems as being a more immediately important goal than helping the child to achieve educational goals in terms of cognitive development.
5. Portage allows the actual level of parental involvement to be matched to individual family dynamics and circumstances. Depressed mothers living in socially debilitating circumstances and beset with marital problems are unlikely to be able to participate as actively as more fortunate couples living in good home environments who are enthusiastic towards the idea of working with their child (p. 23).

In the later sections of the reading the author examines some of the criticisms, or questioning, of the Portage model and its applications, claiming that 'many criticisms reflect, probably correctly, some of the earlier relatively ill-considered and rigid applications of the approach. Portage cannot exist in a vacuum. A specific task-orientated curriculum must be put in the broader context of parents' and other needs and must be backed by general supportive services' (p. 24).

For a recent comprehensive review of research, see Sturmey, P. and Crisp, A.G. (1986) 'Portage guide to early education: a review of research'. *Educational Psychology*, **6**, 139–57.

REFERENCES

Bush, A. (1983) 'Can pupils' reading be improved by involving their parents?'. *Remedial Education*, **18**, 4.

Bushell, R., Miller, A. and Robson, D. (1982) 'Parents as remedial teachers'. *AEP Journal*, **5**, 9.

Carrick-Smith, L. (1982) 'An investigation into the effectiveness of paired reading'. Unpublished thesis, University of Sheffield.

Dyson, J. and Swinson, J. (1982) 'Involving parents in the teaching of reading'. *AEP Journal*, **5**, 9.

Greening, M. and Spenceley, J. (1984a) 'Paired reading made easy'. *InPsych*, **11**, 1. (*InPsych* is the bulletin of the Cleveland County Psychological Service.)

Greening, M. and Spenceley, J. (1984b) 'Shared reading: a review of the Cleveland Project'. *InPsych*, **11**, 1.

Greening, M. and Spenceley, J. (1985) 'Shared reading'. *DECP Newsletter*, 17, March.

Griffiths, A. and Hamilton, D. (1984) *Parent, Teacher, Child*. Methuen, London.

Hannon, P. and Jackson, A. (1987) *The Belfield Reading Project Final Report*. London, National Children's Bureau.

Heath, A. (1981) 'A paired reading programme'. *Edition 2 ILEA School Psychological Service*.

Jungnitz, G., Olive, S. and Topping, K.J. (1983) 'The development and evaluation of a paired reading project'. *Journal of Community Education*, **2**, 4.
Morgan, R. (1976) 'Paired reading tuition: a preliminary report on a technique for cases of reading deficit'. *Child Care Health and Development*, **2**, 13-28.
Morgan, R. and Lyon, E. (1979) 'Paired reading: a preliminary report on a technique for parental tuition of reading retarded children'. *Journal of Child Psychology and Psychiatry*, 20.
Mottram, L. (1985) 'Paired reading'. *Cleveland Learning Support Service Newsletter*, **1**.
Robson, D., Miller, S. and Bushell, R. (1984) 'The development of paired reading in High Peak and West Derbyshire'. *Remedial Education*, **19**, 4.
Scott, J. (1983) 'Process evaluation of paired reading'. *DECP Occasional Papers*, **7**, 1.
Spenceley, J.M. (1985) 'Shared reading: a report on a successful project with parental involvement'. *Cleveland Learning Support Service Newsletter*, **1**.
Tizard, J., Schofield, B. and Hewison, J. (1982) 'Collaboration between teachers and parents in assisting children's reading'. *British Journal of Educational Psychology*, **52**, 1-15.

Reading 3

LEARNING AT HOME: LIVING AND TALKING TOGETHER

B. Tizard and M. Hughes

Earlier we showed how some mothers turned play, games and stories to educational advantage, while a few gave their children formal 'lessons'. But in most families these occasions were relatively rare. A few mothers devoted most of the afternoon to the child, but generally they had housework to do or younger children to care for. In their free moments they often preferred to drink coffee and smoke, while chatting to their child, rather than play with her.

This did not mean that the children were missing out on learning opportunities. One of our strongest impressions from this study was of the amount which children learnt from simply being around with their mothers: discussing what each was doing, or had done, what they would do next, arguing with each other and, above all, endlessly asking and

Tizard, B. and Hughes, M. (1984) 'Learning at home: living and talking together', in *Young Children Learning: Talking and Thinking at Home and at School*. London, Fontana, chap. 4, pp. 73-101. Reprinted by permission of Collins Publishers.

answering questions. In this chapter we will describe some of these contexts of everyday life, and discuss what the children were learning in them.

AN EVERYDAY LEARNING CONTEXT: MAKING A SHOPPING LIST

Making a shopping list is a good illustration of the learning potentialities of an ordinary household event. In the example we quote below, Pauline and her mother had been drinking coffee, and intermittently discussing what shopping was needed. Pauline's mother picked up her shopping list, and started to alter it and add it up. She certainly did not embark on this activity for educational reasons, but she did use the occasion to try to get over to Pauline the message that the contents of a shopping list have to be related to the amount of money available. Pauline was initially curious about what her mother was writing, and assumed it was a note to their friend and neighbour, Irene, who lived upstairs:

Child: What you gonna write? Irene?
Mother: No.
Child: Who?
Mother: Adding up.
Child: Padding up?
Mother: To see how much my shopping comes to.
Child: Packing up?
Mother: Adding up.
Child: I think you said 'padding up'.

Later Irene called round and offered to do some shopping for her in the local Vivo's. The offer was accepted. Irene left, and Pauline's mother started to cross off from her shopping list the items Irene was going to buy for them:

Mother: We've only got that little bit of shopping to get now [shows Pauline the list].
Child: Mummy? Can I have one of them drinks? Can I?
Mother: Get some more drink?
Child: Yeah. Can write it down on there [points to where she wants it written on the list]. Up here.
Mother: I'll get you some when I go tomorrow.
Child: Aw! [Disappointed]
Mother: All right? 'Cause I'm not getting it today.
Child: No . . . In the Vivo's?

Mother: Haven't got Daddy's money yet.
Child: *I've* got no money.

Pauline seems to have misheard her mother at this point. Her mother corrects her:

Mother: No, I haven't got enough to get my shopping. All of it.
Child: Not all of it?
Mother: Irene's just taken five pounds. She'll bring some change back. If she's got some, she'll bring some change back. It's not enough to get all that. Is it? [Points to the shopping list]
Child: No.
Mother: See? So when Daddy gets paid I'll get some more money and then I'll go and get the rest.
Child: Yeah. That's nice, isn't it, Mum?
Mother: Mm . . . I got one, two, three, four, five, six, seven, eight, nine, ten, eleven, twelve [counts items on list].
Child: [Joins in counting] Nine, ten, eleven.
Mother: Fourteen, fifteen, sixteen, seventeen, eighteen bits.
Child: Mum, let's have a look! [Mother shows child the list] Do it again.
Mother: We gotta get rice, tea, braising steak, cheese, pickle, carrots, fish, chicken, bread, eggs, bacon, beefburgers, beans . . . Oh, Irene's gone to get them [crosses off beans] . . . peas, ham, corned beef.
Child: And what's that [points to a word on the list]?
Mother: That's lemon drink [crosses off 'lemon drink']. She's just gone down to get that one. See?

What might Pauline have learned from this conversation? If asked, her mother would probably have singled out the counting activity; when interviewed later, she mentioned that she was teaching Pauline to count. But a great deal more information than this was transmitted. Pauline was learning some basic facts about shopping - for example that planning and foresight are involved and that making a written list is a useful way of organizing this. She was learning that the number of items that can be bought has to be balanced against the money available, and that this in turn may depend upon whether the wage-earner in the family has been paid yet that week. She might even have acquired some idea of what can be bought for a sum like five pounds. In a wider sense, she was learning how women often support each other, and that she and her mother were financially dependent on her father.

What may be less obvious is that Pauline was also acquiring some important knowledge about the nature of written language. It is often suggested that working-class children do not have much experience of their parents engaging in 'literate' activities; yet a shopping list provides an extremely vivid demonstration of the way in which written language may be used within a meaningful human activity. The power of the written word lies in its ability to link up different contexts in space or time, and here it is doing precisely that - forming a link between the home, where the decisions and choices are made, and the shop, where they are carried out. The list can also cope with sudden changes of plan - a friend offering to do some of the shopping leads to some items being crossed off the list. The activity is thus not only emotionally but intellectually more powerful than the labelling of pictures, which is likely to be Pauline's introduction to writing when she starts at infant school. It is not clear from the conversation how much Pauline understood about the nature of written language, but her comments suggest she had a good idea of the basic properties and functions of a list.

LOOKING OUT OF THE WINDOW

Seeing something novel out of the window was a situation which often created an educational exchange. It was not simply that the child was given some new information about what she saw, but that her intellectual horizons were at times extended in unexpected ways. [. . .] The following [. . .] conversation illustrates how a casual conversation about a neighbour could affect the child's thinking.

Susan and her mother were looking out of the window when they saw a man arriving at the house next door:

Child: What has he got a bag on his back for?
Mother: He drives a motorbike. He can't carry it. Needs two hands to steer the bike. [Child laughs]
Child: Is he gonna do it?
Mother: He's just come home from work. It's Dick's lodger. [Dick is the next-door neighbour]
Child: What?
Mother: The man who lives upstairs in Dick's house. The one that you woke up in the middle of the night when you made a noise.
Child: What?
Mother: The one that lives in the room next door to your bedroom.
Child: Does he wake up?
Mother: He can hear you when you make a lot of noise.
Child: What did he say?

Mother: Should think he gets a bit angry.
Child: Not gonna scream.
Mother: You're not gonna scream. I should hope not.

During this conversation Susan has been told, and appears to have assimilated, not simply information about who lives next door, but also that the neighbour's room is in fact adjacent to hers, and that her activities impinge on and annoy him. Information of this kind helps the child to understand her social environment. It may also have more far-reaching implications for her intellectual development. By explaining the way in which the child's activity affects someone of whose existence she had not even known, the mother is helping the child to overcome her 'egocentrism'. [. . .] We [have] found a number of examples of children not yet four who could undoubtedly take another's point of view. Conversations like the one above were probably an important factor in helping this ability to develop.

LIVING WITH BABIES

Nearly half the girls in our study had a younger brother or sister. Often the baby was awake and active for part of the afternoon's recording. The learning situations that this afforded varied from one family to another.

Pauline's mother spent a good deal of time looking after and entertaining the baby. Pauline seemed very fond of her little sister, Ruthie, and was quite happy to spend a lot of time helping her mother. As a result, she was exposed in the course of the afternoon to a rich stream of information and advice about looking after a baby.

Much of this information took the form of a running commentary on the baby's needs and how to meet them. At the very start of the session Pauline's mother was unable to feed the baby because she was crying: 'She's crying so much she don't want any.' Pauline was sent off to get the baby's bottle, and this instantly stopped her crying: 'See how she stopped? Thirsty.' Ruthie finished the bottle and this was pointed out to Pauline: 'Look at that. She's drunk all that now. She *was* thirsty.' Pauline was then shown how to hold the baby, and how to give her a biscuit, and her mother explained how biscuits help teething. Later Pauline helped her mother when the baby's nappy was changed. She fetched a clean nappy, and cream for the baby's bottom, and she was allowed to put cream and then powder on the baby. Finally, she was allowed to give the baby another bottle as she was settled down.

Although not yet four, Pauline was given more information about baby care, and more responsibility for helping with the baby, than many professionals would consider giving to much older children.

None of the other children with babies was so closely involved in their care. Some mothers encouraged the girls to give maternal care to their dolls while they looked after the baby. Others tried to divide their own attention between the older child and the baby. Nevertheless, the presence of the baby inevitably widened the children's horizons. Beth, for example, learned that doctors not only appear when you are ill, but also give babies developmental health check-ups. While at lunch, her mother told her:

Mother: I saw Dr Jones this morning. I took Naomi to see him now that she is one, if she was all right. If she's a nice healthy baby.
Child: And what did the doc, and what did Dr Jones say?
Mother: He said that she was *very* well. Except that she's still got her funny snuffly breathing. He said that would just disappear after a while.
Child: But what, what did you say to him?
Mother: I said I thought she was . . . she seemed very well.

Several mothers used the baby's presence to bring home to the children an understanding that they had once been babies, too. Erica laughed as her baby brother ate with his fingers, and her mother said, 'You used to eat like that when you were a baby. You used to eat chocolate blancmange with your fingers.' Their mothers often interpreted the baby's behaviour – 'I think he wants to get down' – and the children themselves projected into the baby's mind: 'Mummy, I think she wants to go into the garden', 'I don't think he wants any more to eat.'

With the exception of Pauline, who seemed to have entirely taken on a maternal role, the children were ambivalent in their attitude to the babies. At times they played and talked to them lovingly, while at other times they snatched their food and toys, teased and expressed resentment. Mina was the most intensely jealous of the children. At one point in the afternoon, when asked what she would like for her birthday, she replied, 'I'd like Tessa [the baby] put back inside your tummy.' She frequently made fun of Tessa, and although she did not attack her, she did express a death-wish towards another baby:

Mother: You know Phil and Nora? That came round? And she had a baby in her tummy?
Child: Mm.
Mother: Well, it came out yesterday, and she had a little boy!
Child: Oh! Are they gonna come round?
Mother: No, not for a little while yet, I shouldn't think.

Child: Why? Is it gonna die?
Mother: Why should it die?
Child: 'Cause I want it to die. I do.

Mina's mother naturally got very upset by this remark:

Mother: Don't be horrible! What a nasty thing to say! Supposing someone said to you that they'd like Tessa to die, you'd be really sad, wouldn't you? Phil and Nora love their new baby and they'd be ever so sad if they thought you were saying that. Don't really mean it, do you? [Mina shakes her head and changes the subject]

Her mother's comments suggest that she did not realize, or was unwilling to acknowledge, the full force of Mina's angry feelings towards Tessa. Mina herself clearly thought that the baby must reciprocate them. On one occasion Tessa reached out towards Mina:

Mother: She's saying, 'Let me feel your face.'
Child: 'Let me scratch your chin', she's saying.

Mina's mother tried to foster a more friendly attitude in Mina by explaining about the vulnerability of babies and encouraging Mina to put herself in the baby's place. For example, Mina laughed when the baby cried, and her mother said, 'I really don't like to see children laugh when someone is sad, that's not nice. If I were to laugh at you when you were sad you'd be *really* annoyed. And little Tessa can't say, "Don't laugh at me Mina." ' Another strategy of Mina's mother was to point out aspects of the baby's behaviour which might interest her, especially developmental trends ('Have you noticed she's beginning to pick things up?'). What she did *not* do was to involve Mina in the care of the baby.

Thus the mere presence of a baby in the house did not mean that children would have similar learning experiences. While Pauline was virtually serving an apprenticeship in motherhood, for Mina the presence of the baby involved many discussions about kindness and about other people's points of view. We cannot, of course, tell whether Pauline's more loving relationship with her sister was the cause or the result of her involvement in baby care. However, Judy Dunn, in a study of relationships between siblings, found that those children who were encouraged to take a real and practical part in caring for their baby brothers and sisters from the first weeks of their life were particularly interested in, and affectionate towards, them. She also found that this early good relationship tended to persist over a six-year period (Dunn, 1983).

DISCUSSING PAST AND FUTURE EVENTS

One particularly important feature of the home as a learning environment is the fact that mother and child have a wealth of shared experience to draw on in their conversation. For the most part, this is concerned with events which they have shared together in the past. Often, however, it extended into planned trips or outings in the future – as in Rosy's family holiday in France.

The next conversation that we discuss is of particular interest because of the sensitive way in which the mother responds to the child's puzzling over a past event. Joyce is having a sandwich for her lunch, while her mother makes a cup of tea and then starts to prepare the evening meal. The conversation was complex and, after quoting it, we will analyse it in some detail:

1. Child: Mum, it was good to have something to eat while you was at the seaside, wasn't it? [Mother cuts sandwich]
2. Mother: Was good, I agree.
3. Child: Well some people don't have something to eat at the seaside.
4. Mother: What do they do then? Go without?
5. Child: Mm.
6. Mother: I think you'd have to have something to eat. [Kettle boils and mother makes tea]
7. Child: Yeah, otherwise you'd be [unclear] won't you?
8. Mother: Mmmm. When we go to David's school we'll have to take something to eat. We go on the coach that time. [Joyce and her mother are going on an outing with older child's school]
9. Child: Mmm. To the seaside?
10. Mother: Mmm. Probably go for a little stroll to the seaside.
11. Child: Mmm? Yes, I still hungry.
12. Mother: When?
13. Child: When we was at the seaside wasn't I?
14. Mother: We weren't. We had sandwiches, we had apples.
15. Child: But we, but when we was there we were still hungry wasn't we?
16. Mother: No, you had breakfast didn't you?
17. Child: But, we were thirsty when we got there.
18. Mother: Yes, suppose so, yeah we were.
19. Child: What happened? We wasn't thirsty or hungry.
20. Mother: Why weren't we? What happened?

21. Child: Well, all that thirsty went away.
22. Mother: Did it?
23. Child: Mmmm.

This conversation illustrates both the limitation of Joyce's ability to express herself, and the way in which she struggles to express complex ideas despite these limitations. In this she has varying degrees of success. In the first part of the conversation (turns 1–7) she is able to bring out and contrast two separate but related facts: (1) that it was good to have something to eat at the seaside, and (2) that other people didn't have something to eat. These two statements can even be seen as the premises of a logical argument, with the implication being (3) so what do other people do? We will never know if Joyce would have made this step by herself, for her mother makes it for her (turn 4). Later on in the conversation, however, Joyce is less successful in conveying her meaning, despite her mother's attempts to help her (turns 11–23). All the same, one can only admire Joyce's persistence as she struggles to express herself, culminating in the delightful creation in turn 21: 'all that thirsty went away'.

We do not know what prompted this conversation, although it is likely that eating a sandwich in the kitchen reminded Joyce of eating sandwiches at the seaside. For whatever reason the puzzlement arose, the situation allowed her to express it. Joyce and her mother were together in the kitchen, both engaged in their different activities, with time and space for Joyce's musings to be expressed and allowed to develop.

Her mother plays an important role in the conversation. By her support and responsiveness she helps Joyce express her meaning, and follow through some of the implications of what she is saying. Throughout, the mother is sensitive to what Joyce is trying to say: indeed, at one point (turn 12) she shows considerable insight into her daughter's meaning. On the previous turn Joyce has said 'I still hungry', a remark which would seem ostensibly to refer to the present situation in the kitchen: Joyce is, after all, eating her lunch. Yet there is an alternative possibility - that she is still referring to the picnic - and her mother somehow picks up this ambiguity and attempts to clarify it in turn 12. As it turns out, the child *was* still thinking about the picnic, and for the next few turns Joyce's mother tries, albeit unsuccessfully, to discover what is still puzzling the child.

The mother's role, however, is not just a responsive one. In turns 8 and 10 she introduces some new material into the conversation, telling Joyce about a planned trip to the seaside with her brother's school. This information is not of immediate relevance to the child's concern, and it is possible that she sees it as an unwelcome intrusion. The point about this new information, however, is the way it is linked to what has gone before. Through the common elements of 'picnics' and 'seaside' the mother and child are able to link a past event with a future event, thus enabling the shared world of common experience to act as a backcloth to their conversations. The creation of and referral to a shared world is a typical feature of many conversations between mother and child, and we believe that it is of fundamental importance. As we show later, the lack of a shared world between staff and child at school constitutes a considerable barrier to communication.

In the following conversation, Cathie, a much more articulate child, relives a shared past experience with her mother. Cathie is not struggling with an intellectual problem, as Joyce was: the conversation serves rather as an emotional link between mother and daughter, and it also allows Cathie to talk through again what was clearly a frightening experience. The conversation occurs when a trailer comes on TV for the Walt Disney film *The Treasures of Mate Cumbe*. This happened to be a film that Cathie and her mother had already seen at the cinema:

Child: Look, it's *The Treasure of Acka Coombie* [sic].
Mother: Oh, I remember, do you remember it? When they're just about to find the treasure?
Child: Yes . . . but we went with Harriet and Irene.
Mother: That's right. Do you remember this bloke in the storm?
Child: Yes . . . and you thought he was dead, he was drowned, didn't we?
Mother: We thought he was drowned, didn't we?
Child: Mmmm.
Mother: And then he comes back at the end. Do you remember?
Child: Mm . . . he had blood on his arms and all over his face, didn't he?
Mother: Not as much as that, did he? He just had some bruises and a few scratches . . . do you remember? Then he was all right and they all got home safely.
Child: Mm.
Mother: That was a very frightening scene, wasn't it?
Child: Mm.
Mother: Very scary.
Child: And they're only people dressed up with masks and arrows.
Mother: Yes, they were, weren't they?
Child: Pretend arrows.
Mother: Yes.

Child: And bows, arrows and bows, bows and arrows. That one's called Davy, isn't it?
Mother: Yes it is, that's Davy, and he suddenly falls down the pit, doesn't he?
Child: Mm.
Mother: That was exciting, wasn't it?

The excerpt from the film ends, but Cathie and her mother carry on discussing what had obviously been a disturbing experience:

Child: We went with Harriet and Irene.
Mother: Yes.
Child: But Irene was a bit frightened.
Mother: She was very frightened, wasn't she?
Child: Mm.
Mother: You and Erica [Cathie's sister] weren't nearly so frightened.
Child: Not as frightened as Irene and Harriet.
Mother: No you weren't.

Reliving the experience of seeing an exciting and, at times, frightening film seems to have established a closeness between Cathie and her mother, which is reflected in the structure of this conversation. Neither adult nor child is dominating the conversation, but both are equally and independently bringing up their own memories of the event. At the same time, they are both paying careful attention to each other's contributions, and they acknowledge and respond to what the other person says. Through their conversation, and the closeness it established, Cathie re-experienced the fear of the original outing in a secure setting, and perhaps had her anxiety allayed.

Discussion of past and future events could serve another function, that of helping the child to reach a clearer understanding of what had happened, or was going to happen to her. In the following conversation, for example, Samantha's mother tells her about an impending trip to see a speech therapist. Samantha is naturally apprehensive, and wants to know what will happen. Her mother attempts to reassure her:

1. Mother: Oh Samantha, you've got to go and see another lady on Tuesday.
2. Child: What lady?
3. Mother: Another lady wants to hear you.
4. Child: What lady?
5. Mother: The lady at the clinic wants to hear you speaking on Tuesday.

6. Child: [unclear] where [unclear] goes?
7. Mother: No, where you got your ears tested. She's going to learn you how to say your words properly.
8. Child: I don't know all the words.
9. Mother: Yeah. But she's going to learn you. She's going to teach them to you.
10. Child: What's her name?
11. Mother: Em . . . Miss Patrick.
12. Child: And . . . that's where I got my ears tested?
13. Mother: Where you got your ears tested then.
14. Child: That's where I'm going?
15. Mother: Mm-mm.
16. Child: Kevin mustn't make a noise. [Kevin is Samantha's younger brother, who was presumably told to be quiet when Samantha was having her hearing tested]
17. Mother: That was when you were getting your ears tested, he mustn't make a noise.
18. Child: No.

In this conversation both Samantha and her mother link the planned visit to the speech therapist with a previous trip to the clinic. In turn 7 Samantha's mother tells her that she's going back to the same clinic where she got her ears tested, and Samantha herself checks this again in turns 12 and 14. In turn 16 she recalls something that happened on a previous visit - her younger brother was asked to be quiet during the test. Some of the anxiety is thus taken out of this unknown future experience by these links to the shared past.

WATCHING TV

There is a widespread belief that young children nowadays spend much or most of their time at home in unproductive TV-viewing. However, Davie, who observed three- and four-year-olds in Stoke-on-Trent throughout the day, found that they were actually watching the screen on average only sixty-five minutes a day (Davie et al., 1984). This was, admittedly, longer than they spent on other activities, such as listening to stories, but it by no means amounted to 'most of their time'. She found that middle-class and working-class children watched for the same amount of time, although the TV sets were switched on for much longer periods in the working-class homes. There was also no social class difference in the amount of time that mothers watched and discussed TV *with* their children - on average, only seven minutes a day.

In our study, too, we found no evidence of massive TV-watching. Seven middle-class and five working-class children watched TV during our two and a half hours of observation, usually the special early afternoon programme for young children. In half of these cases, the mothers watched with the children for at least part of the time. On average, those children who watched TV spent eleven minutes watching. This compared with the overall average of sixty-two minutes spent in play during the afternoon, and nine minutes spent listening to stories by those children who were read stories.

What might the children have learned from watching TV? TV-watching with their mothers provided the same kind of educational opportunities as listening to stories. The children asked questions about what puzzled them: 'What's the matter with him?' 'Is she going to be cross?' 'Why is he talking so quickly?' Often, as in these examples, the children's questions were concerned with people's motivations. Less frequently, they asked about puzzling objects or events. [. . .] Lynne asked a series of questions about a TV puppet:

Child: How do they make him talk?
Mother: They just talk . . . the man talks in a funny voice.
Child: Is he inside him?
Mother: No, he puts his hand inside, and then makes the puppet move, and then he talks.
Child: What?
Mother: He talks, and it sounds as though the puppet's talking.

However, the children tended to ask fewer questions while watching TV than when listening to a story. Their mothers, on the other hand, tended to ask more. They pointed out things of interest, named letters, asked the children what they could see, or reminded them of parallels in their own experience: 'We saw horses like that in the park with Daddy, remember?' The middle-class mothers, in particular, fed a lot of relevant general knowledge to the children when they watched TV with them, either amplifying the programme or in response to a child's question. Beth was puzzled by a reference to the celebrations for the Queen's birthday:

Child: But it's not our Queen's birthday, because she's had hers, hasn't she?
Mother: Well, this is her official birthday, remember, Daddy was telling you about it. When they have things like this.

Most of the time, though, the children watched on their own. Without a special study, it is impossible to know what the children learned at these times. Sometimes their mothers tried to find out, but even the most articulate children gave unsatisfactory answers. This may have been because the narrative task was difficult for them, or they did not choose to tackle it, but often they seemed not to have understood what they saw. Mary watched TV while her mother prepared dinner, and over dinner her mother asked her:

Mother: What did they do on *Pipkin* [the programme]?
Child: They, they did music and - and Hartley did . . .
Mother: They were singing?
Child: Mm-mm.
Mother: What was the tortoise called?
Child: He's just called tortoise.
Mother: Mm-mm. I saw him singing the last few minutes. What about Granny Pipkin, what did they do there?
Child: I don't know, I think they made a pie.
Mother: I think it was broth, did they make a stew or soup or something?
Child: I don't know, I just don't know.
Mother: What did they put in it?
Child: Things.
Mother: Oh did they?
Child: I don't know what else.

Whether or not their mothers watched TV with them, it seemed likely that the regular occurrence of the programmes helped children to gain some idea of clock time, and of the days of the week. These are concepts which four-year-olds find difficult, but are beginning to grapple with. The children often asked when a favourite programme would come on. The following conversation with Beth illustrates that the most verbally advanced girls had already developed some concepts in this area, admittedly still somewhat confused:

Mother: What day is it today? [Referring to which children's TV programme is shown today]
Child: On Thursday, it's *In the Town*.
Mother: Ah, but it's Wednesday today, isn't it?
Child: It's *Mary, Mungo and Midge* on Thursday.
Mother: Yes, but it's not Thursday, it's Wednesday, I think, isn't it? Yes.
Child: I can hear, I can hear, *Mary, Mungo and Midge*.

The regularity of children's TV programmes also helped to structure the children's lives into a routine. A number of them watched the children's programmes while their mothers prepared or cleared up lunch; Mary was always sent to play in her room on her own after lunch, and called down for the 1.30 programme; Ruth's reading lesson was scheduled for the end of this programme. Routines of this kind probably helped the children by making it easier for them to predict their days, and may have been consciously used by some mothers as a managerial device.

DISPUTES

Professionals who are dubious about how much working-class children learn at home often point to the endless disputes that they believe are characteristic of these families. In our study we found a tendency for working-class families to have either large numbers of disputes or hardly any.

We defined a dispute as occurring when either mother or child made a demand which was refused by the other, and a 'comeback' was then made by the original demander. That is, a dispute must last for at least three turns. In the four most disputatious families, between 30 and 50 per cent of mother–child conversations included at least one dispute. On the other hand, in five of the working-class families less than 5 per cent of conversations included a dispute. By contrast, the great majority of middle-class families (twelve out of fifteen) had a dispute rate of between 10 per cent and 15 per cent, and no middle-class family had a dispute rate of more than 19 per cent.

How did some mothers avoid disputes? It was our impression that in most families where disputes were few the mothers took the initiative in structuring the child's afternoon. These mothers tended to announce their intentions and suggest activities for the child ahead of time, so that one followed another without a hiatus. But not all dispute-free families were of this type. Some mothers were much more passive, and seemed to avoid disputes by good-naturedly acceding to their children's requests. In the disputing families, they generally refused their child's requests and rarely suggested activities for them, or announced their intentions ahead of time. Their children had long unoccupied periods when they did little but argue.

However, we were very struck by the extent to which disputes provided a learning context. In 68 per cent of the disputes in our middle-class families, and 57 per cent of the disputes in our working-class families, the mothers sooner or later gave an explanation for their demand or refusal. *All* the mothers, except those who had very few or no disputes, gave some justifications. [. . .]

In the following dispute, Kelly, who constantly wrangled with her mother, was on the receiving end of a variety of information. This ranged from a discussion of relative sizes to insights into the relationship between her parents and advice as to how to approach her father for help. Kelly's bicycle had stabilizers. She had lent it to bigger boys in the block of flats, and as a result it was now broken, and would not stay upright by itself:

Child: It's not fixed. It's still tipping over. Fix it.
Mother: [Annoyed] Well, you let the big boys ride it, don't you?
Child: It's broken. [Moans]
Mother: [Angry] Go on, it won't hurt you. Oh God you drive me nuts. You let them ride it. So what do you expect? It gets broken and Daddy says he's not going to mend it again. I'm not going to keep paying the price for you, Kelly. I tell you not to let the big boys ride it, and what do you do?
Child: Joan [a friend] did.
Mother: Joan's not too big. Colin and David are. Colin and David are far too long for your bike and they break the stabilizers on it. Now you've got to ask your Daddy to mend it tonight. I bet you he moans. You ask him, I'm not asking him. I did yesterday. You'll have to be good for him tonight and he might do it.
Child: [Seeing younger sister on another bike] Mummy, let me have a go. [The wrangling continues]

We are not suggesting that family disputes should be encouraged; the most disputatious mothers were irritable and may have been somewhat depressed. Our point is rather that disputes are one of the many everyday family situations where the mother has an educational intent - she wants to justify herself, or make clear to the child the implications of the child's actions. The potential of disputes for learning, especially social learning, is therefore considerable.

WRITING TO GRANNY, AND OTHER 'EMBEDDED CONTEXT' TASKS

Earlier [in this book] we saw that some mothers taught writing as a lesson. However, other mothers encouraged their children to write as a way of communicating. To use a term which has recently become prominent in developmental psychology, they 'embedded' writing in a meaningful activity, rather than teaching it out of context. Thus, some children were encouraged to make and write birthday cards, others to write letters.

Over lunch, Cathie's mother suggested, 'We'll write a letter to Grandma after lunch, shall we? She'd like that.' Later in the meal, she said, 'Let's think what we're going to say to Grandma.' Lunch finished, she fetched some writing paper:

Mother: Now, I'll write, what are you going to say to Grandma?
Child: Dear Grandma, I hope you are all right, em . . . love from Cathie.
Mother: I hope [writes 'I hope'].
Child: I hope.
Mother: You [writes 'you'].
Child: You.
Mother: Are [writes 'are']. All [writes 'all'].
Child: Right.
Mother: Love to Grandpa.
Child: Love from Cathie . . . kiss, kiss, kiss.

Cathie's familiarity with letter-writing was evident from the conventional message which she dictated. Her next remarks show that she had a good knowledge of the whole routine:

Child: Mummy, don't you have to, don't you have to put the address, Mummy?
Mother: Mm.
Child: I've got an envelope.
Mother: You've got an envelope, OK.

It was clearly not infrequent for Cathie's mother to write to dictation and then get Cathie to copy her writing, because without any explicit reference to this step, her mother said:

Mother: Shall we write in the garden, or shall we write in here?
Child: Write out in the tent.

They both went into the garden, carrying notepads, and Cathie crawled into her tent. Then she asked:

Child: But what can I press on?
Mother: There . . . [Giving her a book]

Her mother then gave Cathie her notepad to copy from:

Mother: Copy that, and press on there, OK?

Child: Copy what?
Mother: Copy 'Dear Grandma and Grandpa'.
Child: Yes . . . thank you.

Her mother sat in the garden, reading a newspaper, while Cathie copied 'Dear Grandma':

Child: Mummy, look.
Mother: 'Dear Grandma', lovely, 'and', very good, are you putting in 'Grandpa' now?
Child: No, you do Grandpa.
Mother: You make a Grandpa and then I'll show you how to write the next bit.
Child: 'D' is for Grandpa? [She pronounces it 'dee' rather than 'duh']
Mother: 'G' for Grandpa. [Gee]
Child: What is 'G'?
Mother: 'G' for Grandpa like the big 'G' you put for Grandma.
Child: You mean one of these [points to 'G']?
Mother: Yes . . . a nice big 'G' . . . and then you needn't put Grand, you can just put G'pa – so put a big 'G' and then put a 'p'.

The discussion continued, with the whole letter-writing episode in the tent lasting for over ten minutes. It is clear that Cathie, who had just celebrated her fourth birthday, had a good understanding of some fundamentals of literacy – that the written text conveys a message, that it is made up of separate words corresponding to spoken words, that these words are made up of individual letters, and that the written text reads from left to right.

A good deal of '3R' teaching occurred in a much more incidental manner. Counting was the most common number activity. The contexts of the home provided many natural settings for counting. The mothers counted knives as they set the table, counted the items on their shopping list, asked the children to count the number of people coming to tea, or the number of sausages they had put on each plate. The children obviously enjoyed counting and often initiated it themselves. Again, this counting was usually in a very meaningful context, for example counting the coins in their money box. Their skills were still rudimentary. One of the most elementary number skills is to know by rote the number series, but a good many of the children made errors early on, e.g. 'one, two, three, four, five, sixteen'. Their major problem, however, was in one-to-one correspondence, that is, counting objects correctly, without double-counting or missing one out.

Some of the mothers taught more advanced number skills. Susan's mother saw a traditional children's number song as a good context in which to teach subtraction. She and Susan were singing nursery rhymes together. Part-way through the song, which describes a progressive reduction in the number of buns in a baker's shop as they are sold, she stopped singing to teach subtraction in a more explicit way:

Mother: If you've got three currant buns in the baker's shop [holds up three fingers], look, and I take one away [folds one finger down], how many are left?
Child: [Sings] 'Three currant buns in the baker's shop.'
Mother: How many's left if I take one away from three [holds up three fingers and folds one down]?
Child: Two.
Mother: That's right.
Child: 'Three . . .' [Starts to sing]
Mother: No. *Two* currant buns in the shop.

At this point Susan, who seems to have grasped the principle, takes on the role of teacher and begins to instruct her mother:

Child: 'Two currant buns in the baker's shop, round and fat with sugar on the top. Come a boy with a penny one day' [stops singing]. Put your hand up with two fingers. [Mother does so] 'Along come a boy with a penny one day' [folds one of mother's fingers down].
Mother: How many's left now?
Child: [Sings] 'One currant bun in the baker'[stops singing]. Put your finger out . . .[Mother holds up one finger] 'Along come a boy . . . and took it away.' None left.
Mother: None left now!

Susan obviously enjoyed her mastery of this task, and suggested:

Child: Shall we play, shall we play, shall we play three currant buns in the baker's shop again?
Mother: If you want to.
Child: You put your three fingers up [lifting up all five of her own fingers].
Mother: That's more than three. How many's that?
Child: Don't know.
Mother: Count them.
Child: One, two, three, four, five, six, seven, eight [she starts to count her fingers correctly, but goes wrong and screeches with laughter].

Mother: Don't be silly.

At this point it became clear that Susan had not yet an adequate enough grasp of number to master the lesson fully, and she reverted simply to singing the song. We found that other children besides Susan protected themselves from any tendency by their mothers to exert excess pressure, by changing the subject or becoming 'silly' when too difficult demands were placed on them.

[. . .]

Size and shape concepts (e.g. big/little, more/less, bigger than/smaller than, square/round) were used frequently and casually by all the mothers. Conversations about relative size were also quite common. June, for example, tried on an old coat, and her mother pointed out that it was too small, she had grown too fat. Erica and her mother discussed at length which toys would fit into her toy pushchair:

Mother: Jane's legs are too long, aren't they, what about Tommy? He fits in quite well, doesn't he?
Child: And Teddy. And the other teddy.
Mother: I don't know if they will all three fit in.
Child: I'll see.

[. . .] Occasionally, mathematical words were deliberately taught. Susan's mother was getting spoons out for a dolls' tea-party:

Child: Get a bit more 'poons out.
Mother: A *bit* more?
Child: Yes
Mother: A *few* more.

SEX-ROLE TEACHING

It was often hard to determine how much of the teaching in the home was the result of a deliberate intention on the part of the mother. Values and attitudes were sometimes transmitted explicitly, at other times implicitly. We did not make any systematic analysis of the teaching of sex roles, but there were many conversations when the mother's views on this topic were implicitly or explicitly transmitted to her child. Donna's mother's priorities with her time, for example, were a frequent subject for discussion. It was usually made clear, as in the following conversation with Donna, that housework had to come before playing with the child:

Mother: I got washing to do, ironing to do, hoovering . . .
Child: Yes?

Mother: Well, it all takes time.
Child: And then you're finished?
Mother: Yes.
Child: I don't want you to do hoovering and washing.
Mother: I'm sorry, but I've got to.

The way in which roles are shared between mothers and fathers was conveyed in many subtle forms. Fathers were implicitly depicted as powerful people. This power was usually seen as benefiting the family. The children learned that mothers and children are dependent on fathers for ferrying (few mothers could drive, or had access to a car), for money and for mechanical skills ('Oh, you've broken that. Daddy'll have to mend it'). They also learned that an important role for women is to provide household services for men ('Nanny's going shopping. To get Granddad some dinner'; 'I've got to see Daddy has a clean shirt').

The fathers' power was sometimes depicted as potentially threatening as well as positive. As we saw earlier, when Kelly's bicycle got broken she was told, 'Now you've got to ask your Daddy to mend it tonight. I bet you he moans. You ask him, I'm not asking him. I did yesterday. You'll have to be good for him tonight and he might do it.' Ann's mother tore a page out of a notebook for her to write on, and commented, 'You'd better not tell Daddy I gave you a piece of paper out of his book.' These mothers were conveying to their daughters a realistic understanding of relationships and sex-role divisions within their families. In some cases the mothers had internalized these attitudes to such a degree that they became uneasy if even a pretend sex-role change was suggested; as in the case of Elaine's mother:

Child: You be Mummy, I'll be Daddy.
Mother: You be Daddy? OK . . . No, little girls should be Mummies, not Daddies. You be Mummy, I'll be Auntie.
Child: Mm?
Mother: Let's pretend Daddy's at work. OK?

Although we have no quantitative evidence on this, our impression was that sex-role teaching was much more intense in the home, especially in some working-class homes, than at nursery school.

SPECIAL CHARACTERISTICS OF HOME LEARNING

Our study suggests that learning at home occurs in a wide variety of contexts, and that there is no good reason to single out any one context, such as mother–child play, as especially valuable. At the start of the study we had suspected that joint activity of any kind between mother and child might provide the most important learning experiences, but we found no evidence to support this idea. In fact [. . .] the most intellectually challenging conversations tended to occur at mealtimes, or when mother and child were doing nothing in particular, or when the child was watching her mother at work.

What seemed to be important, in fact, was not the particular context, but the mother's desire for the child to learn, coupled with the child's curiosity and wish to learn. Educational considerations, in the broadest sense, were often at the forefront of the mothers' minds. They were dedicated teachers, intent on teaching their child what they thought was important for her to learn. The topics varied, of course, from family to family. However, almost every trivial event could be an occasion for teaching.

This does not mean that home life *automatically* provides rich learning experiences. Some mothers, perhaps if very depressed, or some childminders caring for a child in their home, may have little commitment to education. Equally, in some situations, children may not turn to adults for companionship or to satisfy their curiosity. [. . .] This tends to be the case at nursery school.

A notable feature of learning at home was the large amount of general knowledge that the children were given, especially in relation to the ordinary everyday events of living in a family. The children were particularly interested in people, their motivations and activities, and much of the knowledge that their mothers gave them was concerned with the social world.

Giving young children information and general knowledge is not currently seen as a priority by psychologists. Instead, the central educational task in the pre-school years is seen to be the fostering of basic language and thinking skills. In our view, this is mistaken. The major communication and thinking problems of young children arise, not from inability to reason or compare, but from misinformation, lack of information, and from the lack of a coherent conceptual framework in which to fit their experiences. [. . .]

Further, possession of relevant information can increase children's security and confidence. We have already quoted [. . .] conversations in which the children's anxiety seemed to some extent allayed by being helped to an increased understanding of events. Beth had an amazing amount of general knowledge for a child aged three years and ten months. On one occasion she interrupted a fantasy game with her teacher to announce:

Child:	Do you know, my baby's one now.
Staff:	Your baby's coming here when she's older.
Child:	She'll go to playgroup when she's two, though.
Staff:	Will she?
Child:	Yeah. Because when you're two you go to . . . When I was two I went to a playgroup.
Other child:	So did I.
Child:	That shows you, that people go to playgroup when they're two.
Staff:	Why do they go to a playgroup?
Child:	Because they're not old enough to go to school.
Staff:	I see. And how old were you when you came here, then?
Child:	Three or four.
Staff:	Three or four. Then what happens when you're five?
Child:	You go . . . When I'm five I'll only . . . I'll go to a . . . I expect I won't come to here any more.
Staff:	Where will you be, then?
Child:	Be? In a different school, of course.
Staff:	Do you know which school you're going to?
Child:	Cross Road [her local primary school].

Beth's knowledge of the various stages of early education, and the ages at which transfers between them occur, was better than that of most adults. It seems likely that being able to situate her past and future within the educational system in this way gave her extra confidence in moving through life.

As we have seen, another special characteristic of teaching at home is that it usually occurs in a context of great meaning to the child. While this seems likely to facilitate learning, it also represents a limitation which the child must eventually overcome. Number, for example, must be separated at school from the context of card games or rock cakes if the child is to advance in mathematics.[. . .]

OVERVIEW

In this chapter we showed that many everyday events in family life - for example making a shopping list, looking out of the window, and even irritable wrangling - can involve important learning experiences for children. Mothers are particularly well placed to play an important teaching role because they share the child's world, extending from the past into the future. No single context seemed particularly valuable for learning; it was the mother's desire to teach or clarify, and the child's curiosity, which created the learning potential. We argue that the large amount of information and general knowledge conveyed in the home is important both for intellectual growth and for increasing children's security and confidence.

TOPICS FOR DISCUSSION

1. 'The major communication and thinking problems of young children arise, not from inability to reason and compare, but from lack of information, and from the lack of a coherent conceptual framework in which to fit their experiences.' Discuss.
2. 'Professionals who are dubious about how much working-class children learn at home often point to the endless disputes that they believe are characteristic of these families. In our study we found a tendency for working-class families to have either large numbers of disputes or hardly any.' Discuss the authors' evidence which suggests that disputes provided a learning context.
3. What are 'embedded context' tasks? How, the authors suggest, do mothers use such tasks?

SUGGESTIONS FOR FURTHER READING

1. Tizard, B. and Hughes, M. (1984) 'The gap between home and nursery school', in *Young Children Learning: Talking and Thinking at Home and at School*. London, Fontana, chap. 10, pp. 235–48.

The nursery schools and classes studied by Tizard and Hughes were found to create 'a child-centred play environment in which children had relatively few encounters with adults. When they did encounter the school staff, they found the staff's expectations of them were very different from their mothers' ' (p. 235). The authors examine the range of differences which face the young child on entering nursery school and carefully detail the ways in which children respond and behave to the two very different environments of home and mother and school and teacher. Of particular interest is their discussion of typical effects on working-class children, and the strategies employed by *all* the participants – parents, teachers and children – to bridge the gap between home and school – interestingly, a task that seemed harder for the teachers than for the mothers. How the children tried to bridge the gap is demonstrated in a variety of ways. For example, the authors note that it is obviously necessary that young children should learn how to give teachers appropriate information in a clear and intelligible form. When staff don't ask the right questions, however, there can be quite bizarre results: 'The following conversation failed to establish communication because Lynne did not explain that Polly was her grandmother's dog, who had just spent a night with her, and the nursery assistant did not ask who Polly was, or where her home was:

Child: Polly's back. Polly comed up yesterday, but she's gone home. Polly.
Staff: Polly?
Child: Yeah, my Polly.
Staff: Oh!

Child: We had some biccies up there. When we taked her home. She bringed us some sweeties.
Staff: Oh, that was nice.
Child: A packet.
Staff: A packet? What kind? [Child did not reply, and staff talks to other children]' (p. 238).

Some of the problems which ensue when staff attempt to bridge the home–school gap by asking children questions about their home life are the result of the teachers having no means of evaluating the children's replies. Similarly, it was found that because mothers were familiar with the school routine, conversations at home about school presented fewer problems than conversations about home at school. Tizard and Hughes conclude this very useful chapter with an examination of the implications of the home–school gap.

2. Donaldson, M. (1978) 'Disembedded thought and social values', in *Children's Minds*. London, Fontana, chap. 7, pp. 76–85.

Donaldson reminds us that it is in situations of fairly immediate goals and intentions and familiar patterns of events that we feel most at home. Thus, 'even pre-school children can frequently reason well about the events in the stories they hear' (p. 76). It is when thinking moves beyond the bounds of familiar patterns of meaningful events, to 'formal' or 'abstract' situations or, as Donaldson calls it, 'disembedded' thinking, that there are dramatic differences in the abilities of children to cope. Donaldson illustrates this move beyond the bounds of human sense to the *form* or logical structure of the reasoning (with its attendant difficulties) with the following example:

'Nial (aged 4 years): But how can it be [that they are getting married]? You have to have a man too.' (The book contains an illustration of a wedding in which the man looks rather like a woman. The child thinks it is a picture of two women.)

'(*Premises*: (1) You need a man for a wedding; (2) There is no man in the picture. *Conclusion*: It can't be a wedding.)' (p. 55).

The 'form' or 'structure' of this argument involves breaking the reasoning into separate statements or propositions. Two propositions together with the negations of the two are involved: *there is a wedding* and *there is a man*. The 'pure' form of reasoning, given that

There is a wedding = the symbol *p*, and
There is a man = the symbol *q*, becomes
If *p*, then *q*.
Not q.
Therefore *not p*.

Put like this, Donaldson comments, for many people the reasoning becomes mind-boggling, for we do not easily engage in manipulating meaningless symbols. But note that Nial, aged only four, can very easily *reason* about men and weddings (p. 77).

The author wryly remarks that, in our society, the better you are at coping with problems without having to be sustained by human sense, 'the more likely you are to succeed in our educational system, the more you will be approved of and loaded with prizes'. Donaldson's argument is that you cannot master *any* formal system unless you have learned to take at least some steps beyond the confines of human sense, and that the problems involved in helping the very young child to begin to do this at the very beginning of his or her schooling – or even earlier – have neither been properly recognized nor adequately tackled. The paramount task, then, for teachers of the young, is to teach the disembedded modes of thinking more successfully (p. 82). The lucid discussion of just what teachers *ought* to be doing is of particular importance and relevance to the third topic for discussion in Reading 3.

3. Tizard, B. and Hughes, M. (1984) 'An afternoon with Donna and her mother' and 'The working-class girls, including Donna, at school', in *Young Children Learning: Talking and Thinking at Home and at School.* London, Fontana, chap. 7, pp. 161–79, and chap. 9, pp. 214–34, respectively.

Donna was chosen as an object of study because, the authors assert, she was an extreme example who confirmed the popular, stereotyped picture of a working-class upbringing. However, in spite of the fact that Donna was a demanding child, that much of the time at home was occupied by wrangles and disputes and, in addition, her mother spent little time engaged with her in the kind of educational play so valued by nursery school teachers, Tizard and Hughes maintain that the overall picture did not confirm any stereotypical view of the inadequacies of working-class language. Indeed, the authors claim, Donna's home provided a rich learning environment. Tizard and Hughes present a fascinating vignette of Donna's typical interactions with her mother, demonstrating how the parent was invariably prepared patiently to follow the child's thinking, was concerned to understand what her daughter was trying to say, and offered many explanations which were detailed and specific, giving Donna a clear picture of the constraints and realities of her life. Other episodes demonstrate the mother's concern to help Donna acquire what was considered to be essential learning, namely knowing her letters and numbers. Moreover, Donna's mother was one of a minority of working-class mothers who did not hold the viewpoint that play was important, for she was critical of the nursery school for providing only play, supplementing the school's activities by teaching her child the alphabet and to spell and copy her name. In the afternoon session the authors recorded sixty-nine conversations between mother and daughter, seventy-seven questions – which included twenty-eight 'Why' questions – and noted that Donna and her mother contributed nearly equally to *initiating* and *sustaining* the conversations. As the authors affirm, however, this was a very disputatious working-class family and many of the interactions were to do with discipline so that the range of information given to the child was often relatively limited, given to explanations which were often brief and somewhat implicit. The mother seemed to see her own educational responsibilities much more in terms of encouraging formal school skills than in developing and extending general knowledge or vocabulary.

Chapter 9, 'The working-class girls, including Donna, at school', provides evidence which clearly supports the contention that working-class children are adversely affected by the school setting. Tizard and Hughes teased out the evidence by comparing the way in which the children from the two social classes behaved at home and at school, showing that working-class children were *much more affected* by the demands made on them by the school. For example, whereas at home conversations between mother and child were more evenly balanced, at school the staff did most of the talking. Working-class children contributed only

15 per cent of sustaining remarks in conversation with the staff, and the discrepancy between the proportion of adult talk to child talk at home and at school was significantly greater in the case of working-class children. Such youngsters, in a wide range of situations and behaviours, appeared more subdued and immature at school than at home, and since the teachers adjusted their demands to the perceived immaturity of the children, they in no way *compensated* for any inadequacies in their homes. The authors contend that 'what we *do* know is that the working-class children are already appearing at a disadvantage in nursery school'.

REFERENCES

Davie, C.E., Hutt, S.J., Vincent, E. and Mason, M. (1984) *The Young Child at Home*. Windsor, NFER-Nelson.

Dunn, J. (1983) 'Sibling relationships in early childhood'. *Child Development*, **54**, 787–811.

Reading 4

PAUSE, PROMPT AND PRAISE FOR PARENTS AND PEERS: EFFECTIVE TUTORING OF LOW PROGRESS READERS

K. Wheldall, F. Merrett and S. Colmar

INTRODUCTION

Children with limited reading skills are clearly disadvantaged and this disadvantage will continue throughout their school careers unless some intervention is applied which allows them to improve, and to improve quickly. The secondary curriculum, in particular, will be largely available to slow or poor readers unless they make dramatic progress in reading. They need programmes which will enable them to achieve accelerated improvement in order to catch up with their peer group in reading skills. Given their previous histories of failure in reading earlier on in the primary school, their only real chance to make up ground quickly, in our view, is by:

(a) making a fresh start with a new approach (this includes all the accompanying advantages of novelty);

Wheldall, K., Merrett, F. and Colmar, S. (1987) 'Pause, prompt and praise for parents and peers: effective tutoring of low progress readers'. *Support for Learning*, **2**, 1, 5–12. Reprinted with the permission of NARE.

(b) having a skilled reading tutor hear them read daily for, say, fifteen to twenty minutes to allow opportunities for reading appropriate material; and
(c) employing a powerful and yet readily trainable set of tutoring skills of proven effectiveness.

These are difficult to achieve in most primary and secondary schools, especially the second item. Even given the smaller numbers common in secondary remedial classes, it would be inadvisable, if not impossible, for remedial teachers to attempt this on their own. In any case this would severely limit the broader curricular remit of the remedial teacher. Given this constraint the only other possibilities (apart from classroom assistants) are parents (not necessarily of the low progress readers) and peers (other pupils with more advanced reading skills). Research has shown that both of these groups can be made expert, given thorough training in reading tutoring and can be employed to very good effect, bringing about major gains in their *tutees* (Glynn, 1981; Wheldall and Mettem, 1985). In the case of peers, substantial benefits have been shown to be gained by the *tutors* as well (see, for example, Limbrick et al., 1985). Helping somebody to improve their reading skill leads to improvement in the reading performance of the tutor at the same time.

Without wishing to minimize the importance of the role of parents in the education of their children, we would like to argue the case for the increased utilization of peers for tutoring of reading, in addition to parents. We are using the term 'peer tutoring' here to mean tutoring by other young people of the same age as or older than the tutees; 'cross-age peer tutoring' is sometimes used to indicate the employment of older tutors (Limbrick et al., 1985). Our reasons for advocating the use of peers are as follows:

1. Parents may not always be available in sufficient numbers nor may they be willing to be trained. (In addition, some parents may be too involved emotionally with their own child's difficulties to tutor effectively.)
2. Peer tutors are plentiful, are available for training and can be readily monitored and organized.
3. It has been shown that low progress readers respond readily to peer tutors; as well as, if not better than, to parents.
4. Tutoring has also been shown to be beneficial to the peer tutors and could form a valuable component of a life and social skills course. (Training in tutoring will, of course, also be valuable in the context of training for parenting.)

In this article we will describe a relatively new, powerful tutoring method which may be employed by either parents or peers with low progress readers. There has recently been renewed interest in parental involvement in reading (Topping and Wolfendale, 1985) and 'paired reading' (Morgan and Lyon, 1979), for example, has become increasingly popular. So far, however, there has been relatively little awareness in the UK of the procedure (developed in New Zealand) known as 'pause, prompt and praise', which is, we would argue, at least as powerful a technique as paired reading.

'PAUSE, PROMPT AND PRAISE'

The set of remedial reading strategies known as 'pause, prompt and praise' was developed from research carried out by its authors; Professor Ted Glynn, Dr Stuart McNaughton and Dr Viviane Robinson (McNaughton et al., 1981) and is based on the earlier reading research of Professor Marie Clay (reported, for example, in her book *Reading: The Patterning of Complex Behaviour*, 1979, and operationalized in her 'Reading Recovery Project').

In the 'pause, prompt and praise' model there are two important requirements of reading teachers or tutors. The first is to provide reading material at an appropriate level such that the child is encountering some unfamiliar words but knows enough words to be able to make good predictions, even if these are miscues. The right level of reading material can be broadly assessed by checking the child's rate of reading accuracy. If this rate is below 80 per cent the text is too difficult; if the child is reading at over 95 per cent accuracy it is clearly too easy. At a rate between 90 per cent and 95 per cent accuracy promotion to the next level should be seriously considered. Thus an ideal level for children learning to read, with all the advantages of making mistakes, is between 80 per cent and 90 per cent accuracy.

The second important requirement of reading tutors is that they should provide appropriate feedback as they listen to the child read. It is important to stress that mistakes (errors, miscues) are to be expected. All children learning to read make mistakes; it is an important part of the process of learning to read. In other words, making mistakes is a good thing. By carefully monitoring the child's response to text the teacher can readily work out if the child is making average, or even rapid, progress and if they are using efficient predictive strategies. For example, Marie Clay (1979) suggests that the child's rate of self-correction is associated with good reading progress. Self-correction is seen as an indicator that the child is reading actively in that they are able to 'solve' problem words independently. Similarly, McNaughton's work evaluating the role of attention to reading errors shows that low progress readers, in particular, benefit from receiving feedback following an error. The delaying of attention to errors by five seconds leads to more self-correction and an increase in the child's reading accuracy (McNaughton and Glynn, 1981).

'Pause, prompt and praise' is a technique which stresses that children learn to read by reading, not by learning a large number of separate words or subskills. It assumes three things: first, that the child is provided with an appropriate level and type of text; second, that the child's progress is carefully monitored with respect to the text using running records or simple miscue analysis and, third, that the teacher or tutor listens to the reading and gives appropriate feedback.

Although the whole research project and technique is often referred to as 'pause, prompt, and praise' (including all three of these factors), in fact 'pause, prompt and praise' describes the *third* aspect - that is, the teacher's response to the reading. This is summarized in Figure 4.1.

With reference to Figure 4.1 it is important to note that the praising of correct reading should be in the form of a specific, descriptive comment rather than just a comment like, 'Good boy.' For example, 'Good work David. You corrected "rabbit" all by yourself,' tells David exactly what he is being praised for and so the praise is contingent upon good reading behaviour.

When the child makes an error or hesitates, it is important to pause for at least five seconds. This gives him a reasonable opportunity either to correct his own error or to work out the word independently. Pausing is difficult for most reading tutors, but it is a key factor in responding helpfully to the child who is learning to read.

If, after pausing for five seconds, no response or an error response is made, the tutor then prompts. The type of feedback or prompt given depends on the nature of the miscue. If the child's error has not made sense then the prompt should be aimed at giving clues about the meaning of the story, by asking a question perhaps. The following (real) example illustrates this:

Example one

Text: The other end looked like a pair *of* wings.
Child: The other end looked like a pair *out* wings.
Tutor (*prompt*): The word looks like 'out' but that does not make sense. It would not be a pair 'out' wings, would it?
Child: Pair of wings
Tutor: That's right. Good girl.

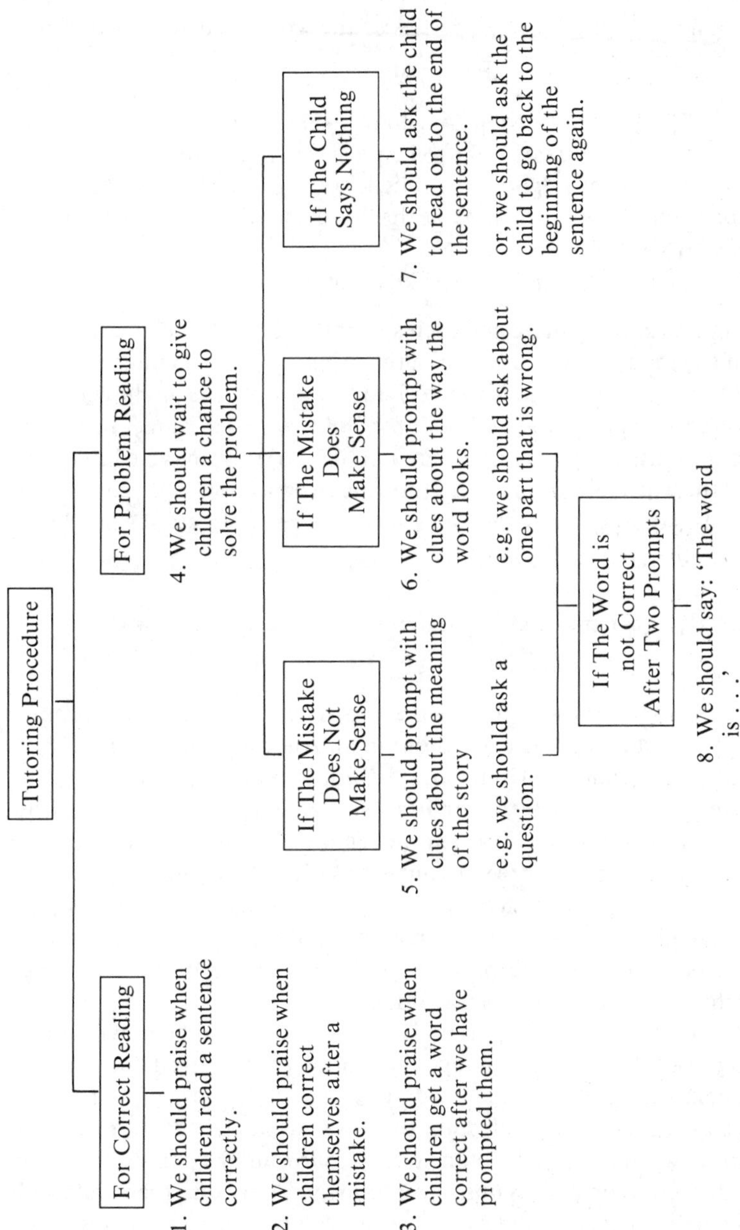

Figure 4.1 Written instruction sheet for use in training parents and peers in the 'pause, prompt and praise' procedures

Often the child's miscue makes sense but the word is still not correct. In these instances the tutor's prompt should be aimed at helping the child to look again at the graphical properties of the word, that is, how it looks.

Example two

Text: 'They *may* not want to help us', said the giraffe.
Child: 'They *might* not want to help us', said the giraffe.
Tutor (*prompt*): That's a very good try. 'Might' fits in with the story but is not quite right. Let's look at the word again (points to word).
Child: It's 'may'.
Tutor: That's right and you worked that out really quickly.

Should the child hesitate and then say nothing, the tutor can either ask the child to read to the end, or from the beginning of the sentence. Often this additional context will help the child to work out the unknown word. In many cases a prompt is sufficient for children to determine the correct word but in instances where they are not able to, it is suggested that they are told the word (given a model) following two prompts. This encourages the fluency of the story and does not unnecessarily stress the child's difficulty in responding correctly.

EVALUATING THE EFFECTIVENESS OF 'PAUSE, PROMPT AND PRAISE'

The first research study evaluating the effectiveness of the 'pause, prompt and praise' technique was carried out in an Auckland suburb in 1978. It was called the Mangere Home and School Project and it involved the intensive study of fourteen families (McNaughton et al., 1981). Low progress readers aged eight to twelve years were tutored at home three times a week for ten to fifteen minutes by either their parent or an older sibling. After ten to fifteen weeks results showed that children, on average, made nearly six months' reading progress, despite the fact that they had been making little or no progress before the project. On average their rate of self-correction nearly doubled.

It was clearly shown that parents were able to change their own natural tutoring style following training. Typically, as untrained tutors, they rarely commented on correct reading or the child's attempts to solve unfamiliar words. They tended not to pause but to provide the child with the correct word as a model immediately following the child's hesitation or mistake. In summary, as untrained tutors working with their child with reading difficulties, they did not pause or prompt or praise. Interestingly, the data collected showed that their untrained tutoring had little effect on their children's reading. However, following training in these methods and regular feedback sessions from the researchers, parents provided delayed attention to errors (i.e. *paused*), provided *prompts* instead of models, and significantly increased their *praise*. The Mangere Home and School Project was so successful that the techniques were subsequently presented on New Zealand Television. A booklet for parents, to accompany the programmes, was also made available (Glynn et al., 1979).

REPLICATION STUDIES

The Mangere study has now been replicated many times. Glynn and McNaughton (1985) review eleven studies which replicate the original experiment, with variations, carried out in New Zealand, Australia and the United Kingdom. Including the original Mangere project the twelve 'pause, prompt and praise' studies have involved a total of over one hundred tutors and ninety-eight children between the ages of seven and twelve. Of these tutors sixty-two were parents tutoring their own children, thirty-one were adults tutoring other children whilst fifteen were older children tutoring younger ones. All the subject children had marked deficits in reading skills which varied from six months to as much as five years with a mean of about two years.

One characteristic of 'pause, prompt and praise' as set up in the original Mangere project was the monitoring of the tutors' and the children's responses by means of audio tapes. This is normally done before the training of the tutors to establish a baseline of skill performance for comparison. Invariably the levels of tutoring response have tended to be low, e.g. for pausing less than 33 per cent, for prompting less than 47 per cent and, perhaps surprisingly, for praising (a much more natural and expected response) less than 8 per cent. Typically these rates improve considerably with training, which demonstrates that the procedures were readily learned by the tutors. The normal procedure is, then, to monitor maintenance of these behaviours through later examination of taped sessions made in private. This was done in six of the replication studies and these gave firm evidence for the continued use of the learned strategies. Overall, it seems that the level of attention to errors did not change much. What did change was the difference in tutor response brought about by the 'pause, prompt and praise' training and this seems to be the critical element.

Five of the studies reviewed by Glynn and McNaughton (1985) involved tutoring at home, four of the studies were carried out in school only, whilst in a further three studies tutoring was carried out both at home and at school. Tutors included parents, teachers, parent helpers, residential childcare workers and peers. The results from these various studies carried out by a wide range of tutors show major gains in children's reading.

The improvements in reading skill cannot be attributed simply to the tutor time given to the children. Baseline measures relating to untrained tutoring have never shown any trend of improvement. Moreover, as Wheldall and Mettem (1985) show, large, additional gains accrue when tutors trained in the 'pause, prompt and praise' procedures are employed, compared with a control group of untrained tutors. The amount of time (length and number of sessions) spent on tutoring appears to be related to improvement. As Glynn and McNaughton (1985) conclude, 'The consistent replication of treatment effects across the twelve studies adds to the growing confidence in the effectiveness of the original Mangere Home and School Remedial Reading Procedures.'

'PAUSE, PROMPT AND PRAISE' IN THE UK

Relatively little research on 'pause, prompt and praise' has been carried out in the UK as yet, apart from Glynn's own work when on sabbatical leave in Birmingham in 1980 (see Glynn, 1981), studies by Wheldall and his students at the Centre for Child Study at Birmingham University (see below) and some pilot work by Winter, formerly in Kirklees but who has now moved to Hong Kong (Winter, 1985). Topping and Wolfendale's excellent book *Parental Involvement in Children's Reading* (1985) should help to encourage more work on 'pause, prompt and praise', however, since it is given favourable support by the editors, alongside chapters on it by Glynn (1985) and Winter (1985). Glynn's chapter summarizes the original Mangere study and the follow-up study he carried out in Birmingham whilst Winter describes his workshops which gave parents a choice of paired reading or 'pause, prompt and praise'.

Wheldall's work, which began in 1981, includes three separate studies carried out with Masters level students (Hilton, Mettem and Walker) using 'pause, prompt and praise' procedures with both parents and peers. The first of these was a pilot investigation of peer tutoring carried out with Josie Hilton. This small-scale study involved three groups of three seven- to eight-year-old children who were about six to eighteen months behind in terms of reading age for accuracy. The peer tutors were six ten- to eleven-year-old pupils from the same school of at least average reading ability. The results of this study were equivocal but it served as a valuable introduction to the rigours of this methodology and the practical problems of its implementation. What became clear was that peers could be effectively trained to use all three components of the 'pause, prompt and praise' procedure.

The second study in this area carried out with Paul Mettem (see Wheldall and Mettem, 1985) was, however, highly successful. In brief, eight sixteen-year-old, low achieving pupils were trained to tutor reading using the 'pause, prompt and praise' method. The effectiveness of training such tutors was investigated through a tutorial programme in which these older pupils tutored eight twelve-year-old remedial children who were on average three to four years behind in reading. The programme consisted of twenty-four tutorial sessions each of fifteen to twenty minutes three days per week over eight weeks. Two matched control groups of remedial readers were also included in the experiment. One consisted of eight pupils tutored by a group of eight untrained tutors, who taught during the same sessions and used the same materials. The second control group consisted of a third group of remedial readers, who read silently, without a tutor.

Analyses of the tutoring sessions revealed important differences in tutoring behaviour between the trained and untrained peer tutors. Attention to errors in both groups was very similar but for delayed attention to errors the picture was markedly different. Whereas a mean of 58 per cent of attention to errors was delayed in the experimental tutors, for the control group such delay was almost non-existent. Prompting almost never occurred in the untrained control group and was never successful whereas trained tutors used prompts in 27 per cent of their attention to errors and were successful in 49 per cent of these prompts. Finally, use of praise was observed on average 8.8 times per tutor per session in the experimental group but hardly ever in the control group. From these results it can reasonably be claimed that the experimental group tutors were trained successfully in the 'pause, prompt and praise' procedures.

Turning next to the performance of the tutees, it was shown that for the children in the experimental group self-corrections were around 20 per cent but in the control group this figure never rose above 10 per cent. Moreover, the experimental group of tutees made a mean gain of six months in reading accuracy by the end of the programme. The tutees of control group I, who had received untrained tutoring, made a mean gain of only 2.4 months whilst the pupils of control group II, who read silently without a tutor, made a mean gain of 0.9 months. In simple terms, half of the experimental group made gains in excess of six months whilst none of the children in either of the control groups made such gains. This study clearly showed that low progress readers could be successfully tutored by peers, provided the tutors had been given adequate training in these rigorous tutoring procedures.

'PAUSE, PROMPT, PRAISE' WITH BETTER READERS

Our third study carried out with Chris Walker evaluated a parent tutoring programme with *high progress young* readers. Three groups, each of seven pupils, were involved, aged from five and a half to seven and a half, with advanced reading ages. One group were an untutored comparison group, one group were tutored by their parents, who were given general tutoring advice, whilst the third were tutored by their parents, who had been trained to use 'pause, prompt and praise'. Pre-training (baseline) and post-training measures of parental tutoring behaviours were obtained from both (tutored) groups.

Briefly, the results again showed that tutors (this time parents) could be readily trained to use the 'pause, prompt and praise' procedures. Before training, rates for pausing, prompting and praising were very low in both groups of parents but, following instruction in the methods, the trained group paused after nearly 90 per cent of hesitations or errors, prompted nearly 50 per cent of the time (with 60 per cent success) and used six times as much praise. The group of parents given only general advice made only marginal gains in these skills. Interestingly enough, however, the results showed that for these young, skilled readers trained parental tutoring using 'pause, prompt and praise' led to no greater gains in reading age than the general tutoring given to the other group parents.

From these three preliminary studies we can begin to draw tentative conclusions. It appears that both parents and peers can be trained to use 'pause, prompt and praise' procedures relatively quickly and easily. However, it seems that young children who have not been reading for long and who are making good or average (or even a little below average) progress do not really need trained tutoring. Simply having someone hear them read appears to be enough. For older, low progress readers about to enter or already attending secondary school, however, it is a different matter. For pupils such as these, trained tutoring using 'pause, prompt and praise' has been shown (specifically) to be extremely effective.

DEVELOPMENT AND DISSEMINATION

Carrying out experimental studies of peer and parent tutoring is one aspect of development but passing on the methods to others (dissemination) is another issue altogether. Informing interested parties *about* the procedures does not, and indeed cannot, train them in *how* to implement them. Our next task is to attempt to pass on the methods to teachers and to evaluate the success of the tutoring programmes they set up. To this end we have been able to borrow training video tapes from Professor Glynn, with whom we are continuing contact. The video tapes detail the tutoring procedures and will form a foundation for the training of teachers in the 'pause, prompt and praise' procedures together with our own material adapting it to a UK educational context. We are hoping to involve teachers and other educationists in designing a suitable training programme.

The purpose of our proposed dissemination programme is, first, to provide a means by which teachers can be taught these new procedures. They will be given the opportunity to find out for themselves how effective they are in improving the reading skills of poor readers, particularly those who have a long history of failure. Second, we need to find ways of training teachers in effective ways of setting up peer and parent tutoring schemes. This will call for examination of the best ways of involving all those concerned, of training tutors, arranging schedules and times when the tutoring can best be carried out and of monitoring the progress of both tutors and tutees.

The project, which is partly funded by the School Curriculum Development Committee, will be directed jointly by the first two authors, who have researched various aspects of the behavioural approach to teaching over the last ten years. The third author, who is consultant to the project, is an educational psychologist who was trained in New Zealand by Professors Glynn and Clay and who is consequently well versed in the relevant theory and methodologies underpinning their perspectives on reading, which are operationalized in the current research.

CONCLUDING COMMENTS

When presenting teachers with the 'pause, prompt and praise' procedures we have often been told that this may be good advice for parents or peers listening to children read but that, 'of course, teachers do this already'. Our subjective observations caused us to doubt this glib assumption and consequently we are currently embarked on a series of data collection exercises with the aim of establishing the truth of this claim. We have begun to record teachers listening to low progress readers aged between about nine and a half and thirteen and a half. Preliminary analyses of some data collected by our Masters level students on about thirty recordings of teachers listening to low progress readers suggest that our doubts may be justified.

For only about 20 per cent of error attention were teachers' responses delayed by more than five seconds; in fact nearly 50 per cent of teachers never 'paused'. About 75 per cent of errors were followed by 'prompts' and about 70 per cent of these were successful. Teachers praised, on average, about four times per session which is certainly more frequently than untrained tutors but at only half the rate of our trained peer tutors. Finally, we were disturbed to find that nearly three quarters of the pupils were reading from books which were too easy for them whilst a few were on books that were too difficult. It must be emphasized, however, that these are only preliminary findings.

We believe this issue of book level to be critical. If a child can read only three or four words from a ten-word sentence there is little chance of him being able to utilize contextual cues whereas if he knows eight or nine of the ten words his chances of predicting the unknown words are much higher, especially when given a contextual prompt. If, however, he can read nearly every word in the book he has little chance to make progress in this important skill of predicting unrecognized words from meaning and graphophonic cues. The implication of this is that book level is at least as important as the tutoring methodology; in fact, the effectiveness of the tutoring methods is contingent upon appropriate book level.

In view of this, our approach to operationalizing peer and parent tutoring using 'pause, prompt and praise' differs slightly from that of its authors. We would emphasize the (in our view) all-important role of skilled, trained teachers in successfully implementing 'pause, prompt and praise' tutoring with parents and peers. We are keen to see tutoring skills 'given away' to non-professional tutors but are reluctant to allow benefits to be 'thrown away' by insufficient attention to detail, especially with regard to initial placement and promotion in book level. In our view, the teacher should be responsible for this; albeit with the full collaboration of parents or peer tutors, for it is too critical to be left open to error. Thus it can be seen that far from demeaning the reading teacher or 'taking bread from the teachers' mouths', there is, in fact, an important, professional and skilled role for the teacher to play in tutoring programmes. Apart from taking the initiative in publicizing the approach and setting schemes in motion the teacher will be responsible for training tutors, for record keeping, for initial placement and subequent promotion of children to appropriate book levels, for giving feedback on tutoring performance and so on. Parents and peers are extremely valuable resources for the effective tutoring of reading to low progress readers but the success or failure of any such tutoring programme will hinge upon the professional skills of teachers.

TOPICS FOR DISCUSSION

1. What are two important requirements of those who teach reading in the 'pause, prompt and praise' model? What very different error-correction strategies are involved in the 'pause, prompt and praise' model and 'paired reading'? What effects on the child might these two different strategies have? (See suggested reading 1 below.)
2. 'In fact, "pause, prompt and praise" describes the *third* aspect - that is, the teacher's response to the reading.' What do the authors recommend the teacher's response should be?
3. 'When presenting teachers with the "pause, prompt and praise" procedures we have often been told that this may be good advice for parents or peers listening to children read but that, "of course, teachers do this already". Our subjective observations caused us to doubt this glib assumption.' Discuss.

SUGGESTIONS FOR FURTHER READING

1. Winter, S. (1985) 'Giving parents a choice: teaching paired reading and pause, prompt and praise strategies in a workshop setting', in Topping, K. and Wolfendale, S. (eds) *Parental Involvement in Children's Reading*. London, Croom Helm, pp. 201–7.

Winter discusses the very different error-correction strategies involved in paired reading (PR) and pause, prompt and praise (PPP) models of intervention and cites evidence to suggest that, despite the differences, a number of studies have shown both techniques to be effective when used by parents with their children. At present, he suggests, there are no grounds for selecting one technique to the exclusion of the other. The author comments, 'in this situation it seems fairer to instruct parents in the use of both methods, give them a chance to use each, and then ask them and their children to select the one they feel most comfortable using and, if they have a view on it, the one they feel is working best for them' (p. 201). The article describes and evaluates a workshop which Winter set up aimed to do all of these things.

2. Topping, K. (1985) 'An introduction to behavioural methods', in Topping, K. and Wolfendale, S. (eds) *Parental Involvement in Children's Reading*. London, Croom Helm, pp. 163–72.

In this very useful reading, Topping discusses four basic methods of parental involvement in reading. All four approaches, the author writes, 'embody a preoccupation with the surface behaviour of the participants, rather than supposing or implying mysterious and intangible cognitive processes. The methods act directly to change the reading behaviour of the participants' (p. 163). Topping discusses the methods of (a) reinforcement, (b) pause, prompt and praise, (c) precision teaching, and (d) direct instructions. With reference to Reading 4, to do with pause, prompt and praise, the author affirms that this technique has strong 'behavioural' features, but owes as much to miscue analysis and a psycholinguistic analysis of the reading process as it does to straightforward behaviourism (p. 165). The technique, developed by McNaughton, Glynn and Robinson (1981) is based on earlier reading research by Clay (1979). Unlike other techniques, PPP takes account of changes in parental tutoring behaviour following training, since there is evidence that 'excessive and immediate adult attention to reading errors *reduces* reading accuracy by limiting processing of contextual clues and inhibiting the facility of self-correction' (p. 165). In discussing the technique, Topping writes that 'parents are asked to pause to allow self-correction, and if this does not occur to make a tripartite discrimination as to the nature of the error made. If the mistake makes no sense, the parent prompts the child with clues about the meaning of the story. If the mistake *does* make sense, the parent prompts with clues about the way the word looks. If the child stops and says nothing, the parent prompts by asking the child to read on to the end of the sentence, or reread from the beginning of the sentence (to search for contextual clues). If the error word is not read correctly after two prompts, the parent tells the child what the word is. Praise is given liberally for correct reading, for self-correction, and for successful reading after prompting' (p. 166). Topping illustrates this three-step procedure with the diagram in Figure 4.2.

3. Sutton, W. (1985) 'Some factors in pre-school children of relevance to learning to read', in Clark, M.M. (ed.) (1985) *New Directions in the Study of Reading*. Lewes, Falmer.

Recent research on how children learn to read has demonstrated the importance of the child's ability to understand and to reason about the communicative functions of reading and writing. This ability develops early for some children - children who read before school, identified as 'early' or 'natural' readers. Sutton asserts that 'when considering ways in which reception class teachers can best approach the early stages of the teaching of reading, it is worth summarizing the personal qualities, abilities and environmental factors which are currently considered to be relevant to the process of learning to read (that is, those most often identified in studies of early, or "natural" readers)' (p. 54). This very useful paper offers summaries of:

(a) personal qualities observed in studies of early readers;
(b) skills and abilities;
(c) environmental and social factors.

In the second part of her paper Sutton considers the problem 'whether it is best to put all children on to the same formal pre-reading and reading programme as soon as they start school, or whether there may be a range of relevant observations and assessments, albeit producing highly individual results, which should be used to determine *each child's* starting point, in terms of, for example, extending experience, involving parents and stimulating interest by the selection of subject matter' (p. 57). The author proposes a number of tests, questions and interview techniques which sample the level of those factors amenable to such quantification which were used in her research with a group of young children (who had received no formal reading instruction and of whom none had begun to read). Of particular interest is the technique of 'probe analysis' which Sutton describes in detail. See Lewis, G. (1983) 'Children's perception of dynamics in narrative prose'. *Midland Association for Linguistics Studies Journal*, **8**, 31–46.

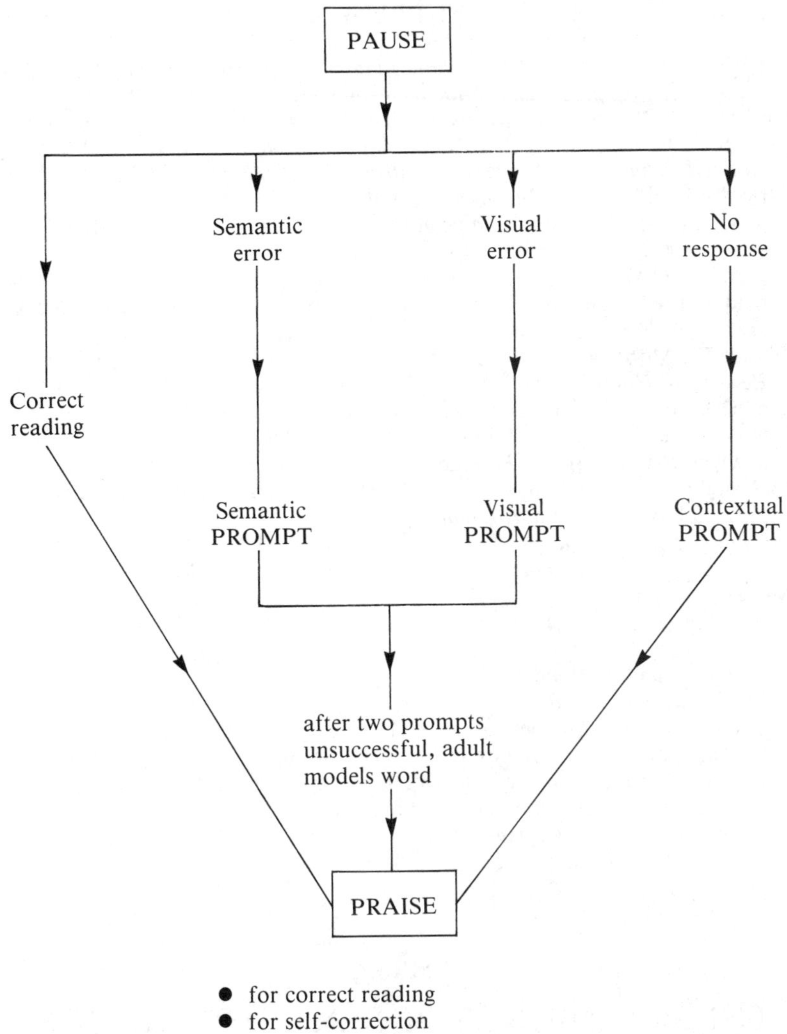

- for correct reading
- for self-correction
- for correct prompted response

Figure 4.2 Topping's (1985) three-step procedure (p. 166)

REFERENCES

Clay, M. (1979) *Reading: The Patterning of Complex Behaviour*, 2nd edn. Auckland, Heinemann Educational.

Glynn, T. (1981) 'Behavioural research in remedial education: more power to the parents', in Wheldall, K. (ed.) *The Behaviourist in the Classroom: Aspects of Applied Behavioural Analysis in British Educational Contexts*. Birmingham, Educational Review Publications.

Glynn, T. (1985) 'Remedial reading at home', in Topping, K. and Wolfendale, S. (eds) op. cit.

Glynn, T. and McNaughton, S.S. (1985) 'The Mangere home and school remedial reading procedures: continuing research on their effectiveness. *New Zealand Journal of Psychology*, **14**, 66–77.

Glynn, T., McNaughton, S.S., Robinson, V. and Quinn, M. (1979) *Remedial Reading at Home: Helping You to Help Your Child*. Wellington, NZCER.

Limbrick, E., McNaughton, S.S. and Glynn, T. (1985) 'Reading gains for underachieving tutors and tutees in a cross-age tutoring programme'. *Journal of Child Psychology and Psychiatry*, **26**, 939-53.

McNaughton, S.S. and Glynn T. (1981) 'Delayed versus immediate attention to oral reading errors'. *Educational Psychology*, **1**, 57–65.

McNaughton, S.S., Glynn, T. and Robinson, V. (1981) *Parents as Remedial Tutors: Issues for Home and School*. Wellington, NZCER.

Morgan, R. and Lyon, E. (1979) 'Paired reading: a preliminary report on a technique for parental tuition of reading retarded children'. *Journal of Child Psychology*, **20**, 151–60.

Topping, K. and Wolfendale, S. (eds) (1985) *Parental Involvement in Children's Reading*. London, Croom Helm.

Wheldall, K. and Mettem, P. (1985) 'Behavioural peer tutoring: training 16-year-old tutors to employ the "pause, prompt and praise" method with 12-year-old remedial readers'. *Educational Psychology*, **55**, 27–44.

Winter, S. (1985) 'Giving parents a choice: teaching paired reading and pause, prompt and praise strategies in a workshop setting', in Topping K. and Wolfendale, S. (eds) op. cit.

Reading 5

THE BEGINNINGS OF SEX STEREOTYPING

P. France

When Kiran, my son, was approaching his second year we started going to a co-operatively run nursery, where he could play with children older and younger than himself. Parents at this nursery take an active role in

France, P. (1986) 'The beginnings of sex stereotyping', in Browne, N. and France, P. (eds) (1986) *Untying the Apron Strings: Anti-Sexist Provision for the Under-Fives*. Milton Keynes, Open University Press, chap. 4, pp. 49–67. Reprinted by permission of Open University Press.

organizing and participating in children's play. One day Kiran and a few other children were playing outside. Kiran's pleasure in his developing running skills became apparent, as he ran about shouting with delight. A., the mother of a two-and-a-half-year-old girl, commented in an approving tone, 'Oh, he's a real boy. So full of energy.' I agreed that he did have energy, but added that many girls can be just as energetic. I then talked about the calm activities, like sharing stories and painting, that Kiran also enjoyed.

A little later A.'s daughter joined Kiran but was quickly warned not to mess up her 'pretty canvas sandals'. Then the girl initiated a new game: kicking a large ball for Kiran to return. Both children enjoyed this collaborative activity so much that they started shouting. Immediately the girl was told to be quiet by her mother, because 'ladies don't shout and make a noise like that'. My very tentative protests that both children were enjoying themselves and that the girl was a skilful ball-kicker did not serve to keep the play going.

This incident highlights the way sex role and behaviour difference are established in the daily lives of very young children. At the time I faced a series of questions and conflicting interests that could be resolved only through regular contact with A. over a period of months.

1. First, I was in a situation where mainly women come with their children in a spirit of equality and co-operation. The talk between adults can be stimulating, friendly, sociable and very supportive. Women have an identity beyond being so-and-so's mother. Naturally I did not want to sour my relationship with any of the women in this setting by challenging ideas in a way that seemed antagonistic. I was aware that, like all of us, A. was trying to raise her child in a patriarchal society, where women and girls are held in check. In-depth discussions are also not practical in a busy nursery.
2. I felt that A.'s comments about Kiran's and her daughter's behaviour needed to be balanced by an alternative viewpoint in front of the children. She was giving voice to a commonplace view: that boys and girls are different and should behave so. This notion can have a limiting effect on both boys and girls by reducing or diverting their options. For a boy to be a 'real boy' he must look and act the part - running, shouting, taking the lead, not caring about appearance or showing any signs of 'weakness'. For a girl to 'act like a lady' she must be the exact opposite - quiet, passive, dependent and careful about her appearance (Browne and France, 1985).
3. I was unsure whether A. intended to stop both children shouting, which is what happened, or whether she honestly believed it was acceptable

for a boy to be noisy. I took the fact that she had already approved of Kiran shouting to be a confirmation that she was reinforcing sex-differentiated behaviour.

4. The way the girl had been dressed meant that she would find it hard to enjoy all the facilities of the nursery. Her open-toed sandals were inappropriate for climbing and might easily be splashed if she engaged in painting or water-and-sand play. She was already learning, like many other girls have and will, that dressing 'prettily' can get in the way of activity and exploration. Girls have to make choices: engage only in activities that suit 'pretty' clothes or attempt to wear more appropriate clothes – a hard choice for any two-year-old.

Why do incidents like this happen all too often in children's lives? What can anti-sexist parents and teachers do to broaden children's experiences and avoid channelling children into narrowly defined and unequal sex roles? The following sections tackle these questions: first, by giving an overview of the various influential theories that tend to describe and explain sex differences; then by considering how a patriarchal society like Britain's is upheld from generation to generation, drawing on my experience as a parent and teacher in London; third, by suggesting some strategies that may help our children grow up with an approach to life that does not rely on sex and race stereotypes.

WHAT THE 'EXPERTS' SAY

Many scientific theories that have attempted to demonstrate and explain differences between people, or between groups of people, have been built on the 'nature/nurture' debate, i.e. on a discussion of whether differences can be accounted for in terms of heredity or environment. John Archer (1978) points out that an adherence to one or other viewpoint has implications for any attempts at change or the development of appropriate social policy:

> For example if one takes the view that criminals are such because of their genetic make-up, the implication is that money spent on improving social conditions as a way of eradicating crime will be largely wasted. However, if one takes the view that some environmental conditions are the important factors, one can then suggest social remedies to prevent crime.

By analogy we can say that the biological explanation for sex-differentiated behaviour means that nothing can be done to change the status quo. An environmental approach allows for change within the growing child's social setting. The biological explanation of sex differences pivots on the assertion that women are intellectually inferior to men. It is believed that women alone possess from birth the personality traits and emotional characteristics that will suit them for their preordained role as carers, housekeepers and dependants. A growing body of research has shown up the flaws in such a theory, which is in reality an expression of the theorists' own biased opinion of women's capabilities and role in society (Archer, 1978; Griffiths and Saraga, 1979; Bland, 1981).

The comprehensive research reviews of Maccoby and Jacklin (1974) and Fairweather (1976) have shown that the extent of proved differences between males and females has been greatly exaggerated. Much substantiated evidence for sex differences in human beings comes from studies of animal behaviour. Griffiths and Saraga (1979) point out that Corinne Hutt's (1972) conclusion that greater male achievement is due to males' greater persistence and single-mindedness is based on evidence from studies of chicks! They conclude that

> the dominant ideology of our society encourages us to believe that the social order is not only legitimate but also 'natural' and hence inevitable. Biologically based explanations of human social behaviour provide an important input into this ideology . . . but how can a biologically based explanation account for very rapid social change, such as the events of the Chinese revolution? (Griffiths and Saraga, 1979)

Given theoretical criticisms of biological explanations it is surprising to find so many people still continuing to promote such ideas. Possibly the support these theories give to current ideology helps to preserve them; also, they are much easier to understand than an analysis based on an amalgam of factors corresponding to the complex reality.

Western society is still experiencing the overwhelming influence of Freud's developmental psychology. Like many other feminists, Marie-louise Janssen-Jurreit (1982) has criticized the patriarchal bias in his theoretical framework and shown that Freudian-orientated anthropologists and psychoanalysts have been responsible for perpetuating the idea of sex-differentiated behaviour. Joan Bean (1978) has pointed out that Freud's theory of sex role development

> assumes the overriding significance of biology and early experience . . . [and] predicts a lifelong stability of masculine qualities for males and feminine qualities for females, ignoring the influences of the cultural environment.

Bean provides a critical view not only of Freud's model but also of two other theories that have been influential in the twentieth century. Both of these focus on the environmental factors that affect sex-role behaviour. The first is a social learning theory based on Skinner's learning theory of stimulus, response and reinforcement. Here the child is in the passive position of acquiring appropriate sex-role behaviour through a series of rewards and punishments from people in the environment. This theory denies any individual choice or the possibility of adopting an alternative sex role. The other theory considered by Bean does place the child in a more active role. This is the theory developed by Kohlberg from Piaget's cognitive stage framework. Kohlberg (1975) considers that a child learns sex-appropriate behaviour as a function of interaction with the immediate environment. Two-thirds of the children that he questioned could tell the sex of a doll shown to them by the time they reached forty months. He concluded: 'as soon as the boy categorizes himself as being male he will value positively the objects and acts that agree with his gender identity'. It is revealing of Kohlberg's own attitudes that he has concentrated his research on the responses of boys.

Sex-identification theories like this have been amply criticized by Selma Greenberg (1979). She shows that one implication of such theories is that boys are assumed to have nothing to learn from women; yet, in a society where women have the major responsibility for early child care, 'A boy is likely to be at home with one adult whom he has neither to walk like, talk like, think like or act like.' Girls, in being discouraged from identifying with their fathers, will be denied 'the world of knowledge, skills and opportunities that greater social access and preferential social treatment have given them [the fathers]' (Greenberg, 1979). From my own experience of boys being raised principally by their fathers and thus seeing men in a caring role, it is still possible to find these boys behaving at times very differently from the male model they have.

A general criticism of all these theories of sex-role development, expressed by various writers (Archer, 1978; Bean, 1978; Rowan, 1979), is that the status quo is upheld uncritically by such theorists. They come from and reinforce the ideology of sexism that permeates the society at all levels.

Alternative models of child development must challenge this rigid adherence to the concept of male and female as opposite sexes, and to the notion of clearly differentiated, unalterable sex roles. They must also take into account that each child is an individual actively involved in her or his development who will profit from being able to develop abilities, interests and personality as broadly as possible, without being restricted into narrow stereotypes. In addition a theory should recognize that there are as many differences between people of the same sex as there are between the sexes (Griffiths and Saraga, 1979).

The preservation of differentiated sex roles is a highly political issue in a patriarchal society. The attributes traditionally assigned to men of being aggressive, competitive and dominating serve to bolster such a society, and violence becomes an important tool to keep 'women feeling fearful, inferior and inadequate so that they do not even contemplate revolt' (Rowan, 1979). Although Rowan confirms that some male psychologists and sociologists, in addition to many feminists, have written about the value to society gained from the breakdown of patriarchy, the question still remains whether their perception has had any impact on child-raising theory and practice.

'DO WHAT I SAY': PATRIARCHY PERPETUATED?

Criticisms of traditional theories have hardly percolated into the lives of people involved in child care in Britain. A child is born into a society bound by rules and standards. These help to perpetuate the notion that there are sex differences. Underlying this idea are certain assumptions, which are transmitted through a range of influential sources. New parents become willing or unwitting upholders of the same values and sex-role stereotypes that have restricted their own horizons. Parents will be given advice from four main sources: the family network, professional advisers, the community (especially the peer group) and the media.

Family network

Value judgements are expressed in homespun truths transmitted from one generation to the next. The authority structure within families, which rests on a sense of allegiances, makes it difficult for new parents to challenge, if they want, the sex-stereotyped views of their relatives. Older relatives may respond to a challenge by referring to their longer-standing experience as parents.

Professionals

Not only is there a ready-made network of advisers created by family and friends of new parents, but industrial society has also created a network of experts and professionals, from the areas of health, education and social services. They form an influential body of opinion, yet in many ways serve to bolster up the status quo, by presenting society as dominated by a white middle-class male élite. Challenging traditional views here can be even more precarious; these people are responsible for decisions that may affect your child's health, social welfare and educational future.

Community and peer group

The power of the community must not be underestimated. A new parent may be drawn into a closer relationship with people, including other parents, in the community and will feel considerable pressure to conform to the norms expressed in that environment. Anyone and everyone feels capable of offering advice and criticism about how to look after a child.

Power of the media

The images of people's roles in society presented by the media are still clearly sex-differentiated. There have been challenges made, especially to advertisers, yet very little has changed. Women are still housewives, mothers and sex objects; men are still busy paid workers controlling the lives of others, being aggressive, adventurous and competitive (Matlow, 1981; McRobbie and McCabe, 1981).

The four assumptions

The major sources of influence on parents described above ultimately have an effect on their children, who also learn about society from their parents and their peers. Underlying the patriarchal outlook, and reflected in social policy and legislation, are the following assumptions, which uphold the notion of sex differences.

Assumption 1: women and men must adopt different roles from each other when they become parents

If, like Lesley Holly (1982), we conduct a survey of the images of parents that are presented by the media and by magazines and booklets from professional organizations such as the British Medical Association, the Royal Society of Medicine and the Health Visitors' Association, we find that the ideology of motherhood, popularized by Bowlby and followers, is enjoying a resurgence. Leading child-care writers, such as Penelope Leach and Gordon Bourne, promote this image. Throughout, the parental model is of a white, heterosexual married couple, who demonstrate sex-differentiated characteristics and undertake different roles serving to maintain a male-dominated family structure.

To be a 'proper mother' a woman is expected to be a warm, loving carer, responsive to the physical and emotional needs of child and father. She must become unpaid 'housewife' as well as mother, married to all the domestic chores involved in running a home. Payment for such work is beyond discussion, yet no paid worker is expected to undertake all the cleaning, repairing and cooking that will happen in the workplace.

Whilst Holly (1982) has pointed out that a new image has been discovered by some social commentators, she considers that it is a token image and that it

> creates an illusion no more liberating than the last . . . so men continue to enjoy their children and family life without having to give up social and economic power, or routinely be involved in the hard work of family life and child rearing.

David Piachaud's (1984) study into the time it takes mothers to care for their pre-school-aged children confirms Holly's view that it is a myth to claim fathers take a full and sometimes equal share in the care of their children. Piachaud found that mothers are responsible for nine out of every ten hours spent on 'life support tasks' (e.g. feeding, washing, nappy changing), whilst fathers take on only one in ten hours.

A man is expected to subordinate any inclinations towards an active role in child-rearing to the demands of providing financially for 'his' family. In return he is acknowledged as head of the household (as assumed in a question still posed on the UK electoral registration form). He can get away with only a token nod at housework - often in the form of maintenance and repair, i.e. jobs that can be done by paid workers if no one in the household is able to take them on.

Within such a rigid framework men and women are both losers, especially in the early stages of raising a child. Women are forced to give up or limit all hopes of a career or job outside the home and of developing their identity as people other than as mothers. Men miss an opportunity to develop the caring side of their character and to enjoy the stimulation (as well as the hard work) of raising a child and forming a close, influential relationship with that child. This sharp division of roles can create tensions between men and women, who become absorbed in their own areas of expertise and may find themselves in conflict where there are clashes of interest.

Women are often in the position of doing an elaborate balancing act with their time to embark on a wage-earning job, in addition to their role as mother and housekeeper. This hard-earned contribution to the family income is rarely given enough credit. For economic reasons many women are forced into employment where they may be exploited and given little control (e.g. in trade union activity).

In my own recent experience of becoming a mother in addition to paid worker, I was made aware of the staggering extent of difference between the role expected from me and that expected from my partner. From the outset of pregnancy I was reminded, in subtle and not so subtle ways, that I was a mother now - even to the point of being called 'mummy' by one Sister in the antenatal clinic. I was overwhelmed from all quarters with advice, information, support, gifts and equipment on loan. My partner got none of this.

The medical profession continued this differentiated treatment. We were disappointed with how much the father's role was marginalized. The hospital's policy of encouraging fathers to attend the birth of their baby meant in practice that men were tolerated as long as they did not get in the way. The hospital, like many others, was insensitive to the needs of many women; for example, it had not recognized that some ethnic-minority women might be used to different cultural practices in childbirth, where the presence of women friends and relatives is preferable to that of prospective fathers.

After my child's birth I perceived a marked change in the way I and the other mothers were treated. Our views no longer counted, and we were rushed into adopting the well-established practices of child care, such as breast-feeding. Fathers were kept at a distance; rigid visiting hours meant that they had less time with their babies and partners and missed the chances of bonding. I asked for Kiran's first bath, described by the nurse as a demonstration, to be delayed until his father was present, since he wanted to do the bathing at home. The request prompted much surprise and was ignored.

Taking Kiran to the local health clinic for weighing and to meet health visitors was also illuminating. Fathers who came with their partners and babies were rarely spoken to directly by staff - the assumption being that they were merely bystanders or 'chauffeurs'. The considerable number of Asian fathers who came were generally treated as interpreters only, so advice was prefaced by comments like 'Tell your wife she must . . .' Over a couple of years I became aware that many of these men were competent and willing carers of their own children. But the stereotyped view of Asian men 'oppressing their women' and having little to do with child care prevailed. This stereotype is harmful and insulting to men and women. I have witnessed more expressions of warmth, kisses and cuddles directed to Asian children by their fathers than I have ever seen shown by white fathers in Britain. I also have considerable experience of strong and assertive Asian women who are helping their own children break free from sex-role stereotypes. A friend told me once of the preferential treatment her husband received when he took their small daughter to the local health clinic for weighing. He was offered a small room to change her in private and congratulated on being 'so brave and clever' when he explained that he looked after their two children full-time and could easily manage a nappy change.

Assumption 2: the male sex is superior, so a boy child is preferred

Though prospective parents are usually concerned about having a healthy, happy, well-adjusted baby who has few sleeping and eating problems, their attention is diverted by others on to one key issue: the desired sex of the baby. Parents are pushed to state a sex preference. Expressing preference for a girl surprises many, although this tends to be attributed to an act of perversity or a wish on the mother's part to have 'someone to dress up' and 'have as a companion'. Preference for a boy is accepted without the need for justification; after all, 'everyone wants the family line to continue'.

Much of the early child-care advice that parents receive hinges on the concept of sex difference and the importance of the male sex. Feeding a boy baby is expected to be done differently from feeding a girl - 'boys need more because they're more energetic'; 'you don't want a fat daughter'; 'he could do with a bit more fat on him, he's so puny'. A young boy who needs little sleep is excused by those not suffering from his wakefulness; after all, it's a sign that he is 'more intelligent and alert' and has an 'active mind'. A similarly wakeful girl is said to be 'difficult' and really must 'get her beauty sleep'.

In the early stages of life a baby may suffer from stomach pains, known as colic. Some specialists have claimed that only boys suffer this,

> as it is likely they are caused by the baby being lonely and tired and the realization that he doesn't have his mother's full attention. Your thoughts have turned to getting a meal ready for your husband, as is natural, and seeing him. (Jolly and Gordon, 1982)

The false assertion that girls do not suffer from this pain presumably stems from the idea that they will have learnt to cope with less attention already!

Elena Belotti (1975), Selma Greenberg (1979) and Judith Arcana (1983), among others, have considered the ways that the male sex is treated as superior in Western society. I shall focus on one way that language is used to this end: the commonplace practice in writing and speech of referring to the unknown child as 'he'. This happened to a friend when she went for an ultrasonic scan, late in her pregnancy. The radiographer used 'he' to refer to the baby and so she assumed the scan had revealed the sex. The radiographer laughed at this and said that it was usual practice to use 'he' because it was 'easier'. He was surprised by her suggestion that this could be misleading and disappointing.

'He', it is asserted by some baby-care writers, is used as a sex-inclusive term, which avoids the tedious use of 'she or he'. The idea of using 'she' like this is far too provocative. Jenny Cheshire (1985) has pointed out that

> there is a wealth of impressive evidence from psycholinguistic experiments that when we are given a sentence containing the pronoun 'he' we interpret it as referring to a male subject, not a female one.

This interpretation is certainly the prevalent one made by young children. The way a baby behaves even in the womb gets interpreted in sex-stereotyped ways. So if that baby is consistently referred to as 'he', any kicking is interpreted as a sign that *'he's* going to be a footballer', never *'he's* going to be a dancer'.

Assumption 3: a child will be treated differently according to her or his sex

This begins with the baby and affects all aspects of child care. Female and male babies and children are treated differently, and the myth of 'opposite sexes' is still prevalent (Greenberg, 1979).

Assumption 4: boys and girls will develop differently from each other in behaviour, temperament, cognitive and physical ability

Once different aspects of a child's character and behaviour are given social acceptance, it follows that children will stick with these aspects in order to maintain a good relationship with people in their environment – both authority figures and the peer group. Table 5.1 illustrates the different ways male and female babies and children are treated and are expected to behave.

Do the children have any say?

By the time children are two or three years old and can talk about themselves and their relationships with others, they have some awareness of the physical differences between people and are interested in how such differences relate to them. In conversation with my two-and-a-half-year-old I have noticed that he has observed differences between people in terms of size, age, skin colour, sex and physical ability. Fortunately he does not yet link these physical differences to judgemental assertion of dos and don'ts, cans and can'ts. Children's attention is drawn to

Table 5.1 Sex-stereotyped treatment of babies and young children

Area	*Boys*	*Girls*
Sleeping patterns	Poor sleeping is excused and attributed to liveliness.	Girls need their 'beauty sleep'.
Crying	Not tolerated, therefore dealt with more readily to stop crying. Boys learn to suppress this expression of emotions early on (Belotti, 1975).	Babies left to cry. Crying expected from girls and continued to a relatively late age.
Feeding	Given more breast-feed and for longer. Concern if they look underfed.	Given less, weaning earlier. Concern if they look overfed.
Physical play	Rough-and-tumble encouraged between boys and with adults. Assumed to be more active (Loo and Wenar, 1971).	Treated with more care. Less adult male play. Assumed to be less active.
Signs of affection	Learn to shake hands not kiss. Affection shown to mother is more criticized the older the boy gets. Not liked if kisses other boys. Can kiss girls and babies.	Encouraged to kiss everyone. Can show affection to mother till quite old. Approved if kisses other girls, babies and boys.
Use of outdoors	Encouraged to use space and be active (Hart, 1978).	Less encouragement to play outside.
Domestication	Help with car care, DIY, gardening; toys reflect this. Can be untidy.	Help with household chores; toys reflect this. Must be tidy.
Dependence/ independence	Encouraged to explore, not be 'tied to the apron strings'.	Kept close till older age (Belotti, 1975; Hart, 1978; Serbin, 1978).
Socializing	Can be rough with other boys; 'like a gentleman' with girls.	Must be 'ladylike' with girls. Not to play with boys – 'they're too rough'.
Aggression/ assertiveness	Encouraged to 'avoid being a wimp'. A boy's aggression to another is a case of 'boys will be boys'.	Restrained, even if standing up for themselves.

differences and opposites by the songs and stories that they hear. Yet whilst promoting such a sense of difference, those involved with young children are coy and evasive in two areas: they tend to be 'colour blind', and avoid discussion of anatomical sex difference, yet happily create sex-role differences (Greenberg, 1979).

In a very busy learning period children are subject to a host of influences that preserve the status quo. The influence of the child's close family is strong, and so is that of the media and the peer group. The following three incidents illustrate some of the experiences my son has had from his contact with other children. In these encounters he is picking up messages about the type of behaviour that is socially acceptable for all children and what is expected of boys in particular, if they wish to join with their peers. Caution is needed before asserting that sex identification operates between peers (see Greenberg, 1979), but we can at least give this source of influence consideration in connection with the adults' reactions and how these affect the bonds developing between children.

1. Kiran and I had been going to a 'baby bounce' for several months at the local leisure centre. Towards the end of one session two four-year-old boys started to fight with another boy, pushing him to the ground and piling on top of him. This boy's carer reproved him for being 'all talk' and 'bottling out'. The adults with the other two just laughed, even louder when a younger brother started to make threatening postures. Kiran was bewildered by all this, but the following week he imitated the boys as he approached others.
2. Children react differently depending on the setting – not only the physical environment, but also who is there. For example, one morning at our nursery co-operative Kiran and two young brothers were playing happily alongside each other with play-dough and animal shapes. Shortly after, two other boys arrived with toy guns (although we have a no-guns policy) and almost immediately started chasing, shouting and shooting each other. The whole atmosphere changed; both Kiran and his two friends reacted till all the boys were running about. There were confrontations, fights and tears, one gun was lost, the other broken.

   We diverted the children's attention into a variety of other activities, and by taking charge and splitting up the children we were able to restore the peace. I was struck by the change not only in Kiran and his friends but also in the others once parted from their guns and involved in more constructive play.
3. Boys and girls in this nursery have marked out territories for themselves. Sometimes the same equipment or space is used in very different ways. A wooden framework that has a door and window is turned into a home or shop by groups of girls and becomes the setting for some imaginative and co-operative play; boys use it to hammer on, bang the doors and windows and fight over occupancy.

It is important to become aware of the conflicting messages that children pick up from their peers and find ways of helping them understand just how complex any individual can be. Voicing concern over the aggression of a boy or the passivity of a girl is not enough. We must help children express their feelings – the whole range – and understand how non-productive aggression or passivity can be. We must also avoid making over-generalizations like 'he's so tough', 'always on the go', 'a good little fighter', 'she's so good-natured', 'home-loving', especially in their hearing. Remember that these are only characteristics children demonstrate some of the time.

We need also to be alert to the images that children are subjected to from the media. [. . .] In addition to children's programmes it is important to consider breakfast-time and early-evening television. Some violent and sexist US imports (*Dukes of Hazard, The A-Team*, etc.) have been screened earlier in the evening to catch a young audience, and this has been linked with the heavy promotion of toys featuring the fast cars, combat gear and guns seen on the programmes.

Over a period of several months' selective viewing of children's programmes (from both the BBC and commercial television) I have noticed a sexist bias in both programmes and advertisements, and a preponderance of violent themes, particularly in cartoons. By contrast, studio-based programmes that have an educational perspective - like *Playschool, Rainbow and Mooncat* - are attempting a positive approach. Both men and women appear as informed, skilled and caring adults. Yet these positive gains are undermined by the cumulative effects of the other programmes on offer. Much of the material is dated, particularly the inevitable American cartoons with their superfluity of heroes or violent 'humanized' male animals, and as a consequence the sexist, racist and élitist values of an earlier generation are openly promoted.

Young children are treated daily to short-story series animated with puppets or illustrations (*Postman Pat*, *Camberwick Green*, *Alfie Atkins*, etc.). The majority of these use a male story-teller and have a male main character - apart from *Heggarty Haggerty*, which features a witch.

Advertisements shown during breakfast-time, early-evening and weekend children's programmes concentrate on toys, food, drinks and sometimes household commodities. They are heavily sex-biased. Dolls, cuddly animals and home-based toys - cookers, vacuum-cleaners and the like - are shown being played with by girls only. Boys alone are shown using cars, highly competitive games, bikes and toys of aggression. In food and drink advertisements boys of all ages are shown as rock stars and dancers; girls, when they are featured, are their adoring fans. Some animated images are openly racist, associating black characters with a jungle setting, rhythmic drum-beat and other such stereotypes. Needless to say, household commodities are still used only by women; they get 'expert' advice from a man, who appears in person or does the voice-over.

STRATEGIES FOR CHANGE

1. Avoid describing characteristics as typically masculine or feminine. See the wide-ranging potential of every child, given encouragement and non-restricting treatment.
2. Remember (and remind others) that diversity between people operates within the same sex.
3. Remember (and remind others) that each individual has a range of characteristics, behaviours, emotions and capabilities and will respond differently in different settings and with different people.
4. Try to offer an alternative, additional viewpoint when sexist comments are made.
5. Remember that you have time on your side. Your views, attitudes and behaviour will become apparent to your child as she or he gets older. You will remain the constant factor in your child's life.
6. Even when your own roles seem to reflect the traditional stereotypes, e.g. for economic reasons, try to point out to your child that alternative roles are possible.
7. Do not trivialize or elevate a role or task just because it is traditionally sex-associated (Bowman, 1978).
8. Talk, talk, talk; share your views with your child, relatives, friends, professionals and other parents.
9. Be careful in the selection of experiences that you organize for your child. But be realistic that you cannot build a shell to protect your child.
10. Find ways to exert influence on the outside world. Unite with other parents and carers to express your view and change practice in shops, libraries, schools, health centres and playgroups. Express views in writing to pressure book publishers and booksellers, toy manufacturers, television programme editors and so on. Find support from established groups like women's centres and community bookshops.

Remember that children are human beings who have a right to express themselves and not just become a walking, talking version of your political beliefs:

> The active/passive, aggressive/submissive distinctions are not only traditional male/female distinctions. They also express values in a capitalist society . . . some parents may feel so strongly about non-sexism that they are prepared to enforce it in their children. Do we really want non-sexism at any price? How can we encourage non-sexism without being authoritarian, without thwarting our children's developing personality and autonomy?

TOPICS FOR DISCUSSION

1. 'Alternative models of child development must challenge this rigid adherence to the concept of male and female as opposite sexes, and to the notion of clearly differentiated, unalterable sex roles. They must also take into account that each child is an individual actively involved in her or his development who will profit from being able to develop abilities, interests and personality as broadly as possible, without being restricted into narrow stereotypes.' Discuss.
2. 'Countering sexism is part of the struggle to extend choices and opportunities for everyone.' Discuss.
3. What are the most important aspects of the school and its organization which need to be considered when attempting to develop an anti-sexist policy?

SUGGESTIONS FOR FURTHER READING

1. Whyte, J. (1983) *Beyond the Wendy House: Sex Role Stereotyping in Primary Schools*. London, Longman for Schools Council.

The author's 'message' is that sexual equality is dependent on eliminating sex bias in the earliest years of education - and that to achieve this goal the commitment and support of primary school teachers is of paramount importance. She describes a wide range of sex-stereotyped practices that are common experiences for many girls and boys during their primary education, emphasizing that such practices 'are insidious because they are unconscious and yet particularly persuasive in their long-term effects on girls' and boys' abilities, aspirations and achievements' (p. 5). Whyte reports that many nursery and reception teachers claim to be able to see differences between girls' and boys' behaviour, interests and attitudes as soon as they first come into school. She asks the question when and how this sex-typing occurs and considers whether it is inherent in the make-up of each sex or whether it is the result of social learning. Certainly it is the case that as children progress through the school system sex differences in 'learning styles' become increasingly apparent. 'The boy's learning style is active, participatory, demanding, lending itself to a confident, independent approach to learning. The girl's is more passive, less participatory, making fewer demands on the teacher's time and attention and leading to an underestimation of her own ability and lack of confidence, especially in science and mathematics' (p. 8).

Chapter 2 of the book considers what children have learned before they come to school, summarizing some of the evidence about ways in which children adapt to the 'appropriate' sex-role behaviour expected of them by parents, teachers and society at large. Of particular relevance is Whyte's account (in chap. 4) of the 'hidden curriculum', which discusses how the experience of school can reinforce traditional sex-role stereotypes and exacerbate the polarization of the sexes. She highlights four aspects of school life which, she claims, constitute a 'hidden curriculum' from which children learn and adapt to different expectations and standards for boys and girls:

(a) the informal interactions between children in the classroom or outside it;
(b) common school experiences (practices and procedures) which divide or distinguish the sexes, often for no sound educational reason;

(c) teachers' expectations;
(d) patterns of teacher–pupil interaction in class.

2. Davies, D. (1984) 'Sex role stereotyping in children's imaginative writing', in Cowie, H. (ed.) *The Development of Children's Imaginative Writing*. London, Croom Helm, chap. 4, pp. 73–87.

Although this reading is not specifically concerned with the pre-school age group, it has been deliberately included to show how sex-role typing in the very early years shapes the attitudes, behaviours and values of children as they grow older. Maccoby and Jacklin (1974) found that 'Boys seem to have more intense socialization experiences than girls. They receive more pressure against engaging in sex-inappropriate behaviour, whereas the activities that girls are not supposed to engage in are much less clearly defined and less firmly enforced. Boys receive more punishment, but probably also more praise and encouragement . . . Whatever the explanation, the different amounts of socialization pressure that boys and girls receive surely have consequences for the development of their personalities' (p. 348). Similarly, Block (1978) found more consistent emphasis in the socialization of sons in the areas of achievement, competition, independence in the sense of personal responsibility, and in the control of emotion. Davies provides a very useful digest of recent research on sex-role stereotyping and discusses at length the subject of sex-role socialization of children by parents. She considers the evidence to show how teachers actively contribute to the process of sex-role stereotyping, describing a number of studies which suggest that teachers differentially encourage sex-appropriate behaviour and evaluate children's performances according to sex-stereotypical dimensions. Discussing sex-role stereotyping of children by the mass media, Davies writes, 'There is wide agreement as to the stereotypic characteristics and behaviour ascribed to males and females, and despite changes in many societal values over the last few decades these stereotypes have maintained an unchanging quality. Further, sex-role stereotypes have for most people been incorporated into the individual's self-concept' (p. 81). The author shows that throughout the media, and in particular children's literature and television programmes, 'males and females are presented in ways consistent with their sex-stereotyped image. Different messages are conveyed as to the appropriate behaviour for males and females, thus providing an important source in both learning and reinforcing existing stereotyped sex roles' (p. 86).

3. Thomas, G. (1986) 'Hallo, Miss Scatterbrain. Hallo, Mr Strong: assessing attitudes and behaviour in the nursery', in Browne, N. and France, P. (eds) *Untying the Apron Strings: Anti-Sexist Provision for the Under-Fives*. Milton Keynes, Open University Press, chap. 7, pp. 104–20.

This reading explores how the sexual inequalities which are inherent in our education system are introduced at a very early age, in fact, during the pre-school years. The crux of Thomas's argument is that sex-typed roles restrict personal fulfilment for *both* males and females by severely limiting the options that each is allowed to pursue. The 'message' is that sexual equality is dependent on the elimination of sex bias in the earliest years of education and that primary school teachers must be committed to this goal. Recent research adds support to earlier evidence that education in the early years is unduly geared towards boys' interests, that boys receive more time and attention from their teachers than girls, and that in the early years of schooling teachers classify children according to their sex and expect sex-stereotyped behaviour from them. In this reading Thomas provides illuminating evidence to suggest that this state of affairs continues.

REFERENCES

Arcana, J. (1983) *Every Mother's Son*. London, Women's Press.

Archer, J. (1978) 'Biological explanations of sex-role stereotypes', in Chetwynd, J. and Hartnett, O. (eds) *The Sex Role System*. London, Routledge & Kegan Paul.

Bean, J. (1978) 'The development of psychological androgyny: early childhood socialisation', in Sprung, B. (ed) *Perspectives on Non-Sexist Early Childhood Education*. Teachers' College Press, University of Columbia.

Belotti, E.G. (1975) *Little Girls*. London, Writers and Readers.

Bland, L. (1981) 'It's only human nature', 'Sociobiology and sex differences'. *Schooling and Culture*, **10**, Summer, ILEA Cockpit Arts Workshop.

Block, J.H. (1978) 'Another look at sex differentiation in the socialization behaviour of mothers and fathers', in Sherman, J.A. and Denmark, F.L. (eds) *The Psychology of Women: Future Directions in Research*. New York, Psychological Dimensions Inc.

Bourne, J. (1983) 'Towards an anti-racist feminism'. *Race and Class*, **XXV**, 1, Institute of Race Relations.

Bowlby, J. (1952) *Maternal Care and Mental Health*. Geneva, World Health Organization.

Bowlby, J. (1953) *Childcare and the Growth of Love*. Harmondsworth, Penguin.

Bowman, B. (1978) 'Sexism and racism in education', in Sprung, B. (ed.) *Non-Sexist Early Childhood Education*. Teachers' College Press, University of Columbia.

Browne, N. and France. P. (1985) 'Only cissies wear dresses', in Weiner, G. (ed.) *Just a Bunch of Girls*. Milton Keynes, Open University Press.

Byrne, E.M. (1978) *Women and Education*. London, Tavistock.

Cheshire, J. (1985) 'A question of masculine bias'. *English Today*, **1**, January, Cambridge University Press.

Clarricoates, K. (1980) 'The importance of being Ernest . . . Emma . . . Tom and Jane', in Deem, R. (ed.) *Schooling for Women's Work*. London, Routledge & Kegan Paul.

Fairweather, H. (1976) 'Sex differences in cognition'. *Cognition*, **4**.

Greenberg, S. (1979) *Right from the Start: A Guide to Non-Sexist Child Rearing*. Boston, Houghton Mifflin.

Griffiths, D. and Saraga, E. (1979) 'Sex differences and cognitive abilities: a Griffiths field of enquiry?', in Hartnett, O., Boden, G. and Fuller, M. (eds) *Sex Role Stereotyping*. London, Tavistock.

Hart, R. (1978) 'Sex differences in the use of outdoor space', in Sprung, B. (ed.) op cit.

Holly, L. (1982) 'Who's holding the baby?'. *Spare Rib*, **122**, September.

Hutt, C. (1972) *Males and Females*. Harmondsworth, Penguin.

ILEA (1982) *Equal Opportunities for Girls and Boys*. Report by the ILEA Inspectorate.

ILEA (1984) *Providing Equal Opportunities for Girls and Boys in Physical Education*. ILEA Study Group.

Janssen-Jurreit, M. (1982) *Sexism: The Male Monopoly on History and Thought*. London, Pluto Press.

Jolly, H. and Gordon, H. (1982) *A–Z Pregnancy and Babycare*. London, Royal Society of Medicine.

Kohlberg, L. (1975) 'Moral stages and moralization', in Lickona, T. (ed.) *Moral Development and Behaviour*. New York, Holt Rinehart and Winston.

Leach, P. (1979) *Who Cares?*. Harmondsworth, Penguin.

Loo, C. and Wenar, C. (1971) 'Activity level and motor inhibition'. *Child Development*, **42**.

Maccoby, E.E. and Jacklin, C.N. (1974) *The Psychology of Sex Differences*. Stanford University Press.

Matlow, E. (1981) 'Advertising, imagery, women and the family'. *Schooling and Culture*, **10**, Summer, ILEA Cockpit Arts Workshop.

McRobbie, A. and McCabe, T. (1981) *Feminism for Girls. An Adventure Story*. London, Routledge & Kegan Paul.

Piachaud, D. (1984) *Round About 50 Hours a Week*. London, Child Poverty Action Group.

Rowan, J. (1979) 'Psychic celibacy in men', in Hartnett, O., Boden, G. and Fuller, M. (eds) op. cit.

Serbin, L. (1978) 'Teachers, peers and play preferences', in Sprung, B. (ed) op. cit.

Spender, D. and Sarah, E. (eds) (1980) *Learning to Lose: Sexism and Education*. London, Women's Press.

Stones, R. (1983) 'Pour out the cocoa, Janet'. *Sexism in Children's Books*. London, Longman for Schools Council.

Whyte, J. (1983) *Beyond the Wendy House: Sex Role Stereotyping in Primary Schools*. London, Longman for Schools Council.

SECTION TWO

HOME-SCHOOL/ COMMUNITY LINKS

INTRODUCTION

Section Two of the sourcebook consists of three readings, the first of which questions whether the information which schools must now statutorily provide about themselves is of interest and value to parents. The author suggests that parents are predominantly interested in different kinds of information about schools from that now on offer, and that by encouraging schools to compete with each other, effective home–school communication is more likely to be constrained rather than promoted.

Munn reviews a number of recent research projects on accountability, concluding that parents are most interested in obtaining information which they can relate directly and specifically to their own children, and that, in parents' views, the mechanisms by which this information is conveyed (report cards and consultation evenings) are in urgent need of reform. The author comments, 'by placing schools in direct competition with each other and emphasizing parents' rights, it [recent legislation] places home–school relationships in a combative framework' (p. 118).

Reading 7 provides illuminating insights into the kinds of communication which take place every day between the home and the school. The letters and notes which schools receive from parents, the author asserts, 'taken together . . . offer a unique view of teacher–parent relationships, of life for the young family at home and, in their assumptions, of life in school' (p. 121). In this very readable account, Roberts concludes that 'an occasional review of letters sent to school has much to offer to teachers. If they become conscious of the difficulties parents still experience with the written word they may become more tolerant and realistic about their children. It may also provide a clearer perception of the problems faced both by parents and by teachers themselves and of the implication of such problems for teacher–parent relationships' (p. 128).

In the last reading in this section Hughes introduces his paper with a succinct review of recent developments in parental involvement, concluding that 'in general terms, then, the principle of involving parents and the wider community in early education has nowdays achieved widespread acceptance' (p. 133), but that the assumptions and philosophies which underlie any particular community or parental involvement scheme will crucially affect the orientation and direction of that scheme. Hughes calls one widespread set of assumptions underlying many approaches to community and parental involvement the 'deficit' model. The author writes that 'the main characteristic of this model . . . is the assumption that particular groups of parents (usually working-class, or ethnic minorities, or isolated rural families) are defective in the educational environment which they are providing for their children. The purpose of involving these parents, then, is to encourage and help them change their child-rearing practices – for example by modelling them on the practices of teachers or other professionals' (p. 133). It is only in recent psychological literature that these assumptions of linguistic deficit have been challenged. Hughes suggests that three recent British studies (see suggested readings 1, 2 and 3) demonstrate that the homes of the vast majority of children provide rich learning environments – often richer than those involving young children and their teachers.

In later sections of this paper the author considers aspects of the community which impinge on the life of the young child and discusses how these aspects influence young children's development and learning.

In the second article which makes up this reading, Watt reaches similar conclusions to those of Hughes, stressing that ways must be found of bridging the gap between home and school by using the community to achieve more successful learning in children. Where Hughes tends to look mainly to teachers to find ways of capitalizing on children's out-of-school experiences, Watt stresses the importance of the complementary process of parents capitalizing on their children's in-school learning, so that 'parents and children could build on the shared experience of school as they went about their daily lives at home and within the community. If we had both processes going on side by side then not only might we achieve better learning in children, but we might also move closer to an understanding of what "community" in early education might mean' (p. 146).

Reading 6

ACCOUNTABILITY AND PARENT-TEACHER COMMUNICATION

P. Munn

A flurry of information about schools has recently become statutorily available to parents. As a consequence of the recent Education Acts in England and Scotland, schools are obliged to provide information about their public examination record and to provide general information about themselves, such as their aims and objectives, the courses they offer, their staff complement and so on. More recently still, HMI reports on schools inspected have become publicly available.

The availability of all this information about schools can be seen as the latest manifestation of a government concern about school accountability which transcends both major political parties. Under Labour, concern about accountability manifested itself via the so-called Great Debate on education initiated by James Callaghan. The diverse issues in that debate, the cost-effectiveness of schools, the coherence and relevance of the school curriculum, the worries about 'standards' and the need for schools to be more responsive to public needs, have been reconstructed by the present government within a framework of market forces ideology. By re-emphasizing the parents' right to choose the school their children will attend, the government is encouraging schools to enter into competition for pupils. It hopes that the information now available about schools will be used by parents in helping them to make this choice. Schools whose examination record is poor, or who receive critical reports from the Inspectorate, or who are not offering the kind of education which parents want, will be forced to change their ways if they are to attract customers, or so the argument seems to go.

The renewed emphasis on parents' rights (the 1981 Act in Scotland is popularly known as 'The Parents' Charter') has highlighted an important aspect of school and teacher accountability, namely home-school relations. Parental interest and involvement in their children's education has long been regarded as important for pupil learning (see, for example, Douglas, 1964; Wiseman, 1964; Newsom and Newsom, 1976). It seems appropriate to ask, therefore, whether the information which the schools must now statutorily provide about themselves is of interest and value to

Munn, P. (1985) 'Accountability and parent–teacher communication'. *British Educational Research Journal*, **11**, 2, 105–10. Reprinted by permission of the copyright holder, Carfax Publishing Company.

parents, and indeed whether this information promotes effective home-school communication. I want to suggest that parents are predominantly interested in different kinds of information about schools from that now on offer and that by placing schools in competition with each other the government is more likely to constrain than to promote effective home-school communication.

ACCOUNTABILITY AND PARENTS' VIEWS

A number of research projects on accountability were funded in the late 1970s by the SSRC, as it was then known. Three of these, which have now reported and which included extensive exploration of parents' views (Becher et al., 1981; Elliot, 1981; Munn et al., 1982) found parental trust in the expertise and competence of teachers to be a pervasive feature of their data. Becher, for instance, concludes that 'Parents' respect for a teacher's professional role and judgement is usually strong and need not normally be doubted' (p. 36). Nias (1981, p. 221) states that in all the Cambridge Accountability Project schools, 'researchers found teachers defending their right to autonomy on the basis of (their expert) knowledge, and parents, governors and employers ready to accede to their claims'. The Scottish research similarly reports that parents saw teachers 'as possessing specialized skills and knowledge which they, as lay persons did not have . . . Parents assumed that teachers were competent in applying skills and knowledge' (p. 18).

From this trust in teachers' expertise and competence certain consequences seem to follow in terms of the kind of information about school which parents were interested in. All three projects conclude that parents seem content to delegate to teachers, decisions on a whole range of matters concerning schooling, on the grounds of teachers' expertise. Thus the availability of general information about the curriculum or about school organization and management seems not to have been a dominant concern of parents. These were matters for expert decisions. Indeed, all three projects report poor parental attendance at meetings organized by schools to transmit information on aspects of the curriculum and report teachers' views that this indicated parents' lack of interest in schooling.

In contrast, parental attendance at consultation evenings was generally high. On these occasions their individual children were the explicit focus of parent-teacher communication. Correspondingly, Becher and Munn both stress that it is information from which children stood to benefit and which seems to be most pertinent to their individual children's education that parents want. For most parents, this meant direct information about what and how their children were doing at school. Consistent with parents' view of teachers as experts, parents wanted to know how their children were responding to the expert instruction they were receiving and the particular curriculum they were following. Becher's (1981) account of parents' 'great thirst for information about what their children are doing at school' (p. 36) makes it clear that it is information which parents can easily and directly relate to their own children, that they want.

Although schools typically provide information about themselves in a variety of forms (Gibson, 1981), it was the inadequacy of the mechanisms by which specific information about pupils' progress was conveyed that concerned parents. Consultation evenings and report cards are mentioned in all three project reports in this context. Parents complained about the lack of privacy in their conversation with teachers and the limited amount of time which was available for such consultation. Report cards were seen as unhelpful both in terms of the language used to describe what the child was doing and in terms of the grades used to describe attainment. It was these aspects of parent–teacher communication which parents saw as being in urgent need of reform. They generally wanted more time to talk to teachers privately about their children and to have more easily understood report cards. It is important to make clear that parents wanted more information about their children's progress at school as a way of helping them through school, not as a means of monitoring teacher competence. Parents did not generally have doubts about this competence.

Belief in teachers' competence was reflected in what parents had to say about their children's attainments. Both Elliot and Munn draw attention to parents' reluctance to ascribe responsibility to teachers for their children's attainments. Elliot (1981) stresses parents' views that the school is responsible for the quality of the 'educational processes' it offers pupils (in terms of 'pushing' or 'stretching' them) not 'educational outcomes' (pp. 50–1). Munn cites examples of parents blaming their own children for poor examination performance, not the teacher (Munn et al., 1982, p. 19).

Paradoxically, however, it is the very trust in teachers as experts which parents have which inhibits the kind of communication parents want every bit as much as procedural arrangements. If teachers are seen by parents, and indeed see themselves as possessing expert skills and knowledge, and are assumed to be competent in applying them, then any request for information relating to these skills and knowledge can be interpreted either as a challenge to teachers' expertise or as illegitimate. Thus parents can feel inhibited about asking for descriptive information about their children's progress at school and the kind of work they are doing, for fear that such inquiries might be interpreted as comments on the inadequecy of the school or teacher and inquiring parents consequently fingered as 'troublemakers'. The Scottish research reports parent-teacher interaction in a primary school where a parent was unhappy about the school's policy on spelling, but did not ask for an explanation of it because it 'wasn't her place' to do so and, as teachers 'are supposed to know what they're doing', the parent 'left it to them' although she corrected her child's spelling at home.

It can be seen that by inhibiting discussion between parents and teachers the 'professionalism' of teachers might promote demands for accountability. If a parent feels unable to talk to a teacher about the school's 'progressive' spelling policy, then politicians' public worries about standards and about the curriculum are more likely to find a sympathetic ear. Becher et al. (1981) similarly argue that unless parental trust in teachers' professionalism is based on understanding, then it is only skin deep.

It seems appropriate to ask, therefore, whether the information now available about schools promotes understanding of the teacher's job. Does it help to break the circle of parental trust in expertise inhibiting effective parent-teacher communication which in turn promotes demands for accountability?

DOES THE INFORMATION PROMOTE EFFECTIVE PARENT-TEACHER COMMUNICATION?

On the evidence of the recent research on accountability mentioned above, it is information which parents can relate directly and specifically to their own children that they are most interested in obtaining. While there is no evidence that parents would positively object to more general information about schools being made available, neither is there evidence that the general information which schools are now statutorily required to produce is the kind which parents would find most useful. It is difficult to see how schools could present information on the school curriculum, for instance, in the particularistic way which would enable parents to relate this information to their children. Indeed, the effects of the Act seem to have been to encourage schools in England and Wales to go beyond the requirements specified in DES (1980, 1982) regulations and provide broader information. This information, however, tends to be of the more general kind which research has indicated is not parents' prime concern.

More important, however, by embedding this information in rhetoric about parents' rights and about accountability, teachers are hardly encouraged to respond to parents' trust in their expertise and competence by being more open about the difficult and multi-faceted nature of the job. Information presented in a hothouse atmosphere of parents' rights implies that teachers and parents are at loggerheads over the education of children. It hardly promotes notions of partnership between home and school. Rather, it encourages teachers to seek refuge in their professional expertise as a means of safeguarding their autonomy and thus inhibits communciation. Yet where teachers have felt able to respond to parents' trust in their expertise by being more open about the difficulties of their job and by actively engaging parental help in their children's learning in direct and specific ways, the consequences are rewarding for teacher, parent and pupil.

In a working paper produced as part of some Scottish research on mastery learning and criterion-referencing (McIntyre, 1983) the efforts of the remedial department in a Scottish secondary school to engage parents actively in their children's learning are described. Here, through a series of group discussions with parents who had children attending the remedial department during the first year of their secondary schooling, problems were identified and strategies for dealing with these problems were worked out. In particular, parental help on pupils' homework was identified as a means by which both teachers and parents could promote pupil learning. A homework form was designed with space both for the teacher to describe the homework to be attempted and for the parent to comment upon; a series of meetings between the teachers and parents was instigated at which homework and other matters were raised and discussed on a small group basis; and further developments included a reading workshop where parents could learn more about how to help their children at home with their reading.

Clearly, this is only one small-scale example of effective parent–teacher communication, effective in the sense that parents and teachers came openly to discuss the problems both of ensuring homework was done and of setting homework. It is surely this kind of communication within a mutually supportive framework that the government should be encouraging.

Another way in which the information constrains effective parent-teacher communication about schools is that it gives parents a thoroughly misleading impression of what schools and teachers are able to achieve. The clearest example of this is the publication of schools' examination records in a form which enables comparison with other schools. Recent research on school and teacher effectiveness has revealed how little still is known about how pupils learn and, therefore, about how schools and teachers can influence pupil learning (see, for example, Kyriacou, 1983; Gray, 1981).

Provision of information on schools' public examination results might, therefore, be thoroughly misleading to parents if they interpret this information in terms of the school best able to maximize their own children's public examination performance. Gray et al. (1983) stress the continued high correlation between school intake measures and public examination performance. In particular, the catchment area of the school and the corresponding social class of pupils continue to correlate significantly with its public examination record. The publication of examination records, therefore, provides parents with fairly reliable information on the social class composition of a school's intake. It does not tell parents at which school their children are likely to achieve good public examination results as it is an unreliable indicator of the quality of the teaching in schools. Thus, as well as being potentially misleading to parents, information on schools' public examination records does nothing to help those schools who are low down on the list of numbers of successful passes to improve their performance. Since the most significant correlation between examination performance and a school is the social class composition of its pupils, all these schools can do is aim to attract more pupils of the 'right' social class.

Perhaps, therefore, the most serious implication of all contained in the information on schools which is now available is that it sets implicit or explicit criteria against which schools are to be judged without any elaboration of whether it is in fact reasonable to expect schools to meet these criteria. The information available rather implies that a whole variety of matters, ranging from the curriculum on offer to its public examination record, are within the total control of individual schools. McIntyre (1977) has argued that there is in fact only a small range of matters which teachers can control or for which they can rationally accept responsibility and, therefore, for which teachers are accountable. Such matters, confined as they are to a teacher's own activities and the overt classroom behaviour of pupils, necessarily offer an impoverished and trivialized view of teaching. Nevertheless, if one's concern is with accountability and through it to improving educational practice, it is pointless to judge schools and teachers against criteria which they are powerless to meet.

A school's public examination record or the courses on offer to its pupils are not entirely within its control, and information about these kinds of matters is helpful only in the context of opening up the difficult and multi-faceted job of teaching to parents and to the public at large in an attempt to engage parents and others more actively in schooling. In a context where schools are in competition for pupils, such information is likely either to encourage what Stenhouse (1977) has called 'beating the accountants without improving the balance sheet' or concentration by teachers on a very narrow range of pupil attainment criteria with all the well-documented disadvantages of teaching to the test and a restricted curriculum (MacDonald, 1979; House, 1973).

CONCLUSION

The kind of information now available about schools seems, on the evidence of recent research on accountability, not to be the kind that would be of most direct use to parents. They would like more direct and specific information about what *their child* is doing at school and how he is progressing. It is the mechanisms by which this information is conveyed, namely report cards and consultation evenings, which are in urgent need of reform, in their view.

Moreover, the available research evidence suggests that parents have considerable trust in the competence and expertise of teachers. By forcing schools to provide information about themselves, recent legislation is doing nothing to encourage either parents or teachers to use that trust as a basis for more open discussion about the difficult and multi-faceted job of teaching. It either ascribes control to teachers over pupil attainments in a misleading way, through publication of examination records, or impoverishes the rich and varied business of schooling by encouraging schools to portray themselves in brochure language. Most important of all, by placing schools in direct competition with each other and emphasizing parents' rights, it places home-school relationships in a combative framework. The information, then, does nothing to promote the kind of interaction between parents and teachers which would facilitate understanding about each other's roles. Far from promoting effective home-school communication, therefore, recent legislation is actively constraning it.

TOPICS FOR DISCUSSION

1. 'I want to suggest that parents are predominantly interested in different kinds of information about schools from that now on offer and that by placing schools in competition with each other the government is more likely to constrain than to promote effective home-school communication.' Discuss.
2. 'Although schools typically provide information about themselves in a variety

of forms, it was the inadequacy of the mechanisms by which specific information about pupils' progress was conveyed that concerned parents.' Discuss.

3. In the light of recent research evidence on 'accountability' what better ways might be employed to improve the quality of teacher-parent communications?

SUGGESTIONS FOR FURTHER READING

1. Wolfendale, S. (1983) 'Parents and schools - an evolving relationship?, in *Parental Participation in Children's Development and Education*. London, Gordon and Breach, chap 4, pp. 44-62.

In this chapter, Wolfendale considers recent developments and current thinking on a numbr of topics associated with the relationship between parents, schools and the education process, demonstrating that it is a relationship which is evolving in positive, closer directions. She charts the progress of what is, in her view, the central issue - that of parental entitlement to have knowledge of, and some access to, educational decision-making, discussing in detail the topic of parents' rights and the Education Act 1980 under the headings of (a) parent governors, (b) choice of school, (c) information and, of particular relevance to Reading 6, (d) accountability.

2. Pugh, G. and De'Ath, E. (1984) 'Parents of school-age children', in *The Needs of Parents: Practice and Policy in Parent Education*. London, Macmillan, chap. 7, pp. 168-82.

The authors comment that 'education and support for parents of pre-school children may be inadequate, but compared with the availability of schemes for parents of school-age children, it provides a richness and diversity that leaves older parents looking back wistfully to the days of health visitors and informal groups' (p. 168). This useful chapter examines some aspects of the relationship between home and school, describing various ways in which the school can help to continue the support which has usually begun informally in the community in the pre-school years. Such approaches involve professionals 'building upon parents' inherent interest in their children and helping to raise their understanding of how their children develop and learn' (p. 169). In a later section of the chapter the authors discuss the quality of the relationship between parents and their school-age children, the areas of relevance for parent education and the types of schemes and projects which offer parents practical and emotional support.

3. Hannon, P., Weinberger, J., Page, B. and Jackson, A. (1986) 'Home-school communication by means of reading cards'. *British Educational Research Journal*, **12**, 3, 269-80.

In Reading 6 Munn contends that 'the kind of information now available about schools seems, on the evidence of recent research on accountability, not to be the kind that would be of most direct use to parents. They would like more direct and specific information about what *their child* is doing at school and how he is progressing. It is the mechanisms by which this information is conveyed, namely report cards and consultation evenings, which are in urgent need of reform, in their view' (p. 118).

Hannon et al. argue that the nature of home-school communication is emerging as a crucial issue, and that whatever the medium of communication the kinds of contact and messages, particularly those from the school to the home, may serve either to limit or to enhance parental involvement. Thus, they argue, 'the more central the educational role allowed to parents, the greater the necessity to find lines of communication which are quick, reliable and easy to use'. Their report describes and evaluates an attempt to use written forms of communication in the hope of encouraging parental involvement in the teaching of reading. The form of communication was by means of reading cards which were carried between home and school each day by children.

REFERENCES

Becher, T., Eraut, M. and Knight, J. (1981) *Policies for Educational Accountability*. London, Heinemann.

Douglas, J.W.B. (1964) *The Home and the School*. London, MacGibbon & Kee.

Education Act (1980). London, HMSO.

Education (Scotland) Act (1981). London, HMSO.

Education Act (1982). London, HMSO.

Elliott, J. (1981) 'How do parents judge schools?', in Elliott, J. et al., op. cit., chap. 3.

Elliott, J., Bridges, D., Ebbutt, D., Gibson, R. and Nias, J. (1981) *School Accountability*. London, Grant McIntyre.

Gibson, R. (1981) 'Teacher-parent communication', in Elliott, J. et al., op. cit., chap. 4.

Gray, J. (1981) 'Towards effective schools'. *British Educational Research Journal*, **7**, 59-69.

Gray, J., Mcpherson, A.F. and Raffle, D. (1983) *Reconstructions of Secondary Education*. Henley, Routledge & Kegan Paul.

House, E. (1973) *School Evaluation: The Politics and Process*. Berkeley, California, McCutcheon.

Kyriacou, C. (1983) 'Research on teacher effectiveness in British secondary schools'. *British Educational Research Journal*, **9**, 71-80.

MacDonald, B. (1979) 'Hard times: educational accountability in England'. *Educational Analysis*, **1**, Summer.

McIntyre, D. (1977) *What Responsibilities Should Teachers Accept?* Seminar paper No. 1. University of Stirling.

McIntyre, A. (1983) *Action Research in the Remedial Department* (unpublished).

Munn, P., Hewitt, G., Morrison, A. and McIntyre, D. (1982) *Accountability and Professionalism*. University of Stirling Education Monographs.

Newsom, J. and Newsom, E. (1976) *Seven Year Olds in the Home Environment*. London, Allen & Unwin.

Nias, J. (1981) 'The nature of trust', in Elliott, J. et al., op. cit., chap.15.

Stenhouse, L. (1977) 'Accountability'. *The Times Educational Supplement*, 13 May.

Wiseman, S. (1964) *Education and Environment*. Manchester University Press.

Reading 7

PARENTS' LETTERS TO PRIMARY SCHOOLS

T. Roberts

INTRODUCTION

Most primary schools require letters of explanation to account for child absences and written requests when circumstances warrant any exception to the normal conventions of school life. Many notes from parents are received in primary schools every day. They are letters with a distinct purpose and once they have served that purpose they are generally filed or destroyed. Yet, taken together they offer a unique view of teacher-parent relationships, of life for the young family at home and, in their assumptions, of life in school.

Primary schools tend to deal with parents who are young, financially unestablished and in the early years of marriage. In many households there will be several children of school and pre-school age. For many young parents, particularly mothers, these are years of considerable stress. Brown and Harris (1978) have shown how vulnerable to psychiatric disorder such mothers may be. In their study of urban women, they found a high rate of depression particularly among working-class mothers with three or more children under fourteen at home. Quite apart from difficult living conditions and their greater exposure to crushing life-events, working-class women appeared to be more vulnerable on account of the personal isolation they experience. Schools are a unique source of contact for such mothers and letters to teachers may reveal critical aspects of their circumstances.

Stress is not confined to parents, however. Much recent work (e.g. Kyriacou and Sutcliffe, 1978) emphasizes the particularly stressful nature of teaching. Cox and Brockley (1984) suggest the possibility that such findings may at least in part be due to teachers' particular ability to define and articulate their problems. The teachers in Fletcher and Payne's (1982) study considered meeting the demands of individual children to be the single most stressful aspect of their job. Parents' letters may shed some light on whether this is a perceived or a real problem since they will give an indication of the kind of requests which parents make for special treatment for their children.

Roberts, T. (1985) 'Parents' letters to primary schools'. *Education 3-13*, **13**, 2, 23-8. Reprinted by permission of the publishers.

Many official publications from the Plowden Report onwards have called for more involvement of parents in their children's schooling. Recent investigations show that some progress has been made. Blatchford et al. (1982) found that teachers who visited the homes of children due to begin school were almost universally welcomed by parents. Cyster et al. (1979) found that there had been a considerable increase in the amount of parental participation in primary schools since the Plowden Report. In both studies, however, parents are shown to be reluctant to make demands on the school.

The implication is that schools should increase their efforts to make parents feel more confident towards them, but there are many situations in which it is the teachers who may lack confidence. Lortie (1975) emphasizes the teacher's genuine vulnerability in being without the status to make parents comply or to withstand their attacks. Each side of the partnership appears to have the power to disconcert the other, and correspondence between them is likely to show signs of how this may happen.

Letters to schools also provide evidence of the standard of literacy current among parents living in the catchment area of the school. The Bullock Report suggests that questions about absolute standards and comparisons with the past are not as important as questions about effectiveness. How effectively for his purpose can a writer communicate; in particular can he convey the facts of a message, adopt an appropriate form of expression and write with accuracy? Interest in questions of this kind is not simply academic for the schools for there is plenty of evidence (e.g. Butler, Davie and Goldstein, 1972) to show a strong relationship between the standards of achievement of parents and those likely to be achieved by children.

Moreover, parents' facility with the written word may in itself influence relationships between parents and teachers. Stubbs (1980) suggests that the written form of language carries considerably more social prestige than the spoken form. In a situation where parents are compelled to communicate by means of the written word with members of an institution devoted to the teaching of the written word, diffidence about writing may well promote particular feelings of inferiority and make it even more difficult for parents and teachers to relate to each other on equal terms.

In short, letters to a primary school can be expected to provide information concerning a variety of issues: relationships between parents and teachers; parents, particularly mothers, who are at risk; demands made for special treatment for individual children; and the standard of literacy achieved by parents. These are the themes which were explored in the present study.

THE STUDY

The study is based on an examination of letters sent to a primary school during the course of a school year. The school is a one-stream, Group IV school with a thriving nursery class. The school serves a well-established urban area. Most fathers who are employed are in skilled manual jobs and the population in the area is predominantly white British.

THE LETTERS

The letters sent to the school are chiefly of two types; those which account for absence and those which request a particular concession for the child. Absence notes generally refer to sickness, accidents or unforeseen events. They reveal a predictable range of common illnesses, which evidently occur with great frequency. They are reported in a variety of styles extending from the terse and uncompromising – 'MRS Simpson Tony as had the flue. Thankeing you MR Dickens.' – to the chatty and informal, where it is assumed that the teacher is positively interested in the child's state of health. Barry is 'still not A1', Pauline 'suffers a lot with her ears in the Winter', Marie has been 'out of sorts and not too well', Karl has been 'running around fine this morning' and Michael's ringworms 'still keep coming'.

Reported accidents frequently involve falls, broken glass and riding bicycles but some are so far from common as to be almost puzzling. It is difficult to envisage, for example, how Jane 'trode on a needle' or where Jean was when, already 'suffering from a very bad tonsils infection', she managed to sustain 'a very nasty bite on her hand from a horse fly'.

Unanticipated events range from short-term disruptions such as holidays and minor family crises, which often appear to lead to oversleeping, to much more fundamental happenings such as death, where the school may share the sense of shock which is communicated through the parent's very need to observe the usual pattern of formalities:

> Dear Miss Wright Tina was off last week because she had an upset stomach. N. Smith (Mrs)

> Dear Miss Wright Tina was sick yesterday N. Smith (Mrs)

> Dear Miss Wright Tina had tonsilitis last week N. Smith (Mrs)

> Dear Miss Wright Tina was off Thursday and Friday as her father had died. 21 Sept she attended the funeral. Tuesday she wasn't well. N. Smith (Mrs)

Letters which request concessions for children tend to focus on the areas of eating, drinking and sport or to be concerned with recovery from illness. So requests are made for children to be excused from drinking milk:

> It makes her feel sick because its warm

> She does not like the milk. I have left it this long thinking she would get used to it, but she has,nt I'm very sorry.

and from eating dinners:

> HE WAS SICK LAST WEEK. AND ALL HIS DINNER CAME UP.

Many reasons are found for asking for children to be excused sporting or PE activities:

> I do not want him to go swimming this week as he is hardly eating anything yet.

> Would you please excuse Margaret from Baths as she has rather a sore throat and I don't think going in the water will help it.

but occasionally a letter displays unusual honesty:

> Please excuse Peter from football, as he does not like the game.

In addition to letters accounting for absence and those requesting concessions, there is a further category of letters which, though few in number, tend to receive more attention than the others. These are letters of complaint or comment on school matters which require some sort of action.

> Other boys instead of getting on with their lessons seem to find more pleasure in ridiculing anyone wearing glasses. I, and Daniel would be glad if a stop could be put to this.

> I would appreciate it if Andrea's earings were not removed when she goes to the swimming baths. I have had endless trouble healing her ears up.

Such letters are not always hostile, however, and may be written solely to express support of school activities even though there may be some uncertainty about what these are:

> My Child Eleanor is Aloud to go to the Chest Club Thank You.

HOME LIFE

Emerging from school letters with particular clarity is a picture of how difficult and stressful life at home must be for many young mothers. Their children at school pick up whatever illness is around.

> Miss Williams, Philip Dunn will be absent from school as from the 10. 12. 79, as he has taken ill with the chickenpotts, and will be back as soon as possible. Mrs Dunn

> Miss Taylor. Martin Dunn will be absent from school as from the 10. 12. 79, as he has taken ill with the chickenpotts, and will be back as soon as possible. Mrs Dunn

Frequently other younger children in the household become ill too:

> Christine . . . was bad with flue along with Lynn.

> This was due to an ear infection, plus the fact that his two brothers had measles.

The mother's own health may suffer, 'I was not well enough to see her to school', and the demands of work on the father may mean that he is not in a position to help:

> As I haven't been well myself since week-end I havn't been able to bring Linda to school. My husband is working away in London which will explain why he couldn't bring Linda either.

> Andrea was absent because there was no-one to bring her and Arthur. David haveing the Mumps. Their Father had changed shifts.

Sick children cause sleepless nights and the family oversleep in the morning:

> Sorry Marie was absent yesterday only Norma kept us all up crying with earache on Monday night.

> We overslept having had a very bad night with his brother, who had pains and kept us up most of the night.

Sometimes children seem to suffer from one illness after another: Janet 'as had a bad cough', 'as had ear trouble', 'as been not to good again with her cheast', 'has got a sore throat and She not talk poperly'. Similarly, some children seem so accident-prone that survival to adulthood must sometimes seem in doubt: Lynette 'has been ill, She split her tonge had stitches last Sunday' and a little later 'fell last week and cut her hand badly, it is stitched'. The tension and stress which such periods of experience cause in a family are difficult to overestimate.

It is not surprising that when epidemics of infectious illness occur, parents hold their breath at the slightest sign of sickness:

> TONY HAS BEEN SICK & HOT THOUGHT HE WAS GOING TO HAVE MEASLES.

> I have sent William into school today . . . He did not have measles just a common cold.

> Frank has now most definitely got measles.

The pressure which many young parents experience sometimes leads to discord between husband and wife and it is not surprising to find that children's absences are from time to time accounted for by a vague reference to 'domestic trouble at home'.

SCHOOL LIFE

The picture of school life to emerge from the letters is in some ways contradictory. On the one hand, there is the image of a rule-bound community where special permission must be sought for a child not to take part in certain activities. Similarly, release is requested from the obligation to eat and drink according to the conventional pattern. Non-attendance must be accounted for and warning given of predictable absences.

On the other hand, there is an assumption that rules will be broken, allowances made and special consideration given to any child whose parents consider he or she needs it. The teacher is asked to act in a paramedical capacity taking on responsibility for storing and administering medicine at the right time.

> She brings with her 2 medinices for this afternoon.

> he will be alright he as his tablets in his pocket which must be taken every four hours but could his teacher please lock them away until he needs one.

Children recovering from illness may require special treatment:

> he hade a Bad tummy with all this cold wether that we are having will you Please keep him in and not let him Play in the Play Ground.

Evidence of lingering illness may remain in odd behaviour:

> if she rushes to the toilet thats what it's for.

> It has left him a bit deaf so you may have to shout sometimes.

> there's not much I can do about the cough.

It is not easy in a school to provide additional playtime supervision and to cope with a class containing children who are coughing, running to the toilet or being sick. Demands such as these can come at a difficult time for the teacher. Usually it is winter when an accumulation of wet playtimes makes the children restless and requires extra supervision from the teacher. At the same time, she herself may not be feeling well, exposed as she is to additional infection. Letters to school can show nothing of these difficulties but they reveal little understanding on the part of parents of the pressures under which the teacher may be working.

PARENT-TEACHER RELATIONSHIPS

The question of mutual understanding and relationships between teachers and parents is one on which the letters do shed light. There is a general assumption by parents that the teacher cares about the children. Indeed that is one of the reasons why they feel able to make demands on behalf of their child. Many more personal details are included than are necessary for the purpose of the letters. There is also an assumption that the teacher is willing and able to sort out problems: 'Will you please have a word with Tina Wilson and our Katy'. At times there is a certain hostility, as with Daniel and his glasses, but this is rare.

Some letters convey a defensiveness, particularly those explaining recurring illness where it is clear that teachers have indicated scepticism about the child's frequent absence from school:

> Sorry to have kept him off yesterday but I could not send him to school when he was ill.
>
> I hope this is the last time he will be off school.

There seems little hope of a solution to this conflict of perceptions for the teacher is committed to the child's educational welfare and will be alert to the possibility of children being kept unnecessarily at home. The parent, already concerned for a genuinely ailing child, however, must find the implicit criticism difficult to accept.

STANDARDS OF WRITING

Writing appears to be an activity with which many parents are not comfortable and often it is done under pressure. It is true that some letters are written on Basildon Bond paper with a matching envelope but these are the exception. The harassed parent is likely to use whatever comes to hand. Squared paper, pieces of paper towel or bag, pages torn from a diary or order book are all made to serve. Often the slip of paper appears to have been prised from the hands of a younger child or else snatched by him or her after the letter has been written, for many are decorated with the whorls and squiggles of a brother or sister too young to come to school. It is clear that in many of the houses concerned, adequate materials for writing are simply not available and it must be assumed that it is not a habitual activity and may therefore be one where parents may feel themselves to be at a disadvantage. This may be one of the reasons why some parents adopt the support of a superficial formality.

Insecurity is likely to arise, too, from the difficulty parents have in expressing themselves in writing. The extracts already included indicate something of the problems presented by spelling. Medical terms are particularly tricky and alternative versions of 'tonsillitis', 'diarrhoea' and 'chicken pox' are rather more common than the conventional forms. Not surprisingly, alternatives flourish - 'a sore throat', 'runs to the toilet all day and sickness' - and mishearing results in novel conditions such as 'chicken spots' and 'anifected throat'.

It is clear in many letters that parents have aimed at a high standard of accuracy in phrasing and punctuation but have over-compensated in areas of confusion.

> It turned out to be an ear infection of which she now seems to be clear of.

> I am sorry Wayne was n't in school last week only he was in bed with Flu. Would you please n't let Wayne do PE or go to the bath's has he has a cought and cold. still,
>
> Yours B. Evan's (MRS)

> REF. MARY ROBSON
> Dear Sir,
> With reference to the above named, I wish to beg to inform you that the reason why my daughter, Mary, was absent from school, 'Tues', she was suffering from a sevvere headache, so I thought it adviseable to keep her home.
> Yours faithfully
> P.D. Robson
> 'FATHER'

It may well be that written communications record an aspect of the relationship between parents and teachers where the parent feels most inadequate and that this accounts for the conciliatory tone of much of the correspondence. In most instances, the rules of the school have required parents to put pen to paper and when they do so, they are aware that their weaknesses will be exposed. It is noticeable that the isolated letters of complaint, where parents have made a positive decision to write, are amongst the most literate in the collection.

CONCLUSION

An occasional review of letters sent to school has much to offer to teachers. If they become conscious of the difficulties parents still experience with the written word they may become more tolerant and realistic about their children. It may also provide a clearer perception of the problems faced both by parents and by teachers themselves and of the implication of such problems for teacher-parent relationships.

From those considered in this study, there is evidence of the extreme pressure to which young parents are often subject, pressure to which the school may add with its demands for conformity and its occasional scepticism. In addition to coping with the demands of family life, the well-intentioned parents must, for the sake of the child, meet the standards of the school. Early parenthood is an exacting phase of adult life.

Teachers may be among the first to see signs of the pressures and events which may lead ultimately to psychiatric breakdown on the part of a young mother, yet the likelihood is that they will be prevented from taking an interest because of the pressures of their own circumstances.

Several stressful factors for the teacher emerge as a reality from these letters. Considerable faith is placed in the teacher's ability to take an almost limitless interest in the children, to sort out their problems, to keep them warm and supervised, to administer their medicines, to take care of them when they are not completely fit, to keep an account of their comings and goings, to judge the case for exceptions to routine and so on. The teacher, occupied as he or she may be in keeping his or her own head above water, is unlikely to be able to offer to a young mother the sort of lifeline which he or she may be in a unique position to see the need for. Indeed, the teacher may even be an agent of submersion.

Finally, the letters bear witness to the contradictory nature of the relationship between parents and teachers. School appears to dictate the conditions and, apart from occasional outbursts, parents conform. On the other hand, parents appear to make considerable demands and teachers to satisfy them.

For the outsider, letters inevitably give a one-sided view of situations. We know nothing of the teacher's response. We also know nothing of the oral communication which takes place between parents and teachers. It may be that those parents who write are the ones who tend not to go into the school in person. Face-to-face communication may be much more relaxed and parents and teachers may meet on more equal terms.

For those working in schools, however, these limitations are less important for they know the situations and the people. The value for them in a more objective and sustained scrutiny of letters is that in a collected form, the letters may reveal elements of the picture which normally, at a day-to-day glance, pass them by.

TOPICS FOR DISCUSSION

1. 'Moreover, parents' facility with the written word may in itself influence relationships between parents and teachers.' Consider this statement in the light of research which suggests that the written form of language carries considerably more social prestige than the spoken form.
2. 'An occasional review of letters sent to school has much to offer to teachers. If they become conscious of the difficulties parents still experience with the written word they may become more tolerant and realistic about their chidlren. It may also provide a clearer perception of the problems faced both by parents and by teachers themselves and of the implication of such problems for teacher–parent relationships.' What do you think are the problems and their implications for teacher–parent relationships?
3. 'Each side of the partnership appears to have the power to disconcert the other, and correspondence between them is likely to show signs of how this may happen.' What evidence does the author offer to support this statement?

SUGGESTIONS FOR FURTHER READING

1. Winkley, D. (1985) 'The school's view of parents', in Cullingford, C. (ed.) (1985) *Parents, Teachers and Schools*. London, Robert Royce, pp. 73–95.

Winkley argues that 'the school, with its special professional, institutional *modus operandi* creates an ambience and identity of separateness' (p. 73), and that 'the history has yet to be written of the traumas created by the resistance of institutions to public accessibility' (p. 73). He cites a number of examples to show that parents not only disrupt routine and 'display disproportionate interest in their own child', but sometimes can be actually seen as threatening to teachers (p. 74). For the teacher, then, the plurality of the clients' demands (i.e. parents) can be catered for only up to a point; in the final analysis some decision must be taken in the common interest (p. 75). The problem, as Winkley sees it, 'is one of accommodating diversity' (p. 75). Added to this is the ambiguity and uncertainty of the teacher's role, which the author sees as one of the central dilemmas of the 1980s. Furthermore, the author claims, teachers' knowledge is necessarily limited because what they know about the child is largely gleaned from within the school; they are inadequately trained in the study of parents and their educative role and have but very limited opportunities to observe the actual working of the child's relationship with his or her family (p. 77). Discussing 'cultural dissonance', Winkley suggests that teachers' 'norms', a curious amalgam of 'cultural, emotional and rational components', may produce, in their relationships with parents, 'a stereotype of the other which is intermittently either confirmed, undermined or complicated', and that such stereotypes invariably begin with the teacher in the position of 'expert', knowing more than the parent about child development and child-rearing techniques. This is the very 'dissonance' which Roberts's paper (Reading 7) exposes in her examples of the letters which parents write to teachers. The author develops what he sees as another underlying problem in the teacher–parent relationship – that 'despite their apparent assertiveness, teachers are often not very self-confident when asked to articulate their views to, or defend themselves against, other *adults*' (p. 77). Yet increasingly the role of the teacher is changing from that of a lone practitioner who operates within the confines of the classroom to that of 'an advisory, supervisory and explanatory one in which the agencies of parent and family assume much more significance' (p. 77). Added to this 'catalogue of demarcation lines', Winkley argues that because of the largely bureaucratic structure and organization of 'education', schools (and teachers) tend to see themselves as accountable to 'the LEA or "management" and beyond them to the DES, rather than, in anything more than a moral sense, to parents and communities' (p. 78).

The rest of Winkley's paper is taken up with a very readable account of how a group of teachers in a school in 'a very low-spending LEA' tried to respond in a practical way to parents in a multicultural, inner-city community. Of particular relevance to Reading 7 is the author's account of the development of the home-school liaison teaching service built up to promote more effective teacher-parent communication and co-operation.

See also Bastiani, J. (1978) *Written Communication between Home and School*. School of Education, Nottingham University.

2. David, T. (1986) 'One picture is worth a thousand words: a proposal for communication with parents'. *Education 3-13*, **14**, 23-7.

David writes that 'at the stage when communication between home and school should be at their most straightforward, namely the nursery and reception class years, research reports suggest that misconceptions still abound' (p. 23). The author examines the nature of misunderstandings between home and school and suggests that these largely result from poor communication. She asks the questions: 'How often do staff actually ask parents coming to enrol a child why they want a place at the nursery or what they expect the child to learn in the reception class? Do we just assume that we know what parents want and expect? Do we even ask parents to tell us as much as they can about their child, or discuss targets with the parents of current pupils, so that parent and teacher have some idea of what is going to be seen as fruitful for each individual child?' (p. 24). David examines the problem of diminution in the self-confidence of both parent and child when away from the home environment, and goes on to discuss the differences in parents' and teachers' views about preparation for the infant school. The last section of the reading considers the use of video recordings as a means of effectively communicating to parents the work and life of the school, its aims, organization and approaches, and the types of developmental activities the teachers use to promote the learning of the children.

3. Farquhar, D., Blatchford, P., Burke, J., Plewis, I. and Tizard, B. (1985) 'A comparison of the views of parents and reception class teachers'. *Education 3-13*, **13**, 2, 17-22.

The study by Farquhar et al. highlights important discrepancies in parents' and teachers' views on what sorts of academic-related activities are felt to be appropriate *for parents* to engage in with their children at home. The differences in parents' and teachers' views are striking. Most teachers place clear restrictions on the range of 'academic-related' activities they think parents should attempt. They tend to favour *alternative* forms of parental involvement, for example reading *to* children at home rather than encouraging direct parental teaching of reading. Moreover, teachers have low expectations concerning the number of parents who will engage in activities involving general language developments. Parents, on the other hand, while generally subscribing to the view that schools and teachers make the most significant contribution to children's educational progress, nevertheless *actively engage* in many academic-related activities with their children, *even before* they start school (p. 22). The authors report that 'of great interest is the fact that, *despite* a belief in the major influence of schools, many parents in the study not only stated that they intended to help their children at home once they started school, but also saw such help as part of their role as parents. If this is a reflection of the active role that a majority of parents take in their children's early education, then this is indicative of an important, and influential, educational resource' (p. 22).

REFERENCES

Blatchford, P., Battle, S. and Mays, J. (1982) *The First Transition: Home to Pre-School*. Windsor, NFER-Nelson.

Brown, G.W. and Harris, T. (1978) *Social Origins of Depression*. London, Tavistock.

Butler, N., Davie, R. and Goldstein, H. (1972) *From Birth to Seven*. London, Longman.

Cox, T. and Brockley, T. (1984) 'The experience and effects of stress on teachers'. *British Educational Research Journal*, **10**, 83–7.

Cyster, R., Clift, P.S. and Battle, S. (1979) *Parental Involvement in Primary Schools*. Windsor, NFER.

Fletcher, B. and Payne, R. (1982) 'Levels of reported stressors and strains amongst schoolteachers: some UK data'. *Educational Review*, **34**, 267–78.

Kyriacou, C. and Sutcliffe, J. (1978) 'Teacher stress: prevalence, sources and symptoms'. *British Journal of Educational Psychology*, **48**, 159–67.

Lortie, D.C. (1975) *Schoolteacher: A Sociological Study*. University of Chicago Press.

Stubbs, M. (1980) *Language and Literacy*. London, Routledge & Kegan Paul.

Reading 8

EARLY EDUCATION AND THE COMMUNITY (1)

M. Hughes

INTRODUCTION

Since the middle of the 1960s those concerned with early education have been regularly urged to take greater account of the community in which young children are growing up – and in particular to look for ways of involving children's parents in the work of the school. An early impetus in this direction was the Plowden Report (1967), which set out specific

Hughes, M. (1986) 'Early education and the community (1)'. *Scottish Educational Review*, **18**, 1, 31–67. Reprinted by permission of the publishers.

objectives that in retrospect seem quite modest: schools were asked to provide parents with a welcome to the school, meetings with teachers, open days, information and reports. Many aspects of the Plowden philosophy were taken up and extended by the EPA (Educational Priority Area) projects of the early 1970s, where parent involvement and the idea of the community school became central to many schemes (e.g. Halsey, 1972). Out of some of the EPA projects grew a further initiative, that of educational home-visiting schemes (e.g. McCail, 1981). In these schemes teachers and other professionals did not rely on parents coming into school of their own accord, but instead set out to visit them in their own homes, usually with the aim of improving the educational environment which was being provided there. In the 1980s parent involvement has taken on a new emphasis – that of involving parents in specific areas of the curriculum, particularly reading (Topping and Wolfendale, 1985).

In general terms, then, the principle of involving parents and the wider community in early education has nowadays achieved widespread acceptance. As Joyce Watt points out ('Early education and the community (2)', p. 145) the word 'community' is a 'good' word with many positive associations: few would want to argue *against* involving the community. There is much less agreement, however, as to exactly why this involvement should be desirable and how it can best be achieved. Some would argue, for example, that parents are needed primarily as an extra resource inside and outside the classroom – 'an extra pair of hands'. In contrast, there are others who see parental involvement within a wider remit of 'community education', and a commitment to lifelong adult education for its own sake. Clearly the assumptions and philosophies underlying any particular community or parental involvement scheme will have a crucial bearing on the orientation and direction of that scheme.

One common set of assumptions underlying many approaches to community and parent involvement has been what might be termed the 'deficit' model. The main characteristic of this model – which underlies many of the schemes mentioned above – is the assumption that particular groups of parents (usually working-class, or ethnic minorities, or isolated rural families) are defective in the educational environment which they are providing for their children. The purpose of involving these parents, then, is to encourage and help them change their child-rearing practices – for example by modelling them on the practices of teachers or other professionals. Despite protests from educationists and sociologists in the 1970s, this set of assumptions has persisted. It has surfaced with particular frequency in the area of language, where it has often been claimed that working-class children, for example, receive a severely restricted linguistic input from their parents. This viewpoint usually obtained its theoretical justification from the work of Bernstein (1971) or Tough (1977), although in practice its support often came from anecdotal observations of parents interacting with their children when they brought them to or collected them from school.

Until recently these assumptions of linguistic deficit have remained virtually unchallenged in the psychological literature (with a few notable exceptions such as the work of Labov, 1969). In the last few years, however, three independent British studies have been published which cast doubt on many of these assumptions (Davie et al., 1984; Tizard and Hughes, 1984; Wells, 1984). All three studies point to similar conclusions - namely, that the homes of most (if not all) young children provide a rich learning environment, and that the conversations which take place between young children and their mothers are in many respects richer than those involving young children and their teachers.

These conclusions have major implications for many aspects of early education. In this paper, however, I want to focus on their implications for one particular area - the relationship between early education and the community. More specifically, I want to approach this relationship from a point of view that is often given insufficient emphasis - that of the young child. In particular I want to ask three questions. First, I want to ask what aspects of the community impinge on the life of the young child. Next, I want to consider how these aspects of the community influence young children's development and learning. Finally, I want to look at how the kind of learning which takes place in school fits into the overall picture. In answering these questions I will draw heavily on the findings of one of the three studies mentioned above (Tizard and Hughes, 1984).

WHAT ASPECTS OF THE COMMUNITY IMPINGE ON THE LIFE OF THE YOUNG CHILD?

The first problem is to define what is meant by 'the community'. My dictionary suggests that three related elements are involved: a geographical area or locality, the people who inhabit or have dealings with that locality, and the purposes and interests that bring people together in the locality. Let us consider each of these elements in turn.

For the young child, the community as a geographical area undoubtedly starts with the home. This is the first community into which young children are introduced, and it is the base from which excursions are made into the wider community outside. The wider community can be seen as a series of progressively widening circles starting with the home, then gradually encompassing neighbouring houses or flats, local shops, the park, the library and so on. As children grow up, they will become increasingly familiar with this locality, and the area within which they feel 'at home' will gradually widen.

Next, consider the people who make up the child's community. For young children, the most important people are clearly their family: parents, brothers and sisters, elderly relations – whoever shares their home and with whom they have close daily contact. But families do not exist in isolation: close at hand will be friends and neighbours, with other relatives possibly a bit further afield. Then there are the people who are regularly encountered outside the home, such as shop assistants and fellow customers, other children and parents met at the swings or swimming baths, fellow passengers on buses and perhaps just familiar passers-by. There are also those people who service and regularly visit the family, such as the postman, the milkman and the window cleaner. It is these people who will come to constitute the 'social community' for the young child.

Finally, consider the various purposes and interests which connect these members of the community. Some of these are relatively obvious, such as those involving the postman or shopkeepers, while others are more haphazard and coincidental. A good example of the latter comes from the following conversation between four-year-old Susan and her mother. They were looking out of the window and saw a man arriving at the house next door. Susan's casual inquiry about this man led to the interesting discovery that her life and his were more closely connected than she might have expected (from Tizard and Hughes, 1984, pp. 76–7).

Susan: What has he got a bag on his back for?
Mother: He drives a motorbike. He can't carry it. Needs two hands to steer the bike. [Susan laughs]
Susan: Is he gonna do it?
Mother: He's just come home from work. It's Dick's lodger. [Dick is the next-door neighbour]
Susan: What?
Mother: The man who lives upstairs in Dick's house. The one that you woke up in the middle of the night when you made a noise.
Susan: What?
Mother: The one that lives in the room next door to your bedroom.
Susan: Does he wake up?
Mother: He can hear you when you make a lot of noise.
Susan: What did he say?

Mother: Should think he gets a bit angry.
Susan: Not gonna scream.
Mother: You're not gonna scream. I should hope not.

During this conversation Susan was reminded that her activities not only impinge on this stranger but might actually annoy him. This kind of knowledge, together with the need to modify her activities to take account of the lodger's possible reactions, are of course an integral part of what it means to be part of a community.

Most of us live within an elaborate network of people who interact and whose lives are linked together in a variety of different ways. The child's life, although perhaps more focused on home and family, inevitably develops within and as part of this complex. Of course, the importance of the wider community is not equally strong for all families and all children. Some families are more self-sufficient than others. Some families may be physically isolated from the rest of their communities - for example by living at the top of a high-rise block of flats. Other families may be isolated by feelings of alienation - for example if they belong to an ethnic minority, or because the child's mother is too depressed to make much contact with the outside world. Nevertheless, the fundamental point remains the same: young children do not grow up in a vacuum, but are part of an interconnected and responsive community.

HOW DOES THE COMMUNITY INFLUENCE CHILDREN'S DEVELOPMENT AND LEARNING?

One of the major changes which has taken place in developmental psychology over the last ten to fifteen years is that increasing recognition is being given to the role of the community, particularly of the people immediately surrounding the young child, in early development and learning. This represents a substantial shift away from the view of development associated with Jean Piaget, for instance, who repeatedly stressed the importance of young children's interactions with the physical world - the world of sand, water and bricks. The new approach is exemplified by the recent work on children's language by Jerome Bruner and his colleagues (Bruner, 1983). Bruner emphasizes the way that children's language evolves out of their interactions with an adult care-giver - usually but not always the mother - as they strive to communicate with each other about their needs, or play games such as 'Peekaboo' to amuse each other. Another example of this new approach can be found in the recent work of Judy Dunn (1984) as she explores the major effects that young children's brothers and sisters can have on their lives. Both these researchers emphasize the importance of people around young children in shaping their whole learning environment.

Barbara Tizard and I came to very similar conclusions in our own study of four-year-old children at home and at nursery school. We were greatly impressed by the richness of the homes as a learning environment, irrespective of social background. All the children were observed engaged in a good deal of talking, questioning and thinking as they discussed and argued about various aspects of their world. Much of this learning was embedded in everyday tasks, particularly those which linked the home to the wider community outside.

This point is well illustrated in the following conversation between Pauline and her mother. Pauline's mother was making a shopping list, explaining to her what she was doing. At that point a neighbour, Irene, dropped by on her way to the shops and asked if she could get anything for them. Pauline's mother accepted the offer, and Irene went off with some money to get some of the items from the list. Pauline's mother then showed Pauline the amended list.

Mother: We've only got that little bit of shopping to get now.
Pauline: Mummy? Can I have one of them drinks? Can I?
Mother: Get some more drink?
Pauline: Yeah. Can write it down on there [points to where she wants it written on the list]. Up here.
Mother: I'll get you some when I go tomorrow.
Pauline: Aw! [Disappointed]
Mother: All right? Cos I'm not getting it today.
Pauline: No . . . In the Vivo's? [the local shop]
Mother: Haven't got Daddy's money yet.
Pauline: [seems to misunderstand] *I've* got no money.
Mother: No, *I* haven't got enough to get my shopping. All of it.
Pauline: Not all of it?
Mother: Irene's just taken £5. She'll bring some change back. If she's got some, she'll bring some change back. It's not enough to get all that. Is it? [Points to the list]
Pauline: No.
Mother: See? So when Daddy gets paid I'll get some more money and then I'll go and get the rest.

Close examination of this quite ordinary and unremarkable conversation reveals the many ways in which it may contribute to Pauline's developing awareness and understanding. For example, from it Pauline might acquire some ideas about the usefulness of making a list, of planning and budgeting. She might learn that written words can be a valuable link between one context (the home) and another (the shops). She might learn something about money, and about the number of items that can be bought for five pounds.

She might also learn about the way in which neighbours can help each other, or about the dependence of the family on her father's weekly pay-packet. Her grasp of all these things may still be tentative, but they are a real part of her ordinary everyday life.

Conversations like this one reveal that much of children's learning before they go to school is embedded in the network of people, and their purposes and interests, that make up the community. While the extent and nature of this learning will obviously vary from one child to another, the importance of the community in early learning is clear.

HOW DO SCHOOLS FIT INTO THIS PICTURE?

Schools, like families, are communities in their own right. They are busy, crowded places where young children must come to terms with a large number of other children and adults. There are many differences between what is acceptable at home and at school, and children must come to terms with these new rules and expectations. For example, they must learn to accept the way in which time is structured - not according to the patterns generated by the natural requirements of family life, but as determined by the teacher. Moving from home to school is probably the biggest single event in a young child's life.

One major difference between the home and the school is that the links between schools and their immediate communities are often not as strong as the links between home and community. Teachers do not as a rule pop out to the shops to buy their milk, nor do neighbours drop in to the school to see if they can do some shopping or to ask if they can leave their child for a few minutes while they go to the doctor's. Indeed, many children do not go beyond the boundaries of their school during school hours from one week to the next, and many schools are in real danger of becoming isolated from the communities they serve.

One consequence of this isolation is that many of the links which children have built up with their community before they start school may not be recognized or even acknowledged by the teaching staff. All children bring to school their own individual understandings of the world, much of which is derived from and embedded in their own communities. Teachers, even if they might wish to, cannot possibly known all the details of each child's individual background. Nevertheless, the fact that they know so few details may cause severe communication difficulties between children and teachers.

These communication difficulties often make their presence felt when young children want to tell their teachers about something that is important to them. This is well illustrated in the following conversation which we recorded in a nursery school. Four-year-old Lynne is trying to tell the nursery assistant about her grandmother's dog Polly. This dog had been staying in Lynne's house overnight, and this had been a major event for Lynne.

Lynne: Polly's back. Polly comed up yesterday, but she's gone home. Polly.
Staff: Polly?
Lynne: Yeah, my Polly.
Staff: Oh!
Lynne: We had some biccies up there. When we taked her home. She bringed us some sweeties.
Staff: Oh, that was nice.
Lynne: A packet.
Staff: A packet? What kind? [But Lynne does not reply and the nursery assistant goes off to talk to some other children]

Clearly, the nursery assistant had little idea what Lynne was talking about. But we should not blame her for the lack of communication: she had upwards of twenty other children to look after, and she could hardly be expected to know the name of every child's grandmother's dog! Nevertheless the conversation reveals that there may often be a considerable gap between, on the one hand, the child's interests and concerns and, on the other hand, what is known about the child in school.

It might be argued that what children bring to school is irrelevant to the main purposes of school. For example, it might be argued that the main aim of early education is to provide children with some basic skills - such as in reading, writing and mathematics - which are relatively independent of children's individual backgrounds. After all, a teacher might well wonder whether she really needs to know the name of a child's grandmother's dog if her main aim is to teach that child to read.

It certainly cannot be denied that one of the aims of school is to give children knowledge and skills which help them go beyond their immediate horizons. Indeed, Margaret Donaldson (1978) argues that one of the main purposes of education is to free children's thinking from the initial contexts in which it was originally 'embedded'. The crucial question, however, is whether school can really achieve this aim if it does not take account of and build on the knowledge and learning which children have acquired, slowly and laboriously, through their everyday interactions with family and community. For it is this learning and knowledge which provide the framework within which school learning will be interpreted and made meaningful. If school does not connect with this aspect of children's lives, then what children learn in school may well be seen as artificial and unreal - and certainly irrelevant to children's 'real' life in their communities. And if this happens, then school will surely have failed.

To conclude: I have argued that children grow up within a closely linked network of people, based on their family, which makes up their community. Much of children's early learning takes place within this network. When they start school, children find themselves in a very different world, from which there are few links either to their own community or to the kind of knowledge they have acquired within that community. One of the tasks of school must be to help children create these links. I do not pretend that this is anything but an immensely difficult task.

EARLY EDUCATION AND THE COMMUNITY (2)

J. Watt

Martin Hughes [see p. 132 this volume] has presented early education with a major challenge - how to rethink its community role in relation to children's learning. At one level, the findings he outlines and his conclusions are non-controversial. Few, for example, would deny his point that

> much of children's learning before they go to school is embedded in the network of people and their purposes and interests that make up the community.

As he himself points out, other contemporary writers have come to much the same general conclusions. Katz (1985), in particular, reflects many of Hughes's assumptions when she suggests that the principles underlying communicative competence in young children are: interaction; content which is 'ecologically valid' ('related in meaningful ways to their own

Watt, J. (1986) 'Early education and the community (2)'. *Scottish Educational Review*, **18**, 1, 39-44. Reprinted by permission of the publishers.

interests, perceptions and backgrounds, rich in association and optimally familiar to them'); and 'experiencing others' responses to them as contingent upon their own'. Like Hughes she is also critical of some of the patterns of communication which she has observed in teachers talking with young children in school and she outlines what she sees as some of their 'inhibiting practices'.

Where the Tizard and Hughes (1984) study is distinctive is that it specifically compares the communication patterns of a group of children with their mothers at home and with their teachers in school. On the basis of that comparison they conclude:

> The kind of dialogue that seems to help the child is not that currently favoured by many teachers in which the adult poses a series of questions. It is rather one in which the adult listens to the child's questions and comments, helps to clarify her ideas and feeds her the information she asks for.

Their contention is that teachers of young children cannot play the more educational role because they cannot relate to children's 'out-of-school' learning. Hughes (above) goes on to claim that this 'mismatch' is grounded in what he sees as one of the basic weaknesses of today's schools, their relative neglect of their 'community'. The paradox is that although they are 'learning institutions', schools by neglecting their role within the community are denying the first principles of learning. Hughes does not deny that the task for schools in developing the kind of community role which would facilitate learning is ill-understood, and he acknowledges the likely complexity and difficulty of what this might involve.

Nevertheless, in presenting his argument he makes two basic assertions about schools and communities. First, that:

> One major difference between the home and the school is that the links between schools and their immediate communities are often not as strong as the links between home and community.

Second, that 'many schools are in real danger of being isolated from the communities they serve'. Let us examine the apparent implications of both these statements. If we accept Hughes's interpretation of 'community' as the interaction of locality, the people in that locality and the interests and activities which bring those people together, then I would regard the first statement simply as fact. The links between schools and their immediate communities are not, cannot be, and should not be as strong as the links between home and community. In the same way, teachers cannot be like parents and they should not feel that they have failed because the school cannot emulate the home in the essence of what 'home' is about. While Hughes would probably agree with that, this first statement does carry the clear implication that in order to fulfil their educational functions schools must try to develop much closer links with the community as he defines it. How might schools answer this?

Certainly those who work in schools would agree with Hughes that, given the existing staff:child ratio (especially in primary schools), there are huge practical difficulties involved in going out to spend large amounts of time in the school locality. Those in nursery schools might also point out that many children travel considerable distances to attend, and the immediate locality of the school might not always be particularly relevant for their learning. Again, many teachers would emphasize two points partly conceded by Hughes himself: first, that it is the purpose of schooling at any level to encourage and develop children's thinking beyond what is experienced and known in the context of everyday life; second, that it is impractical to relate school learning to each individual child's experience of home and community.

Finally, some teachers, I suspect, would also claim that in many schools there are stronger links with the locality than Hughes allows and that visits to local parks, shops, libraries and building sites are a regular part of school life. They might also claim that common household activities such as baking, cooking, tidying and sweeping are part of everyday school life; and that just as postmen, window cleaners and neighbours are an intrinsic part of the experience of home, so older children, health visitors, traffic wardens and policemen are part of the experience of school. However, despite these reactions, most teachers would probably still concede that even where such community links exist more could be done to exploit their potential for learning.

The implications of Hughes's second statement ('many schools are in real danger of being isolated from the communities they serve') are possibly, however, more serious, for here a different and even more complex dimension of community seems to be emerging. Where the first statement seems to emphasize community as locality and the interaction of people brought together by common interests and activities within the locality, the second stresses 'relationships' through the notion of 'service'. It is important to note here that Hughes does not include 'relationships' explicitly in his own tripartite definition of community, and we must therefore look elsewhere for our starting point.

'Community' is, of course, a notoriously difficult concept to define or analyse satisfactorily. In his study of organizations, however, Silverman (1970) presents us with a useful distinction between 'attachment', which symbolizes the functional and instrumental links which an individual has with an organization, and 'social bonding', which develops out of attachment through shared experiences and the building up of mutually reinforcing affective relationships. 'Social bonding' by whatever name, is the notion of 'belonging' which most associate with the concept of community. An extension to this notion (Nisbet et al., 1984) is that, on this dimension, community is achieved to the extent that within the social group or organization individuals are valued as active contributing members and find a personal significance through their membership.

It is important then to ask, first, whether schools do encourage this 'bonding', this sense of belonging for those whose lives impinge on them, or whether schools are, for many people, simply organizations which they use for their own short-term purposes with little more than a passing 'attachment'; second, if there is a little or no sense of belonging, even in a few, why might this be? Halsey (1972) saw pre-schooling, for example, as '*par excellence* a point of entry into the community school'. Has early education really achieved little towards that end in the intervening years?

I would argue that in some ways a great deal of progress has been made since the early 1970s. There is little doubt that at the policy level, for example, nursery schools are being actively encouraged to develop a more dynamic community role. Strathclyde Region in particular, through its recent policy statement on under-fives provision (Strathclyde Regional Council, 1985), has put the community firmly at the centre. 'Community nurseries' with their strong implications for both 'locality' and 'belonging' will be the linchpin of what is probably the most radical plan for pre-school education in Britain today.

More generally there are already many examples of both nursery schools and infant schools, which are centres of 'belonging' in their area, offering a permanent 'open door' for parents and others to use the school and its resources on their own terms. Some use it casually and informally as a drop-in centre, others for more organized purposes such as adult education classes, health and welfare clinics, discussion groups, toy libraries, senior citizen lunches or social functions. It is easy to point to these striking examples of developments in early education which have acted as a stimulus and even an inspiration to the community school idea, but it must also be conceded that a few schools have resisted any serious move in that direction and many have explored the idea only tentatively. The reasons for the lack of development in some schools are no doubt complex and varied: some will be highly individual but others, I suspect, are more general. Let me consider briefly three possible general factors.

First, I suspect that many schools are still ambivalent about the role to be played by parents. Given all the research evidence of the last twenty years and the huge pressure to redefine home–school relationships, most have moved beyond the once standard traditional patterns of parent involvement (outings, open days and fund-raising activities) and now also try to involve parents in a variety of ways in the classroom as well as in adult educational and social events. But it must be said that few promote the role of parents as active, contributing members of schools with the responsibility of helping to shape the school's programme or policy. The range of mutually shared experiences which are the prerequisite of 'social bonding', and therefore of community in 'belonging' terms, is therefore often limited and exercised only within a traditional model of teacher–parent relationships. The result is that often parents find little 'significance' for themselves within the school setting.

Some of the reasons for limited parent involvement may well be practical. In nursery education parents may be geographically remote from the school; children may spend only a very short time in the nursery school; parents may work or have pressing family commitments; some may simply not be interested, or the sheer numbers involved may make more fundamental forms of involvement impractical. Certainly a recent study which looked at the involvement of parents as children moved through their pre-school years into primary school (Watt and Flett, 1985) concluded that many parents failed to find a significant role for themselves in this process.

One of the reasons that parents experienced little feeling of significance in schools was that, justifiably or not, they felt that professionals saw only a broad and rather vague supportive role for them: in the early stages of primary schools, in particular, some felt that any involvement they had with the school had little significance for their children's learning. And although the transition process was often sensitively and sympathetically handled for children as they moved from playgroup to nursery school and into primary school, it was a process in which parents often felt they played no significant part.

The second point relates particularly to the staff of nursery schools. Let me consider it in the specific context of teachers, although for different reasons it is probably also applicable to nursery assistants. To what extent are nursery schools institutions where teachers find a sense of belonging, places where they themselves find 'significance'? Certainly most find great satisfaction in their work with children but some at least find little sense of belonging in the wider adult context of nursery education. The reasons are not hard to find.

Society in general and governments in particular have been ambivalent towards nursery education and, except for a brief period in the 1970s when substantial expansion was envisaged (White Papers, 1972a, 1972b) it has had to struggle for legitimacy and sometimes fight for its very existence.

Nor has nursery education fared well even within the education sector. In times of economic stringency it has always been one of education's casualties and even within the profession its aims and methods are often ill-understood and its institutions cut off from the rest of the system.

Misunderstandings abound among parents too. In areas where children may attend first a playgroup and then a nursery school before they enter primary school, many parents find it difficult to understand the purpose of nursery schools although they are happy to use them as a preparation for primary school. Playgroups are believed to be about socialization, primary schools about 'real learning', but that leaves the nursery school rather uncomfortably in between (Watt and Flett, 1985). Nursery schools do try to explain their educational function but there is often a failure of communication perhaps because, to return to an earlier point, the message is probably understood better through practical involvement than through verbal explanations.

For several reasons, then, nursery schools can be isolating places for teachers and their sense of community of 'belonging' is derived from their relationships with the children. It is in the learning experiences of children in the contained environment of the nursery school where teachers take full responsibility, that they find their professional satisfaction.

Finally, we return to the nature of community itself. Community is a 'good' word: its overtones are of warmth, friendliness, co-operation and 'belonging'. But it is at least arguable that community is a dynamic concept in which relationships are continually tested and realigned, where tension, competition and conflict are just as natural as agreement and co-operation. Poulton and James (1976), quoting Simmel, argue that 'conflict is a necessary means of expression in order to establish identity and that it plays an important part in all human affairs'. Furthermore, 'an analysis of conflict shows that community disagreements may be used as a measure of community life'.

While no one would argue that schools should be places of constant open conflict among adults, it may well be that 'community' is less than dynamic in early education since few want to risk the tension, competition and conflict which would inevitably arise in more open flexible adult relationships. Many see all conflict as negative, are ill-equipped to handle it and would need considerable persuasion to believe that, if handled well, it could be a constructive and educational element in any institution with pretensions to community status. Some indeed would argue that, in minimizing discord artificially, where all is equable, pleasant and unthreatening, schools and particularly nursery schools have become 'benign' places, remote from the realities of life, not just for adults but for children (BBC, 1975).

We have come full circle. My conclusion is very similar to that of Martin Hughes. Ways must be found of bridging the gap between home and school through the community to achieve more successful learning for children. But where he looks mainly to teachers to find better ways of capitalizing on children's out-of-school experiences, I would go further and also stress the complementary process of parents capitalizing on their children's in-school learning. If ways could be found to achieve that, parents and children could build on the shared experience of school as they went about their daily lives at home and within the community. If we had both processes going on side by side then not only might we achieve better learning in children, but we might also move closer to an understanding of what 'community' in early education might mean.

But no one should minimize the scale of the community task. Those who work in early education may have the opportunity to provide '*par excellence* a point of entry into the community school', but few in any sector of schooling have as yet been spectacularly successful in showing us just what a community school is all about. We are asking a lot.

TOPICS FOR DISCUSSION

1. 'One common set of assumptions underlying many approaches to community and parental involvement has been what might be termed the "deficit" model . . . Despite protests from educationists and sociologists . . . this set of assumptions has persisted.' Discuss.
2. What aspects of the community impinge on the life of the young child and how do they influence young children's development and learning? What are the implications for teachers and schools?
3. 'The links between schools and their immediate communities are not, cannot be, and should not be as strong as the links between home and community. In the same way, teachers cannot be like parents and they should not feel that they have failed because the school cannot emulate the home in the essence of what "home" is about.' Discuss.

SUGGESTIONS FOR FURTHER READING

1. Davie, C.E., Hutt, S.J., Vincent, E. and Mason, M. (1984) 'Language', in *The Young Child at Home*. Windsor, NFER-Nelson, chap. 8, pp. 129–52.

In studying the language environment of the young child at home the authors selected a small number of specific measurements which they considered were of theroretical importance. Because they felt that a measurement of the *total amount* of speech exchanged by the subject with both adults and children with whom he or she had contact was essential, Davie et al. recorded all speech between the subject and other people, identifying the speech recipient, and defined the subject's general speech as *Communication* - any form of speech except moaning or aggressive speech to another individual.

They recorded separately:

1. *Auto-talk* - the subject talking to him or herself.
2. *Singing*- singing, humming and whistling.
3. *Telephone* - telephone talking.

The authors were interested to see how auto-talk related to the amount of general social communication, wondering, for example, whether high levels of communication to and from a child would increase his or her 'chattiness' and therefore increase the likelihood of the child talking to him or herself or, conversely, whether children tend to talk to themselves in the absence of social communication. Following Bernstein's (1975) contention that language must be examined in different contexts and the predominant use, exposed in these contexts, can assign the subject to having access to a particular code (the contexts Bernstein specifies being: the regularitive, the instructional, the imaginative or innovative, the interpersonal), the authors defined two categories, 'instructions' and 'abstracts', in order to study patterns of language interaction of the young child in the home:

1. 'Instructions' - giving of information, which may be used outside the child's own home, and which does not involve elaboration or expansion of a concept, such as specifically naming objects by drawing the child's attention to them, making statements of fact without justification, correcting the child's speech to the individual's own speech criteria.
2. 'Abstracts' - statements or questions which involve abstractions to a class of individuals, objects or events, i.e. which include a general principle.

The research team included an aspect of communication which they considered would be important in guiding and changing the child's behaviour, sustaining his or her interest in an outgoing activity or suggesting a new one. This they classified as an 'option':

3. 'Option' - an invitation, a suggestion to the subject that he or she does something - includes non-verbal communication.

Finally, they distinguished the two categories of negative speech and positive speech:

4. 'Negative speech' - direct verbal punishment and aggression and threats.
5. 'Positive speech' - approval, praise, affection and promise of treats.

Important findings of the research are as follows.

Speech from the subject to adults did *not* vary with social class, age or sex, but showed differences according to family position. Only children spoke more to adults than either eldest or youngest children, and eldest spoke more than youngest, i.e. youngest children were having least general conversation with adults. In particular, youngest children talked much less to their fathers than did either of the other two groups. Where speech to other children is concerned, the situation reverses: youngest subjects spoke far more to other children than either of the other two groups (p. 137).

Speech from other people to the subject showed a similar pattern to expressed speech, and again, although there was no difference between groups according to social class, sex or age, adult speech did tend to decline with age, and family position exerted an influence. Only children were talked to by adults far more than either of the other two groups, but eldest children did receive more adult speech than youngest. The authors found that although social class differences were apparent on some of the speech measures used in the research, they were not as widespread or as striking as those found by other researchers. Similarly, sex differences were not apparent – the girls were not interacting verbally more than the boys either generally with adults or specifically with their mothers. There were, however, some social class differences in the qualitative speech measures designed to assess speech that would increase the child's vocabulary, classificatory ability and concept formation. Middle-class adults were found to be more likely to provide their children with 'instructions' and their children were *significantly more likely* to ask for 'instructions'.

Abstract explanations proved to be genuinely very rare events, probably because an abstract explanation is an extremely difficult thing to give to a young child, and parents of both social class groups tend to avoid attempting them. 'Options' and adult 'positive' and 'negative' speech showed consistent social class differences (pp. 148–9). The analysis of 'auto-talk' revealed that children who displayed frequent social talk did not also engage in high levels of auto-talk, which tended to occur when children had less opportunity for social speech from both adults and other children.

2. Tizard, B. and Hughes, M. (1984) 'Learning at home: play, games, stories and "lessons" ', in *Young Children Learning: Talking and Thinking at Home and at School*. London, Fontana, chap. 3, pp. 37–72.

Tizard and Hughes examine what children are learning from their mothers at home and, specifically, the contexts in which this learning takes place. They dismiss the widely held view that many children – particularly in working-class areas – learn little or nothing at home, and spend most of their time watching TV. Parents are frequently exhorted by professionals to play and talk more with their children in order to develop intellectual and linguistic skills. The authors set about examining whether these opinions and advice are offered in the absence of any real knowledge of what 'typical' parents actually do at home in 'educating' their children. Tizard and Hughes did this by asking parents what they believed they were teaching their children at home, and found that *all* the parents they interviewed had definite ideas about what they were teaching their children. The answers parents gave were compared with detailed observations of what mothers actually talked to their children about and, in order to examine what the mothers were teaching, the authors scanned each of the mothers' turns of talk to see what kind of information was being conveyed. Thus, they looked at whether the information was about control (what the child should or shouldn't do) or about other kinds of knowledge. Information not concerned with control was coded under one of twenty-seven categories ranging from basic information about colour and size, through information about time relationships, family relationships, social interactions, to general knowledge and school-type subjects such as history, science and geography (pp. 38–9). The authors provide a fascinating account of how the children in the study received, on average, 150 turns an hour of information of all kinds, most of which was information that was *not* to do with control. Of particular importance is the examination of the contexts in which this vast amount of information was being transmitted and acquired – learning through play, for example, was seen as valuable by parents in helping the child understand the adult world by acting out roles - 'it's practice in life', 'she learns by copying adults', 'it brings us closer together' being typical parent responses to the question of whether they thought play was important and for what reasons (p. 41). The authors offer numerous examples of children learning through imaginative play, through games with rules, games for fun, through stories and 'lessons', demonstrating the very wide range of topics and learning contexts found in most of the homes of parents involved in the study.

3. Davie, C.E., Hutt, S.J., Vincent, E. and Mason, M. (1984) 'Summary and conclusions', in *The Young Child at Home.* Windsor, NFER-Nelson, chap. 11, pp. 177-86.

The final chapter of this important study summarizes the major differences in children's behaviour and experience attributable to the four independent variables on which the sample selection was based: social class, sex, age and family position. The authors then go on to review and discuss more general observations about the young child's life at home and relate this to the parents' attitudes to their children's care and education.

In many ways the research team found that social class did not operate as strongly as the earliest literature and research would suggest. The differences they did find were subtle and qualitative. Working-class parents, for example, spent as much time talking and interacting with their children as middle-class parents. But middle-class parents were more likely to provide their children with toys of educational value, and middle-class children were also more plentifully supplied with books and were encouraged to spend more time on activities likely to develop pre-reading, writing and number skills. There were also qualitative social class language differences (p. 178). For example, middle-class parents offered more praise to their children and working-class parents used higher rates of 'negative' or punishing speech with their children. However, in the home, social class differences in speech and style of interaction were not so marked. But the authors make the very important point that the pre-school setting may have the effect of constraining and inhibiting the young working-class child so that, for example, his or her speech and fantasy play are curtailed, enhancing differences in the pre-school setting that are not apparent at home (p. 178). Furthermore, the authors suggest, working-class parents also seemed to be influenced by their feeling that teachers, not parents, were the experts, and therefore 'teaching' the young child was the responsibility of trained teachers and not of parents. Sex differences were marked where traditionally sex-linked toys were concerned, and the authors suggest that the sex differences found in pre-school group settings such as boys showing more aggressive and rough physical play, girls more affiliative and caring behaviour, are enhanced when the child is with a large group of children of mixed sexes, and can choose children of the same sex as play partners. An interesting finding was that parental expectations of young children's competence varied enormously and were not consistent with social class or the sex of the child. Family position, to the surprise of the research team, had a more potent influence than either social class or sex on social interaction between the subjects and both adults and other children. Thus, youngest children received far less attention from adults and spent far more of their time playing and talking to other children than the other two groups. Fathers, particularly, ignored their youngest children, concentrating their attention on older siblings when they returned from work. In the concluding section of their summary, the authors provide a brief account of the studies which show that involving parents in the child's nursery or school life is vital to his or her educational success.

REFERENCES

Bernstein, B. (1971) *Class, Codes and Control*, Vol. 1. London, Routledge & Kegan Paul.

Bernstein, B. (1975) *Class, Codes and Control,* Vol III. London, Routledge & Kegan Paul.

British Broadcasting Corporation (1975) *State of Play*. London, BBC.

Bruner, J.S. (1983) *Child's Talk: Learning to Use Language*. New York, Norton.

Davie, C.E., Hutt, S.J., Vincent, E. and Mason, M. (1984) *The Young Child at Home*. Windsor, NFER-Nelson.

Donaldson, M. (1978) *Children's Minds*. London, Fontana.

Dunn, J. (1984) *Sisters and Brothers*. London, Fontana.

Halsey, A.H. (ed.) (1972) *Educational Priority*, Vol. 1: *EPA Policies and Practice*. London, HMSO.

Katz, L. (1985) 'Fostering communicative competence in young children', in Clark, M. (ed.) *Helping Communication in Young Children. Educational Review*. Occasional Publication No. 11, University of Birmingham.

Labov, W. (1969) 'The logic of non-standard English', in Giglioli, P.P. (ed.) (1972) *Language and Social Context*. Harmondsworth, Penguin.

McCail, G. (1981) *Mother Start*. Edinburgh, SCRE.

Nisbet, J., Hendry, L., Stewart, C. and Watt, J. (1984) *Participation in Community Groups*. Mimeo, Department of Education, University of Aberdeen.

Plowden Report (1967) *Children and their Primary Schools*. London, HMSO.

Poulton, G.A. and James, T. (1976) *Preschool Learning in the Community: Strategies for Change*. London, Routledge & Kegan Paul.

Silverman, D. (1970) *The Theory of Organisations*. London, Heinemann.

Strathclyde Regional Council (1985) *Under Fives*. Glasgow, SRC.

Tizard, B. and Hughes, M. (1984) *Young Children Learning*. London, Fontana.

Topping, K. and Wolfendale, S. (eds) (1985) *Parental Involvement in Children's Reading*. London, Croom Helm.

Tough, J. (1977) *The Development of Meaning*. London, Allen & Unwin.

Watt, J. and Flett, M. (1985) *Continuity in Early Education: The role of Parents.* Mimeo, Department of Education, University of Aberdeen.

Wells, C.G. (1984) *Language Development in the Pre-school Years*. Cambridge University Press.

White Paper (1972a) *Education: A Framework for Expansion*. London, HMSO, Cmnd 5174.

White Paper (1972b) *Education in Scotland: A Statement of Policy*. Edinburgh, HMSO, Cmnd 5175.

SECTION THREE

PARENTS, TEACHERS AND SPECIAL EDUCATIONAL NEEDS

INTRODUCTION

Each reading in Section Three of the sourcebook has been selected on the basis of the practical insights and advice it offers to hard-pressed teachers (and parents). Reading 9 attempts to draw together various recent and current projects and initiatives in the field of primary education and special education which bear powerful testimony to the importance and effectiveness of parental involvement and co-operation in the education of their children. Wolfendale writes that the 'ideology' of her paper 'explicity embraces the view that it is the responsibility of teachers, schools and LEAs to ensure that all adults who have care of children and control over them, and responsibilities for their education and welfare work together for their benefit' (p. 154). The author proposes a viable framework within which parents, teachers and those from other agencies can operate, discussing the notions of empowerment, partnership and responsibilities towards the propagation of parental involvement in contemporary multicultural communities where schools and teachers, homes and families are located.

Pugh's contribution in Reading 10 explores the notions of 'parental involvement', 'parent-professional partnership' and 'parents as educators', terms which, she asserts, have become fashionable in recent years, but which tend to be thrown about with scant regard to their true meaning. The author discusses the extent of parental involvement in Britain, commenting that despite the increasing commitment on the part of many pre-school workers to involve parents more fully, the tendency is still for professionals to invite parents to join them on *their* terms, a situation which falls short of a notion of *partnership*. Partnership, she suggests, involves 'an acceptance of equal skills and experience, and a sense that each partner brings something different but of equal value to the relationship' (p. 178). Thus there has been a tendency to treat parents as deficient in some way, which obscures the fact most parents, as well as receiving services, are well able to contribute to them. The main section of this reading is taken up with a discussion of Portage, which the author evaluates in the context of other home-based schemes, considering advantages and disadvantages, and stressing that no approach is without its limitations. For example, Pugh reminds us that intensive home-visiting programmes can put intolerable pressures on some families, that home-based programmes are only as good as the home visitor, that working in people's homes is a skilled and difficult task, that there is a danger in a cook-book approach based on recipes rather than principles, that home is not always ideal, and that home-based programmes do not solve problems of loneliness and isolation, nor do they provide an exhausted parent with any time off (p. 183).

In the last reading of the sourcebook Widlake asserts that it has been demonstrated beyond all reasonable doubt that the performance of children with special needs in mainstream schools can be dramatically increased when parents are drawn into the educational process. Moreover, the author suggests, 'when teachers and parents acknowledge their "complementary expertise" and arrange to share it, the result can be an educational institution richer in experience, innovative in its day-to-day practice, more responsive to the pressures for change in a democratic society' (p. 190). Widlake describes a survey of the reading and oral language achievements of primary age boys and girls in Coventry schools which were considered to have effective parental involvement programmes. The study covered eight schools and nearly a thousand pupils, and revealed high levels of achievement in oral and written language and in reading comprehension: 74 per cent of infant and 86 per cent of junior age children showed positive attitudes towards reading. The author reports, 'something unusual was happening in these schools. It seems clear to me that infants' schools which keep an open door to adults can be expected to produce children who are confident in talking to adults, who speak clearly and develop their active vocabulary because they are encouraged to express themselves freely. As they move on through junior schools with a similar atmosphere, these qualities can be expected to reveal themselves in their free writing. Sure enough, samples collected from cohorts of seven-, eight- and nine-year-olds showed very high scores on legibility, fluency, accuracy and originality' (p. 191). Widlake describes several other experiments which have improved the educational opportunities of children through various forms of collaborative learning, noting however that 'whatever definition of special educational needs we like to favour there is a considerable mismatch with educational practice. The system discriminates in favour of certain social classes, racial groups, geographical areas and types of ability or disability. Hundreds, thousands of these community-oriented schools are required' (p. 196).

Reading 9

HOME AND SCHOOL MILIEUX FOR MEETING CHILDREN'S NEEDS

S. Wolfendale

The latter half of the 1980s is an opportune time to look back and chart developments in home-school links since the publication of the Plowden Report and its seemingly simple assertion 'by involving the parents, the children may be helped' (Plowden, 1967, para. 114). In fact, that assertion was based on the early findings from the American programme Head Start, as well as a heartfelt conviction by the Plowden committee that, as parents are children's 'primary educators', then professionals' support of their direct involvement with their children's development and education could only be beneficial.

What constitutes 'benefit' to children in these terms was closely examined in a review of developments in parental involvement (Wolfendale, 1983). In that book, I set out a rationale to this growing area and put forward recommendations for the development of LEA and school policies on working with parents.

This chapter sets out to draw together a number of recent and current prime initiatives within primary and special education that bear testimony to the effectiveness of such co-operation. They also provide us with clues as to how successfully to instigate and maintain a way of working which had traditionally been alien to the British educational system but which can, and perhaps should, routinely be part of schools' provision. In so doing, there will be an intentional match between principles and practice for this is the pre-eminent area that links education with the community and the wider society.

Wolfendale, S. (1987) 'Home and school milieux for meeting children's needs', in *Primary Schools and Special Needs; Policy, Planning and Provision*. London, Cassell, chap. 2, pp. 15-35. Reprinted by permission of the publishers.

The 'ideology' of this chapter explicitly embraces the view that it is the responsibility of teachers, schools and LEAs to ensure that all adults who have care of children and control over them, and responsibilities for their education and welfare work together for their benefit. The belief system propounded in this chapter eschews exhortation, however, and has a bias towards a presentation of current thinking and work that illuminates and substantiates these views.

Parental involvement is a contemporaneous issue that reverberates in national and local political circles. All the main political parties have declared a commitment to increase significantly parental input into decision-making, and advocate an extension of consumer choice into educational spheres. 'Parent power', a phrase used in the media and by politicians, however, refers to different faces of the same coin, depending upon party dogma. The enthusiastic espousal of parental rights by politicians of all shades may be less inspired by genuine conviction than by the fact that there has been a demonstrable and impressive groundswell of action and commitment by 'ordinary' people, parents, teachers and other practitioners. Thus it behoves politicians to endorse the electorate in this way. I have participated in various parental involvement initiatives over several years and so the chapter will draw upon some of this work, as it is seen to be central to the spirit of this book.

Children's special educational needs are best appraised within a whole-school context and each child has equal, though uniquely differing, access to curriculum and other opportunities offered by the school. Thus, a school that includes parental involvement as part of its provision potentially offers all children on its roll the chance to benefit. [. . .]

THE ATTITUDES OF TEACHERS AND PARENTS

A certain circularity characterizes arguments about parental involvement in schools, that are based on partial information. That is to say, how do we know if innovative practice comes about as a function of changed attitudes or whether attitudes are changed as a consequence of trying it out? Can teachers and parents be coerced into co-operative ventures by those with the influence to instigate (head teachers, advisers, educational psychologists, for example) when their conviction and enthusiasm are lacking?

The nature of innovation and the persuasive effects these ventures can have may mask, even obliterate, latent resistance. The information we have to hand as to the extent and enthusiasm of parental involvement can only be partial, since we are describing dynamic forces that are already operational, and so the task of keeping a check upon evolving practice becomes well-nigh impossible. It is difficult to keep an accurate and updated chronicle on initiatives that are taking place all over Britain and, sometimes, in schools where teachers and parents may be unaware that their work represents a phenomenon of our times. [. . .]

Now, as we move towards the end of the 1980s, we can attest to manifest change in attitude in the existence of many well-maintained parental involvement ventures and smoothly functioning home-school links, whatever the genesis and the original impetus were. Their success buries myths that earlier attitude surveys uncovered concerning parents' perceptions of teachers' inaccessibility and teachers' perceptions of parents' indifference. Views recently expressed have been within contexts of some degree of active and viable parent-teacher co-operation. These are briefly exemplified below, and demonstrate some commonality in views between teachers and parents in mainstream and special education settings. Since views can be held about and expressed on any number of educational issues, only a brief, selective dip will be made into parents' and teachers' views pertinent to the areas with which this book is concerned.

PARENTS' VIEWS

Some studies on parental involvement in reading (Griffiths and Hamilton, 1984; and see Topping and Wolfendale, 1985) have sought parental views as part of evaluation. Notwithstanding a perhaps predictable halo effect, their attitudes to this particular form of parental involvement with the curriculum have been positive and enthusiastic – they feel that their knowledge of the reading process (teaching and learning) has been enhanced, they are clearer about schools' own methods and goals, they endorse the ways in which they are welcomed into school (e.g., the provision of a parents' room).

The Thomas Report (1985, chap. 4) into primary education in the Inner London Education Authority canvassed the views of parents concerning the curriculum and confirmed parents' interest in their children's schooling and endorsement for schools' curriculum aims and objectives. Yet parents felt that they did not always know 'by what standards to judge their own child's achievement; they have difficulty in understanding modern methods' (para. 2.8, p. 13). Clearly this information - the reported good will and the need to be given up-to-date, precise information are starting points. Indeed, one LEA has now provided this very database to promote effective communication between home and school. The London Borough of Croydon Education Authority, late in 1985, produced a *Guide for Parents: Primary Education in Croydon*. It includes the following: standards and performance, aims and objectives of primary education, the curriculum areas, and a short, half-page section entitled 'Education for a changing world'. [. . .]

Turning now to the views of parents of children with special needs, those who have been or are in receipt of Portage attest unequivocally to its specific benefits *vis-à-vis* the child's acquisition of skills and developmental progress, as well as to the wider advantages (Jordan and Wolfendale in Cameron, 1986). Portage evaluation studies (Bendall, Smith and Kushlick, 1984; Myatt, 1984) include feedback of 'consumer' views. It is therefore likely that the endorsement of the Portage model (its technology, methodology, structure and multi-disciplinary and partner emphases) by parents contributed to the present government's explicit backing of Portage via the Education Support Grant to such under-fives home-based intervention. (See also references in Table 9.1.)

Other parental feedback from joint work was reported in Pugh (1981), and chapter 7, 'Parents and special educational needs', in Wolfendale (1983) provides extensive references to successful joint intervention work (pp. 115–19 and see References List B, pp. 127–30).

On the broader front of access to information and support whilst their children are going through assessment procedures, representative parent groups expressed their views to the Warnock Committee (1978, chap. 9) and to the Fish Committee (1985). Both of these major reports on special education contain recommendations for closer working links based in part on parents' views. The Parents' Campaign for Integrated Education in London, one of the organizations that gave evidence to the Fish Committee, includes in its aims the fostering of a dialogue with professionals.

Finally, a reference to a survey (Sandow and Stafford, 1986) the findings of which reflect just how much more there is to do in establishing effective working links despite the encouraging evidence. This is particularly pertinent in the arena still quite new to all involved in special education, namely the processes associated with the 1981 Education Act and especially the nature of the collaboration between parents and professionals. Sandow and Stafford uncovered an apparent mismatch of perceptions between parents and professionals and the worrying fact that so many parents had not received clear explanation of and guidance through the procedures (although they had voiced their needs to the Warnock Committee more or less ten years ago!). Some of these points are picked up later in this chapter.

TEACHERS' VIEWS

A similar picture is painted in this section. That is, where there are already viable and active forms of parental involvement the benefits are so evident and so clearly outweigh the perceived disadvantages as to be reflected in the positive, enthusiastic attitudes of teachers. Again, this can be exemplified in parental involvement in reading (Griffiths and Hamilton, 1984; Topping and Wolfendale, 1985). Likewise, the attitudes of several hundreds of teachers (head teachers, class teachers, advisory and support teachers, other responsible post-holders) sampled via a face-to-face questionnaire that I carried out (Wolfendale, 1985a) over the period 1984–1985 (and which continues still) into parental involvement showed a clear connection between a lively amount of parental involvement in schools and a confident belief in its benefits to all concerned.

Winkley (in Cullingford, 1985) discusses the sources of misperceptions of teachers and parents referred to above and goes on to document the programme of parental involvement in the junior school of which he was head teacher. He captures an evolving situation and changing attitudes in these words:

> schools' relationships with parents develop slowly, artfully, over a period of time, to the point where it virtually becomes a tradition, an unspoken expectation for both teachers and parents to behave in certain ways . . . new teachers and the parents of new children tend to accept, absorb and develop the

> tradition. The key factor is that the participants find the time spent worthwhile and enjoyable. (p. 83)

In a survey of replies by head teachers to a questionnaire asking about parental involvement in schools, one head teacher remarked that it is the consistency and strength of a school's appeal to parents rather than any single approach that leads to a marked change in their attitudes (COPE, no date).

Within the setting of a school for children with moderate learning difficulties, Marra (1984) sets out some of the requisites for successful parent–teacher interaction and a functioning relationship within the school of which he is head teacher. 'Warts and all' are described in the process and he concludes:

> What has been described . . . reflects parental involvement in its infancy, the objective of educational involvement and the goal of partnership have yet to be reached. However, what have been described are some of the principles for a possible partnership based on experience. (p. 145)

That teachers and parents have a great deal in common is an intrinsic part of the rationale of parental involvement programmes, as is spelled out in Topping and Wolfendale (1985) in chapter 1 and summarized in these words: 'This complementarity of "role" is less a neat formula than it is perceived to constitute a framework for co-operative working' (p. 12).

This commonality was explored on a parent–teacher in-service course described by Davies and Davies (in Cullingford, 1985), the aim of which was to identify the extent to which these parties agreed and disagreed on certain issues seen as fundamental if the dream of parent–teacher partnership were ever to become a reality. These authors, like Marra, on the basis of this and other experiences set out requisites, which, for them, include pre- and in-service training in part to avoid enthusiastic but hasty adoption of parental involvement schemes that do not rest on carefully thought-through systems of planning, execution, management and evaluation. As one model for such planning, in the area of parental involvement in reading, Topping and Wolfendale (1985) put forward one schema (chap. 32). For parental involvement in other curriculum and learning areas Topping proposed another model (Topping, 1986).

Another example of the way in which survey findings can be used as a basis for planning took place in South West Hertfordshire (1984). The views of teachers and parents were sampled; 'negative' opinions were explored, and these were found often to be based on lack of explanation, blurred lines of communication, fears and stereotyped expectations of teachers' and parents' 'roles'. The surveyors used their findings to point the way to building upon present activities and providing an even more secure foundation for joint operations.

It is likely, too, that under the formalized banner of co-operative ventures, some of the misperceptions, anxieties, defences cited in Dowling and Osborne (1985) are reduced if not eliminated. For example, conjoint problem identification and problem solving can be facilitated. To some extent, parental involvement can be viewed as a 'preventive', approach in that 'problems' can be 'caught' and dealt with before they exacerbate. [. . .]

DEVELOPMENTS IN PARENTAL INVOLVEMENT: AN OVERVIEW

In the earlier discussion there was some reference to current work in parental involvement. The purpose was to show a juxtaposition in time between the earlier uncharted territory where first steps were tentative and the many active programmes of today. This is such a fast-burgeoning area that no one chapter can do justice to the initiatives. Yet, I shall try in this chapter to present an overview of the field. Another main reason for this is to demonstrate the many rich and varied ways in which integrated educational settings can foster productive and rewarding relationships with the parents of all children; so that 'special needs' children are as integrated as the rest by virtue of their parents' involvement in the routines of their schools.

The reader is referred for main overview texts into parental involvement to: Craft, Rayner and Cohen, 1980; Wolfendale, 1983; Cullingford, 1985; Beattie, 1985. In order to assist the reader to pursue specific areas, Table 9.1 provides key references to work in hand.

PARTNERSHIP - THE REALITIES

The amount of current work is indeed impressive and, to date, testimony from participants is positive. There are signs that some of the work is taking root within schools as part of routine provision. Some schools are even evolving a policy on involving parents that becomes the official imprimatur to ventures that may have started in an *ad hoc*, modest way. That is, some of the realities were tested out prior to formal acceptance at 'policy' level.

Some of the work is multi-disciplinary, wherein parents contribute and these ventures are seen as part of a wider network of service provision for meeting special needs which is regarded as cost-effective and egalitarian (McConkey, 1985). Portage, in which parents are the educators and therefore play the central role, is seen as coming the nearest to a model of parental partnership, and even then some would argue that the final power of decision-making (in terms of resource allocation, personnel deployment) is retained by professionals.

There are writers who cast doubt upon the possibility of 'true' partnership coming about. Potts (1983) sees partnership as tokenism, a kind of window-dressing without parents ever really sharing power. Gliedmann and Roth (1981) are of the view that partnership cannot come about until parents oversee and orchestrate the services that professionals provide for their children. They question the almost 'God given' self-perception of professionals about the omnipotence of their expertise and aver that

> parents of all races and social classes should be able to pick and choose among different experts, obtain outside opinions when dissatisfied with the services or advice provided by a professional and constantly evaluate the professional's performance in terms of the overall needs of the growing child.

Another writer (Hester, 1977, p. 266) makes the observation, and this applies to educational and other services for children, that 'citizen participation in particular citizen power, in program policy and management is important in warding off inequitable treatment'.

The possibility of this sort of central managerial role within education and child-focused services is also raised by Beattie (1985), who sees the potential of much more direct participation by parents/citizens in power sharing as constituting a challenge to traditional tenets about 'where' power should properly reside and who wields it, including control over the curriculum. [. . .]

In order to demonstrate that partnership need not remain an ideal, an aspiration, some writers with first-hand experience of working as practitioners at the 'interface' with parents have attempted definitions of

Table 9.1 Major areas of parental involvement in the 1970s and 1980s: some examples

	Areas of involvement	*Key sources*
Parents coming in to school	Helping with reading	Stierer, 1985; Griffiths and Hamilton, 1984; Topping and Wolfendale, 1985; Young and Tyre, 1983
	As para-professionals in the classroom	Wolfendale, 1983, chaps 3 and 4; Rennie, 1985; Long, 1986
Parents as educators at home	Parental involvement in reading, language, maths learning and 'homework'	As above, also Topping, 1986; Wolfendale and Bryans, 1986
	Parent–teacher workshops	Wolfendale, 1983, chap. 7
	Portage	See below
	Parent education	Pugh and De'Ath, 1984
Home–school links	School reports	Goacher and Reid, 1983
	Written communication (newsletters) in English and community languages	Bastiani, 1978
	Moves to open files	NUT policy and some LEAs
	Home–school council	Hargreaves Report, 1984
	Parent–tutor groups	Hargreaves Report, 1984
	Curriculum plans to parents	Hargreaves Report, 1984
	Home visiting	Raven, 1980
	LEA parents' handbooks	L.B. of Croydon, 1985
Community education/community	Parents' rooms in school	
	Parents and others attending classes in school	Liverpool Parent Support Programme Coventry, Newham
	Multi-disciplinary work	Fitzherbert in Cullingford, 1985
	Local and national parents' associations	ACE, CASE
	Parents' support groups	Pugh, 1981
	LEA community education	Coventry, Newham
	Parent governors	
Parents and special needs	Parental involvement in referral	Brent LEA
	Parental involvement in assessment	Wolfendale, 1985b and c; Cunningham and Davis, 1985
	Parental involvement in behaviour and learning programmes	Carr, 1980; Westmacott and Cameron, 1981; McConkey, 1985; Mittler and McConachie, 1983; Newson and Hipgrave, 1982; Wolfendale, 1983, chap. 7
	Portage	Cameron, 1982; Dessent, 1983; Daly et al., 1985; Copley et al., 1986; Cameron, 1986

knowledge, skills and experience (Mittler and McConachie, 1983) 'complementary expertise' (Cunningham and Davis, 1985) and 'equivalent expertise' (Wolfendale, 1983).

These are the key operational concepts which are embedded within an equal dialogue. I have explored how operational these elements can be as, for example, 'equivalent expertise', 'a reciprocal relationship', leading to 'mutual accountability, mutual gain' (Wolfendale, 1983, chap. 2) in an exercise in which parents make an equal contribution to the assessment processes under the 1981 Education Act (Wolfendale, 1985b). I remain optimistic that equality in these enterprises can, if sought, be obtained. However, I acknowledge the transitional, evolving nature of working towards such aims, as expressed by Davie (1985):

> a rational understanding of the dynamic of partnership and collaboration in these terms would not *guarantee* a closer and more effective relationship in working for children, but it might help to structure situations or shift attitudes in ways which could promote progress. (p. 7)

This echoes remarks made by Marra that were quoted earlier in this discussion [. . .]

THE RESPONSIBILITIES OF LOCAL EDUCATION AUTHORITIES

Most innovative work on parental involvement has been initiated by people working within LEA contexts and employed by LEAs, such as teachers, advisers, educational psychologists. Many school-based projects have 'taken off' as a result of corporate endeavours and many localities have provided in-service training to promote further take-up. The field of parental involvement in reading has been particularly fertile. In these ways LEAs have demonstrated their backing, if not commitment, and have therefore exercised some responsibilities in terms of plant, personnel, materials.

There are signs that an increasing number of LEAs are prepared to take on board and implement policies on parental involvement. The few examples to date of the LEA commitment show variation between them as to how far they are currently prepared to go and in what particular areas they are actively pursuing these ideas.

Table 9.2 is a list of several development areas, matched with selected examples of LEAs.

Another development area, one already touched upon but relevant again at this point, is the training provided by some LEAs for school governors (George, 1984), who of course include parents. Training varies from day courses to the local adoption of the Open University course 'Governing Schools'. I have been involved in one LEA's School Governor training that utilizes a mix of these approaches, backed up by other types of support, e.g. tutoring. Pertinent to the theme of this book has been an LEA-instigated day training course during 1986 on special educational needs. Governors were provided with an information pack to help them in regard to their responsibilities for special educational needs.

Thus we have evidence that a number of LEAs are taking seriously their responsibility for ensuring an informed citizenry who themselves have definite responsibilities for and within schools. Brighouse (in Cullingford, 1985), based in part on his experience in Oxfordshire, sets out a number of practical strategies LEAs could initiate to promote the partnership between schools, homes and the community and, as he says, 'the ideas and possibilities are legion' (p. 171).

THE RESPONSIBILITY OF SCHOOLS FOR PARENTAL INVOLVEMENT

Using much of the preceding discussion in this chapter as a frame of reference, and drawing upon the now considerable body of reported work (see Table 9.1), this section aims to set out a model for primary schools to further develop their home-school links within their overall policies on children with special educational needs. The philosophy is very much in tune with the principle [. . .] that [. . .] there can be no separate policy on parental involvement for special needs. However, it is consistent with the insistence that children's special educational needs can and should be met within ordinary schools that due attention should be paid by schools to the development of forms of parental participation that promote, if they

Table 9.2 Areas of development in parental involvement in selected LEAs

	Development area and approximate dates	*LEA examples*
Parental involvement	Setting up working parties; seconding teachers 1983	Lancashire
	To report back to Ed. Dept., Ed Committee 1984	Oxfordshire
	Appointment of adviser for home-school links, 1985	Oldham
	Home-school liaison from end 1970s	Buckinghamshire
	Educational home visitors since mid-1970s	(Milton Keynes) L.B. Waltham Forest
	Portage	From 1986 via Education Support Grants
Parental involvement in reading	Urban Aid/LEA project into paired reading, since 1984	Kirklees
	PACT since 1980	L.B. Hackney (ILEA)
Community education	Since 1970s	Coventry
	'Going Community' since 1985	L.B. Newham
	Parents' support programme since 1970s	Liverpool
Written information to parents	Primary curriculum booklets 1986	L.B. Brent, L.B. Croydon
	Booklets on primary, secondary and special needs	Many LEAs since 1980

do not guarantee, meeting children's needs. Research findings from America and the United Kingdom and other European countries unequivocally point to demonstrable gain by children from any one or more identifiable groups (Wolfendale, 1983; Macbeth, 1984; Mittler and McConachie, 1983; Topping, 1986 and McConachie, 1986).

Practical guidelines and planning checklists abound for the introduction, implementation, maintenance and evaluation of parental involvement and home-school links. Here is a list of several (details in References at the end of this chapter).

- *Keeping the School Under Review: The Primary School* (ILEA, 1982).
- Cunningham and Davis (1985).
- McConkey (1985).
- Topping (1986).
- NARE Guidelines No. 7.

Even though these guidelines tend to be presented in sections, conceptual or taxonomic frameworks are less common. I have attempted (Wolfendale, 1983, chap. 10) to provide one that makes a match between the abstract concepts and their applications in practice. This is reproduced in Table 9.3 as an exemplar.

IMPLEMENTING A POLICY ON PARENTAL PARTICIPATION

The many elements that go to make a comprehensive parental involvement programme are presented in Figure 9.1 in the form of a wheel. The purpose of this form of representation is severalfold; it aims to:

1. Demonstrate the intimate connections between the school, the home, and the community, indeed, the 'reciprocal' nature of the interaction.
2. Make the point to readers that in most schools some form of parental contact and involvement has been well established over a number of years.
3. Reiterate that this represents a comprehensive programme, possibly goals towards which schools might work.
4. Illustrate how policy, practice and provision on special needs can be incorporated into general parental involvement structures.

The five texts listed below are British sources, each of which describes in various ways many of the ideas set out in the wheel from first-hand experience.

- Tizard, Mortimore and Burchell (1981).
- Mittler and McConachie (1983).
- McConkey (1985).

Table 9.3 Abstract concepts and practical applications

	Parents into schools	
Area	*Type*	*Focus*
Concrete and practical	Basic help with learning; fund-raising and support; practical skills; social meetings	Classroom and school
Pedagogical and problem-solving	Syllabus design and planning; co-tutoring of school and home-based learning (general education, remedial, special education needs); school-based discussion of progress	Curriculum
Policy and governing	Educational decision-making; parents as governors	School as institution
Communal	Groups for parents and children (workshops, classes, courses, talks, demonstrations)	School and community
	School to home	
Area	*Type*	*Focus*
Information	Verbal, written communication – letters, reports, newsletters, booklets, check and recording systems	Home and parents
Support	Home visiting (inquiry, counselling, relations-fostering); imparting information; discussion of child progress	Home and family
Instruction	Educational home visitor/teacher brief (handicap, special educational needs disadvantage, pre-school)	Home, child and parents
Representation	Input by schools into rest of community (resource sharing, resource loan, local meeting place, focal place for co-operative learning)	Home and community

Reproduced from Wolfendale, 1983, Tables 3 and 4, p. 184.

- Thomas Report 1985, chap. 8.
- Long (1986).

Also recommended are the following texts, which are obtainable in the United Kingdom and which are packed with practical suggestions based on theory and research findings:

- Morrison (1978).
- Rutherford and Edgar (1979).
- Paul (1981)

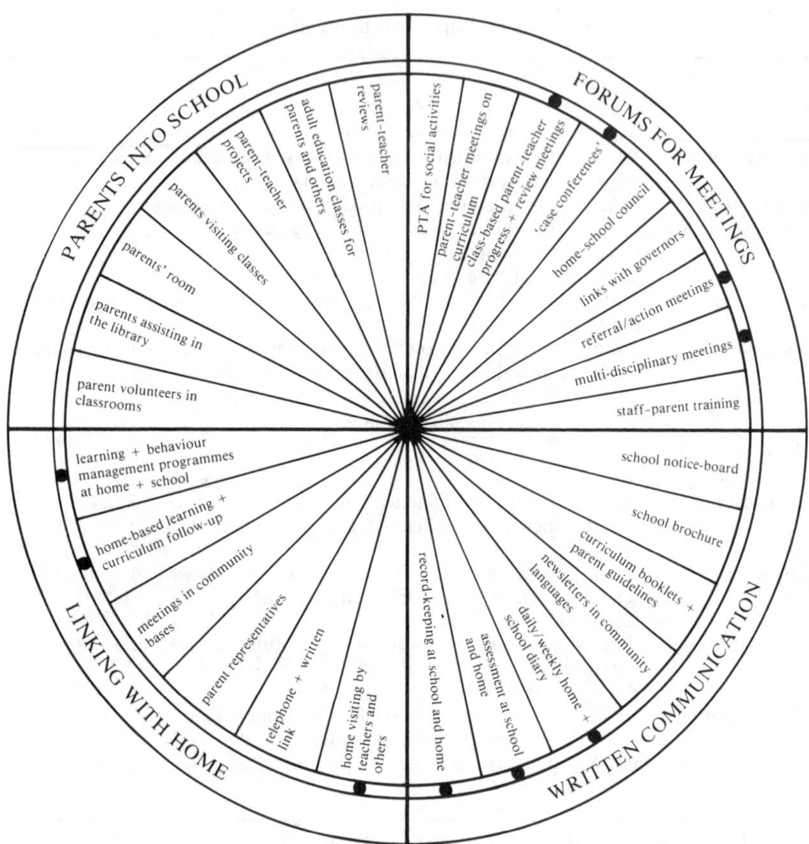

● = part of special needs policy and provision

Figure 9.1. The wheel: a programme of parental involvement

- Berger (1983).
- Lombana (1983).

It is proposed that primary school staff, in conjunction with parents and other support staff, formulate a threefold plan of action to involve:

1. reviewing existing parental involvement;
2. reviewing current policy and provision on special educational needs;
3. reformulating parental involvement to incorporate special educational needs.

This may necessitate devising a goal plan and setting out a timetable for achieving short and longer-term goals.

As can be seen, the wheel includes some elements that can routinely be part of parental involvement yet could also be applicable to working with parents of children with acknowledged special educational needs as and when this is appropriate. To effect these working links in practice involves equating 1 + 2 (above) to equal 3. Thus, from summing 1 + 2, it is possible to abstract these elements from those activities which are denoted on the wheel:

- noting and sharing concerns
- referral
- assessment
- action and intervention
- recording
- review.

[. . .]

SCHOOL IN THE COMMUNITY

It was announced at the outset of this chapter that there would be an explicit commitment to the involvement of parents in their children's development and education. The rationales for this stance have been more fully discussed elsewhere (Wolfendale, 1983; McConachie in Coupe and Porter, 1986) and the chapter abounds with references to research and practice in this area.

The ecological perspective has always been central to these rationales (Bronfenbrenner, 1979; Hobbs, 1978) and there are those who, like this author, aver that it is more or less axiomatic that parental involvement is synonymous with an approach that sees school as being centrally part of the child's world, along with home, family, peers, friends, social institutions, and the neighbourhood. Writers like Apter (1982) perceive the 'problems' of the children not so much as 'within child' problems as problems within these wider systems. The moves towards parental participation/partnership and community education exemplify ecological principles in practice.

It is imperative now, within a multicultural society (Tomlinson, 1984; Swann Report, 1985) that can no longer lay claim to monotheistic religious practice, to incorporate into schooling cultural perspectives and customs that reflect pluralist practice. A schism between home and school is no longer tenable in our communities where there is more than one neighbourhood language, where shops sell produce from all over the world, where dress reflects cultural diversity. Young children are entitled, as they grow up, to feel that there is a rapprochement between home and school and that their teachers and parents share common goals on their behalf.

TOPICS FOR DISCUSSION

1. 'Can teachers and parents be coerced into co-operative ventures by those with the influence to instigate (head teachers, advisers, educational psychologists, for example) when their conviction and enthusiasm are lacking?' Discuss.
2. Discuss the characteristic features of parental involvement ventures which the author suggests 'bury myths that earlier attitude surveys uncovered concerning parents' perceptions of teachers' inaccessibility and teachers' perceptions of parents' indifference'.
3. 'To some extent, parental involvement can be viewed as a "preventive" approach in that "problems" can be "caught" and dealt with before they exacerbate.' What practical strategies does the author suggest to bring this about?

SUGGESTIONS FOR FURTHER READING

1. Laing, A.F. and Chazan, M. (1984) 'Young children with special educational needs', in Fontana, D. (ed.) *The Education of the Young Child*, 2nd edn. Oxford, Blackwell, chap. 8, pp. 128–47.

The authors offer a detailed examination of the effect that various forms of handicap have on the functioning of young children, particularly the effect which their developmental difficulties have on their ability to learn. Many of the learning needs of these children are, however, the same as those of all children. For example, they need opportunities to explore their environment and to come to terms with it, under the guidance from adults who can assist them to develop their comprehension or understanding by structuring these opportunities and matching them to the children's abilities. Laing and Chazan suggest that the normally accepted aims of nursery and infant schools would appear, therefore, to be well suited to children with special needs. They document various forms of handicap (socio-cultural disadvantage, low intellectual ability, physical handicap, behavioural disturbance, communication difficulties and multiple handicap) and discuss the forms of special educational provision which attempt to cater for these disabilities. Of particular relevance to Wolfendale's paper (Reading 9) is the consideration of the role of the parents with regard to the child with special educational needs. The authors conclude with the observation that the child will benefit even more if the parents are aware of their own potential as educators.

2. Wadsworth, J., Burnell, I., Taylor, B. and Butler, N. (1985) 'The influence of family type on children's behaviour and development at five years'. *Journal of Child Psychology and Psychiatry*, **26**, 2, 245–54.

The proportion of one-parent families in Great Britain is increasing. In 1971, 8 per cent of all families with children were headed by single parents and this was estimated to have increased to 12 per cent by 1981. In addition to the financial hardships faced by many single-parent families, there are often difficult emotional demands to meet, which may result in some children from such families exhibiting behaviour and emotional problems or developmental delay. This study investigates the influence of family type on the behaviour and development of five-year-old children. Because there are economic and social as well as emotional pressures on single parents to form new relationships, the authors compared children of step-parent families as well as children of one-parent families with children living in two-natural-parent families. The results of the study show some of the *social* and *biological* associations of different family types. One-parent families and step-parent families were consistently different from two-parent families for each of these variables. Children in atypical families were more likely to live in poor urban neighbourhoods and have a young mother with low educational attainment; children in one-parent families were more likely to be *only* children, children in step-parent families were more likely to have younger siblings. Children from one-parent families and step-parent families had 'anti-social' scores *significantly higher* than children from two-parent families. The children's scores on the developmental tests also showed striking differences according to family type. Developmental test scores of children from one-parent families were a third of a standard deviation below those of children from two-parent families. After the child's total behaviour score, maternal age and education, the child's sex, birth rank, birthweight, and type of neighbourhood had been taken into consideration, a reduced but still highly significant ($P < 0.001$) difference remained.

3. Topping, K. (1985) 'Parental involvement in reading: theoretical and empirical background', in Topping, K. and Wolfendale, S. (eds) *Parental Involvement in Children's Reading*. London, Croom Helm, chap. 2, pp. 17–31.

This scholarly contribution criticizes much of the academic research into the processes of reading, viewing it as fragmentary, circular and trivial. Topping suggests that the 'medical model of human functioning, with its emphasis on a plethora of pseudo-explanatory categories and its preoccupation with purported intra-cranial events is gradually being flushed out of education by more sophisticated and practical ideas, which have much more relevance to life in the classroom and the actual business of teaching children to read' (p. 17).

The author discusses various aspects of research on reading, emotional and behavioural factors associated with reading failure, and considers the relative influence of home and school on educational outcomes. Of particular relevance to Wolfendale's paper (Reading 9) is Topping's analysis of factors involved in the effectiveness of parental involvement on children's reading behaviour (practice, feedback, reinforcement and modelling). The final part of the paper examines changes in parental behaviour as a result of their involvement in reading, specifically explaining the processes involved in training parents and the relative effectiveness of a number of techniques.

REFERENCES

Apter, S. (1982) *Troubled Children, Troubled Systems*. Oxford, Pergamon.

Bastiani, J. (1978) *Written Communication between Home and School*. University of Nottingham, School of Education.

Beattie, N. (1985) *Professional Parents*. Lewes, Falmer.

Bendall, S., Smith, J. and Kushlick, A. (1984) *National Study of Portage-type Home Teaching Services: A Research Report, No. 162*. Health Care Evaluation Research Team, University of Southampton.

Berger, E. (1983) *Beyond the Classroom, Parents as Partners in Education*. London, C.V. Mosby.

Bowers, T. (ed.) (1984) *Management and the Special School*. London, Croom Helm.

Bronfenbrenner, U. (1979) *The Ecology of Human Development, Experiments by Nature and Design*. Harvard University Press.

Cameron, R.J. (ed.) (1982) *Working Together: Portage in the UK*. Windsor, NFER-Nelson.

Cameron, R.J. (ed.) (1986) *Portage, Parents and Professionals: Helping Families with Special Needs*. Windsor, NFER-Nelson.

Carr, J. (1980) *Helping your Handicapped Child*. Harmondsworth, Penguin.

COPE (Committee on Primary Education) (no date) *School-Home-Community Relationships*: examples of how some Scottish nursery and primary schools relate to parents and members of the wider community. Moray House College of Education.

Copley, M., Bishop, M. and Porter, J. (eds) (1986) *Portage: More than a Teaching Programme*. Windsor, NFER-Nelson.

Coupe, J. and Porter, J. (eds) (1986) *The Education of Children with Severe Learning Difficulties: Bridging the Gap Between Research and Practice*. London, Croom Helm.

Craft, M., Rayner, J. and Cohen, L. (eds) (1980) *Linking Home and School*, 3rd edn. London, Harper & Row.

Cullingford, C. (ed.) (1985) *Parents, Teachers and Schools*. London, Robert Royce.

Cunningham, C. and Davies, H. (1985) *Working with Parents*. Milton Keynes, Open University Press.

Daly, B., Addington, J., Kerfoot, S. and Sigston, A. (eds) (1985) *Portage: The Importance of Parents*. Windsor, NFER-Nelson.

Davie, R. (1985) *Equalities and Inequalities in Working Together for Children, in Partnership with Parents: A Contrast in Stress*. Partnership Paper No. 6. London, National Children's Bureau.

Dessent, T. (ed.) (1983) *What is Important about Portage?* Windsor, NFER-Nelson.

Dowling, E. and Osborne, E. (eds) (1985) *The Family and the School, A Joint Systems Approach to Working with Children*. London, Routledge & Kegan Paul.

Fish, J. (Chair) (1985) *Educational Opportunities for All?* The Report of the Committee reviewing provision to meet special educational needs. London, ILEA.

George, A. (1984) *Resource-based Learning for School Governors*. London, Croom Helm.

Gliedman, J. and Roth, W. (1981) 'Parents and professionals', in Swann, W. (ed.) *The Practice of Special Education*. London, Basil Blackwell and Open University Press.

Goacher, B. and Reid, M. (1983) *School Reports to Parents*. Windsor, NFER-Nelson.

Griffiths, A. and Hamilton, D. (1984) *Parent, Teacher, Child*. London, Methuen.

Hargreaves, D. (Chairman) (1984) *Improving Secondary Schools*. London, ILEA.

Harris, J. (ed.) (1986) *Child Psychology in Action; Linking Research and Practice*. London, Croom Helm.

Hester, P. (1977) 'Evaluation and accountability in a parent-implemented early intervention service'. *Community Mental Health Journal*, **13**, 3, 261–7.

Hobbs, N. (1978) 'Families, schools and committees: an ecosystem for children'. *Teachers' College Record*, **79**, 4, May.

ILEA (1982) *Keeping the School Under Review: The Primary School*.

Lombana, J. (1983) *Home-School Partnerships: Guidelines and Strategies for Educators*. New York, Grune and Stratton.

London Borough of Croydon Education Authority (1985) *Guide for Parents, Primary Education in Croydon*.

Long, R. (1986) *Parental Involvement in Primary Schools*. Basingstoke, Macmillan.

Macbeth, A. (1984) *The Child Between: A Report on School-Family Relations in the Countries of the European Community*. Brussels, EEC.

McConachie, H. (1986) *Parents and Mentally Handicapped Children: A Review of Research Issues*. London, Croom Helm.

McConkey, R. (1985) *Working with Parents: A Practical Guide for Teachers and Therapists*. London, Croom Helm.

Marra, M. (1984) 'Parents of children with moderate learning difficulties', in Bowers, T. (ed.) op. cit.

Milton Keynes Home-School Link, Report (1981).

Mittler, P. and McConachie, H. (eds) (1983) *Parents, Professionals and Mentally Handicapped People*. London, Croom Helm.

Morrison, G. (1978) *Parent involvement in the Home, School and Community*. London, Charles E. Merrill.

Myatt, R. (1984) *Report of the Independent Evaluation of the South Lakeland Advisory Service*. University of Exeter.

NARE Guidelines No. 7: *Guidelines for Involving Parents in Special Projects Concerning the Education of Their Child*. Stafford, National Association for Remedial Education.

Newson, E. and Hipgrave, T. (1982) *Getting Through to Your Handicapped Child*. Cambridge University Press.

Paul, J. (1981) *Understanding and Working with Parents of Children with Special Needs*. New York, Holt, Rinehart & Winston.

Plowden, B. (Chair) (1967) *Children and their Primary Schools*. London, HMSO.

Potts, P. (1983) 'What difference would integration make to the professionals?', in Booth, T. and Potts, P. (eds) *Integrating Special Education*. Oxford, Basil Blackwell.

Pugh, G. (1981) *Parents as Partners*. London, National Children's Bureau.

Pugh, G. and De'Ath, E. (1984) *The Needs of Parents*. Basingstoke, Macmillan.

Rennie, J. (ed.) (1985) *British Community Primary Schools*. Lewes, Falmer.

Raven, J. (1980) *Parents, Teachers and Children: A Study of an Educational Home Visiting Scheme*. Sevenoaks, Hodder & Stoughton for the Scottish Council for Research in Education.

Rutherford, R. and Edgar, E. (1979) *Teachers and Parents, A Guide to Interaction and Cooperation*. Boston MA, Allyn and Bacon.

Sandow, S. and Stafford, P. (1986) 'Parental perceptions and the 1981 Education Act'. *British Journal of Special Education*, **13**, 1, 19–21, March.

South West Hertfordshire Teachers' Centre (1984) *Parents and Schools*. Tolpits Lane, Watford.

Stierer, B. (1985) 'School reading volunteers: results of a postal survey of primary school head teachers in England'. *Journal of Research in Reading*, **3**, 1, 21-31.

Swann, Lord M. (Chairman) (1985) *Education for All*. Report of the Committee of Inquiry into the education of children from ethnic minority groups. London, HMSO.

Telford (Shropshire) *Home and School Link Project* (1977-1984).

Tizard, B., Mortimore, J. and Burchell, B. (1981) *Involving Parents in Nursery and Infant Schools*. London, Grant McIntyre.

Thomas, N. (Chair) (1985) *Improving Primary Schools*. Report of the Committee of Inquiry on Primary Education. London, ILEA.

Tomlinson, S. (1984) *Home and School in Multicultural Britain*. London, Batsford.

Topping, K. (1986) *Parents as Educators*. London, Croom Helm.

Topping, K. and Wolfendale, S. (eds) (1985) *Parental Involvement in Children's Reading*. London, Croom Helm.

Warnock, M. (Chair) (1978) *Special Educational Needs*. London, HMSO.

Westmacott, E.V.S. and Cameron, R.J. (1981) *Behaviour Can Change*. Basingstoke, Macmillan.

Wolfendale, S. (1983) *Parental Participation in Children's Development and Education*. New York and London, Gordon and Breach.

Wolfendale, S. (1985a) 'Questionnaire to teachers on parental involvement: results from a survey', unpublished documents. Psychology Department, North East London Polytechnic.

Wolfendale, S. (1985b) *Parental contribution to Section 5 (1981 Education Act) Assessment Procedures*. Spastics Society.

Wolfendale, S. (1985c) 'Involving parents in assessment: exploring parental profiling and the parental contribution to the 1981 Education Act Section 5 Assessment and Statementing Procedures', in *NCSE (National Council for Special Education) Research Exchange*, **4**, September.

Wolfendale, S. and Bryans, T. (1986) *WORD PLAY: Language Activities for Young Children and their Parents*. Stafford, National Association for Remedial Education.

Young, P. and Tyre, P. (1983) *Dyslexia or Illiteracy: Realising the Right to Read*. Milton Keynes, Open University Press.

Reading 10

PORTAGE IN PERSPECTIVE: PARENTAL INVOLVEMENT IN PRE-SCHOOL PROGRAMMES

G. Pugh

WHY PARENTAL INVOLVEMENT?

The terms 'parental involvement, 'parent–professional partnership' and 'parents as educators' have become fashionable in recent years, and tend to be thrown about with little regard to their true meaning. Many of those who work in health, education and social services are being urged to work more closely with parents, and looking at how services have developed it is indeed illogical to imagine that schools should feel they can educate, or hospitals cure, children without the close collaboration of those children's parents.

Yet if we look at the reasons given for working more closely with parents, these tend to vary depending on whether the benefits are seen to accrue to the child, the parents or the professionals. As far as children's educational development is concerned, the research, from the 1960s onwards, has confirmed the crucial role that parents play in their children's development. In Britain we have been particularly influenced by the American Headstart programmes which showed (despite a few hiccups early on) that early intervention programmes for socially disadvantaged children, which involved parents, had a greater long-term effect than those which did not (Bronfenbrenner, 1974). The view that the family is the most effective system for fostering and sustaining the long-term development of children, lay behind parallel developments in behavioural programmes for handicapped children. These simple truths have influenced the thinking behind most of the major government reports concerned with children in the last twenty-five years (Plowden, Bullock, Court ('we have found no better way to raise a child than to reinforce the ability of his parents to do so'), Taylor and Warnock).

The logical extension of this growing view of parents as educators of their children has been to devise programmes which have attempted to sustain parents in their educational role, through a variety of educational

Pugh, G. (1987) 'Portage in perspective: parental involvement in pre-school programmes', in Hedderly, R. and Jennings, K. (eds) *Extending and Developing Portage*. Windsor, NFER-Nelson, pp. 93–103. Reprinted by permission of the publishers.

home visiting schemes attached to schools, home-based intervention schemes (such as Portage) and parent education programmes. I will return to some of these later. At a more general level, research such as that by Tizard and Hughes (1984) confirmed what most of us knew anyway - that without any special programmes at all, young children learn more from talking to their parents than ever they do from talking to busy nursery teachers.

These developments have stressed the benefit to the children, but there is also a growing recognition that parents too may benefit from a closer working relationship with pre-school workers, and a greater involvement in planning and determining services. Evidence from our study of the needs of parents showed that parents tended to feel confused and lacking in confidence in the face of professional expertise. They were aware of the crucial part they played in the early years of their children's lives, and were made to feel that there must be a 'right' way to bring children up if only they could work out which expert to believe. This was particularly acute for parents of children with special needs who wanted help in teaching their children to do things that others did naturally, leading some (as Cunningham and Sloper's earlier study (1978) had shown) to feel very isolated from their child. 'They also think they should not try what they intuitively feel is right, unless an "expert" has advised it. The result is non-activity and usually slower development in the infant.'

Our own work led us to believe that if parents were enabled to contribute to as well as receive services, thus building on their skills and developing their self-confidence, this would provide a firmer base for a more equal relationship between them and professional workers. Many parents in this country, of course, do set up and run their own groups - playgroups, opportunity groups, parent and toddler groups, community nurseries. These have not only given parents greatly increased insight into how children grow, behave and develop, but also the skills and confidence of working in the community.

The other development from the parents' point of view is the move towards making services more accountable to those who pay for them through taxes and rates. Although we are still a long way behind some of our European and American colleagues, the 1980 and 1981 Education Acts have opened the door to parents. Greater availability of information, choice of school, and the inclusion of parents on school governing bodies (at present still something of a token gesture) are an important start. Potentially the 1981 Act has more far-reaching implications, if the rights it affords to parents - to be involved in assessment procedures and in decisions regarding placement - are extended to all parents.

From the professional's point of view a closer relationship with parents offers opportunities for overcoming some of the many discontinuities between home and school. Whether the professional is working with a child with a particular problem or developmental delay, or running a pre-school group, the experience will be of greatest value if it relates to what happens at home and can complement it. There is also the hope that services will be able to respond more directly to need; that problems can be shared and more accurately identified; and that a greater trust can be created.

THE EXTENT OF PARENTAL INVOLVEMENT

It is of course quite impossible to gauge the exact extent to which parents and professionals are working together, but my feeling is that despite the recommendations of countless government reports, parental involvement is not as widespread as it might be. It does, however, depend on how it is defined, as I shall show shortly. The recent report from the Child Health and Education Study (Osborn, 1984), based on 13,000 children, makes disappointing reading. Contrary to popular opinion less than half of the mothers with children at playgroups had helped in the group during the previous term and only a quarter helped once a month. In LEA nursery schools, only 13 per cent helped once a term, whilst day nurseries found difficulty in generating any kind of parental or community activities.

As far as home visiting is concerned, as cuts begin to bite educational home visiting schemes appear to be dwindling, although an increasing number of teachers are visiting homes as part of their work in nursery and infant schools. The main growth points seem to be Portage (which I gather now has 150 schemes) and Homestart, the scheme which trains parents as home visitors and is now in fifty different locations.

In our own inquiry we asked all local authorities and health authorities to what extent services for families with children under five were planned, implemented and delivered in partnership with those for whom they were intended. Very few of those who replied could point to any examples, though there were many references to involvement. Interestingly, a surprising number assumed that we must be interested only in children with special needs and told us of Portage and similar schemes.

In concluding her study of parental involvement in nursery and infant schools, Tizard et al. (1981) suggested that 'there is a discrepancy between the approval in principle of parent involvement in early education and the extent to which it is realised in practice . . . The most enthusiastic advocates seem to be furthest from the coal face.' My feeling is that there is a lot of support and interest at the coal face, but that unless it can be married to support from middle and top management, so that resources and training are made available, there will be very little further progress.

PARENTAL INVOLVEMENT OR PARTNERSHIP?

Despite the increasing commitment on the part of many pre-school workers to involve parents more fully in the services they provide, the tendency is still for professionals to invite parents to join them on *their* terms. Yet a true partnership suggests an acceptance of equal skills and experience, and a sense that each partner brings something different but of equal value to the relationship.

The tendency to treat parents as deficient in some way, and in need of treatment or advice, has perhaps obscured the fact that most parents are well able to contribute to as well as receive services. As the Warnock Report recognized, 'Parents can be effective partners only if professionals take notice of what they say and how they express their needs, and treat their contributions as intrinsically important.'

Speaking at a study day at the National Children's Bureau, Hilton Davis (1985) put it like this:

> Partnership is a relationship in which the professional serves the parents, by making appropriate expertise available to them for their consideration. The relationship is, therefore, one of *complementary expertise*, since the expert knowledge of the parents, on themselves, their aims, their situation generally, and their children, complements what the profession has to offer including professional knowledge and the skills to communicate it. Using this framework of partnership therefore, the professional accepts his/her expertise and limitations; perceives parents as knowledgeable; acknowledges that many of the problems are not easily resolved; and believes that the best approach is to pool their expertise and to experiment together in mutually agreed ways. Although the parents are seen as having ultimate executive control, the professional's role is to offer for discussion alternative ways of viewing the situation and intervening. Decisions, therefore, are made on the basis of negotiation.

DIMENSIONS OF PARENTAL INVOLVEMENT

In order to put parental involvement and partnership into context, I would like to show briefly a typology that we have devised to illustrate the various dimensions of parent involvement. This is based on work we have done in more than 100 pre-school schemes and centres, and on research done by others in this field. It should not be seen as a progression from one end of the spectrum to the other, but simply as a way of describing the different ways in which parents relate to pre-school services.

Non-participation

In some schemes, particularly those providing substitute care for children of working parents, parents are unlikely to be involved on a daily basis (although they may be involved in management). But there are also many parents who do not participate for other reasons - because they lack confidence, are tired or depressed, or feel that a language barrier presents too many problems, or because they do not understand the value or relevance of what is on offer (for example a language stimulation programme).

External support

This is perhaps most relevant to groups and schemes which parents may support from the outside, without actually becoming involved. For example, through fund raising, attending social functions, offering moral support when services are threatened by cuts, etc.

Participation

There are many ways in which parents can participate in pre-school services, under the supervision of professional staff. They can provide an 'extra pair of hands' for busy nursery teachers, either by working with small groups of children or by servicing the group - mending toys, making tea, washing paint pots. Parents can be asked to welcome other parents to the group; they may enjoy sharing in their own children's learning; they may be able to run a toy library or mother and toddler group. Parents may also be able to participate in observation and assessment of their child; attend review panels; or enjoy nominal participation in users' committees or governing bodies.

Partnership

Partnership suggests a sharing of power, resources, knowledge and decision-making between parents and professionals. It can be seen in three different ways.

1. Partnership between an individual and a professional

This is the kind of partnership to which Hilton Davis was referring, and it suggests mutual respect, a sharing of different but equivalent expertise, and a sharing of information. Portage offers an ideal framework for developing skills in assessment, in writing reports, in evaluating the effectiveness of services, in negotiating appropriate placements and in working their way round the system. It gives them the tools and the confidence to 'take on' professionals, and it offers professionals the tools for working with parents on a more equal footing.

But if parents are really to be able to negotiate they are also going to have to understand professional jargon and find a way of communicating their own views. The 'parent profile' that Sheila Wolfendale has been developing provides a simple format for parents to use in describing their child at home, under appropriate developmental headings. The information can then be used as a basis for dialogue, to explore different perceptions and aspirations between parent and professional for a given child (Wolfendale, 1985).

2. Partnership between parents in general and a particular group or scheme

If parents are to be partners in running a service, this implies an equal sharing of power over resources, over knowledge and information, and over decision-making. Although there is some parent involvement in management of schools, and parents are often on the management committees of Portage projects, whether or not this can be defined as partnership depends very much on whether anyone listens to what they have to say. My feeling from talking to a number of parents of children with special needs is that often their problems are such that they are happier to leave the management to someone else.

Partnership is also implicit in the growing number of schemes in which parents are taking on roles as workers – visiting homes (for example the fifty or so Homestart schemes, some Portage schemes, or the parents who are home-school liaison workers in Coventry); offering counselling and support to parents of newly diagnosed handicapped infants (the Southend scheme, and Kids in Camden); convening groups (Scope in Southampton, or the Riverside Health Project in Newcastle); or setting up and running toy libraries and parent and toddler groups.

3. Partnership between parents/clients/consumers and policy makers

This is still all too rare, but is perhaps best illustrated by the important part parents play in Strathclyde's link up groups; and by the growing involvement of parents in community health councils, under-fives committees, district handicap teams, patients participation groups in general practice, neighbourhood health projects and occasionally district health authorities and local council committees.

Control

These would be services in which parents both determine and implement decisions, and are ultimately responsible and accountable. For example, community playgroups, parent and toddler groups and community nurseries.

These groupings should not be seen as progressive, and in any one centre or service different parents will relate in different ways, but they have helped us distinguish between how professionals think they are relating to parents, and what is actually happening.

HOME-BASED SERVICES: SOME ADVANTAGES AND DISADVANTAGES

I would now like to put Portage into the context of some other home-based schemes, and consider briefly some advantages and disadvantages of an approach which theoretically offers considerable opportunities for partnership.

The survey of home visiting schemes undertaken by the National Children's Bureau (Aplin and Pugh, 1983) revealed a marked shift from the earlier emphasis placed on children's cognitive and social performance, towards a focus on supporting families in the vital role they play in children's overall development. Schemes were obviously very different depending on whether they were based on schools, or were funded by adult education, or were run by voluntary organizations - but the general feeling was that the work is most effective when it is directed as much to the parents as to the children. Perhaps the three aims of the Inner London schemes can best illustrate this:

(a) to develop the parent/child relationship;
(b) to encourage the personal growth of the parent;
(c) to develop effective links between the family and the wider community.

So perhaps in contrast to Portage, most home visiting schemes have become less directly educational and highly structured, and more generally supportive to the family as a whole.

SOME ADVANTAGES

1. The service offered can respond directly to the parents' needs, and parents can select priorities.
2. A working partnership is inevitable, if goals are planned together and assessed together.

3. Parents can be helped to develop skills in a way that does not undermine their self-confidence. It can confirm that parents are doing all right, as this London mother says, 'It's really good having someone to talk to - someone who listens to you. Lots of the time you were doing the right thing for the children, but talking it over makes you feel more sure' (Aplin and Pugh, 1983). It provides also some structure when there are particular problems: 'We can do a certain amount by instinct, but you reach a stage when you need more' (mother at Kids).

   The evidence on the effectiveness of home visiting schemes is in fact rather more compelling for the parents than it is for children, showing improved morale, and a greater understanding of and interest in their children (e.g. McCail, 1981; Burden, 1980).
4. Schemes can provide a basis for developing skills in assessment, joint planning and decision-making.
5. Many schemes are able to forge closer links between home and school, not only helping parents to understand what teachers are trying to do with their children, but also giving teachers an insight into the homes and families of the children they teach.
6. The programme and the level of involvement can be matched to other demands and commitments within the family and other family members can be involved.
7. Programmes can deal with problems where they occur, and behaviour can be learned in context. There is a greater chance of long-term gain if the programmes are based on existing skills and are restructuring what is already happening.
8. Home visitors can reach out to parents who may not seek help. Shinman's study (1981) showed that even if there were clinics and playgroups on every corner of every street, depression, alienation and lack of confidence would prevent up to a quarter of all mothers from using them.
9. Home visitors may also be able to help to establish community networks. A study of Homestart (van der Eyken, 1982) found that those who were not coping either did not have or were unable to use social networks. The home visitors were able to help families reach the point where, for the first time, they could use networks and cope adequately on their own.

DISADVANTAGES/LIMITATIONS

No approach is without its limitations, and I would like to remind you briefly what some of these are.

1. An intensive home visiting programme can put intolerable pressures on some families.
2. One of the myths that Tony Dessent exploded was that anyone can visit homes. Home-based programmes are only as good as the home visitor, and working in people's homes is a skilled and difficult task.
3. If parents are made to feel responsible for their children's success as they acquire new skills, so too will they feel they must take responsibility for failures. As previous Portage conferences have recognized, there is danger in a cook-book approach based on recipes rather than principles. And there is danger too in using the child's performance to measure the parent's success.
4. Unless home-based schemes involve fathers as well as mothers, they can become divisive, giving one parent skills and techniques that are not shared.
5. Home is not always ideal. Cold floors for physiotheraphy or the constant accompaniment of the television when a language programme is in progress can be frustrating. As Sandow and Clarke (1978) reminded us: 'The home may be so elegant and the mother so concerned with its effect on the visitor, that the purpose of the visit becomes obscured. Alternatively one may be required to work in a room ten feet by eight, surrounded by three generations of a mutually hostile family, in an atmosphere composed of equal parts smoke, sweat and old chip papers.'
6. And finally, home-based programmes do not solve problems of loneliness and isolation, nor do they give an exhausted parent any time off.

ISSUES AND DILEMMAS

The various points I have made raise a number of issues and point to some unresolved dilemmas.

1. Are we able to start from where parents are at, rather than where we would like them to be? Can we recognize that unless parents' own problems are resolved, then to present a structured programme that depends on their involvement and commitment may increase feelings of guilt and anxiety. Two years ago, Jo Cameron spoke of her needs as a parent for counselling and support, and suggested that there are times when the needs of the rest of the family or of the parent must take precedence. This is supported by the experience at Honeylands, for example (Burden, 1980), and by many of the educational home visiting schemes, which stress the need to work through family problems before

focusing on the child. The Inner London scheme, for example, analysed the content of 200 home visits and found that 200 out of 500 topics that came up during visits were to do with problems of health or marital relationships or housing and were beyond the original aims of the scheme (Aplin and Pugh, 1983).

2. We need to be conscious of the dangers of 'professionalizing' parenthood, and of increasing parents' guilt and anxiety by overemphasizing the need for their commitment to a home-based programme. Partnership suggests discussion and negotiation and the possibility of saying 'No, I can't cope with any more at the moment'.
3. Is partnership possible when professional values are the ones that are operational? Most parental involvement is dictated on professionals' terms - 'you help us in the ways we think fit, and we will help you bring up your children better'. But even in schemes which affect a partnership, there are difficulties. I have been able to observe many home visitors at work - as part of Portage schemes, or the health visitors working with the child development project, or educational home visitors. I am constantly struck by the conflict between the need to give guidance and enforce a structure, and the wish to respond to the parents' needs. Sarah Sandow (1984) [. . .], discussing the mutual selection of objectives, writes: 'care must be taken that this does not mean careful massaging of parental ambitions to fit the tutor's own view of the case. If the parent is to have true power, she must have more than the right to admiringly agree to the tutor's suggestions. But can the professional take a back seat if the selection of objectives seems inappropriate or even perverse?'

   I feel that this issue presents very real problems, that are far from being resolved.
4. Our study of the needs of parents revealed the importance of flexibility and of having a range of services in a community that might give parents some choice. The needs of individual families obviously vary enormously and will change over a period of time, and whilst Portage is clearly meeting a very real need, it may not be the perfect answer to every parent's problems. [. . .] There is still no adequate evidence on the comparative value of home-based and centre-based services, and as I have shown there are some inadequacies in a purely home-based scheme. I have been doing some work in the Kids centre in Camden, where the home learning scheme is linked both to developmental play sessions, where five or six children and their parents come together on a weekly basis in the centre, and to individual counselling and support from the centre staff. The parents seem to appreciate this combination of individual work in the home and the experience of a group.

5. Appropriate training is another key issue. I have already referred to the essential qualities required for home visiting. The first home visiting scheme in Britain (in the West Riding of Yorkshire as part of the EPA project in Denaby) describes a home visitor as needing to be 'unbiased, non-judgemental, able to work under any conditions, knowledgeable without being dictatorial, helpful without being patronizing, able to listen, and sensitive to people's needs without appearing [to intrude] into their private affairs' (Smith, 1975).

   These qualities could equally refer to anyone working with parents, and yet our study of parent education programmes (Pugh and De'Ath, 1984) concluded that the training of most pre-school workers seemed to pay little attention to developing skills in listening, in self-awareness, in understanding and accepting values different from one's own, and in expressing ideas in language that is not riddled with jargon.

   If we are asking professionals to work with parents as partners, to listen to what they say, to be prepared to negotiate and discuss and plan together, and occasionally to admit to not knowing the answer - then this does, I suggest, have considerable implications for initial and in-service training.
6. In our experience, a more open relationship with parents reflects a greater sharing and participation (a) between members of staff in a team or a unit; and (b) between the many professionals who are working with families in a neighbourhood.
7. And finally, to conclude on a note of caution, I think we should ask whether the current emphasis on parental involvement always implies a more open relationship and shared care, or whether sometimes responsibility for children's welfare and education is being shifted from professionals to parents and self-help groups. It is important that at this time of cutbacks and economic recession we look at the rationale for parent-professional partnership. Some, for example, are seeing parents in classrooms and hospitals as cheap labour, releasing teachers to do 'proper' teaching and nurses to do the 'real' caring. Similarly, in promoting self-help and community activities are we simply supporting a cutback in expenditure on state support for families? These are important questions that need answering. Participation of parents can just be a way of passing problems back to those parents.

IN CONCLUSION

In principle, we can I think justify the concept of partnership between parents and professionals, for the long-term benefits it brings to the children; for the increased self-esteem and self-confidence and knowledge it brings to parents; and for the opportunities it offers professionals to respond more directly to need and provide a service based on mutual trust and respect.

In practice, I would suggest it is a great deal more difficult. It requires appropriate attitudes and skills, sufficient time and resources, and a willingness on the part of both parents and professionals to share - information, decision-making and mutual respect. But ultimately it is a question of overall philosophy - do we really believe in working *with* parents to meet their needs, rather than always doing things to them?

My feeling is that Portage provides the right framework for taking this partnership forward, and that you could with advantage spread your ideas and approaches beyond the world of special education.

TOPICS FOR DISCUSSION

1. 'Yet if we look at the reasons given for working more closely with parents, these tend to vary depending on whether the benefits are seen to accrue to the child, the parents or the professionals.' Discuss.
2. 'At a more general level, research . . . confirmed what most of us knew anyway - that without any special programmes at all, young children learn more from talking to their parents than ever they do from talking to busy nursery teachers.' Discuss.
3. What are some of the most important differences between the idea of 'parental involvement' and 'parental partnership'? How do teachers' attitudes and behaviour reflect these differences?

SUGGESTIONS FOR FURTHER READING

1. Williams, B. and Paulson, E. (1986) 'Sounds like Portage', in Bishop, M., Copley, M. and Porter, J. (eds) *Portage: More than a Teaching Programme?*. Windsor, NFER-Nelson, pp. 38-43.

The authors describe a scheme set up in schools in inner-city areas of Liverpool, designed to help break the cycle of deprivation which is a predominant feature of such areas. It was, the authors assert, 'an attempt to bring together the child's two backgrounds - home and school. If we could make a partnership between these two the child would very much benefit both emotionally and mentally' (p. 39). The scheme, 'Parent School Partnership' (PSP), although appearing straightforward and easy to establish in theory, proved in practice to be a much more difficult task. To build up relationships with parents is often a slow process because in inner-city areas school is traditionally an alien place where many parents have unhappy memories of their own experiences in school. The article describes a Portage scheme which one of the authors used to involve parents whose children attend a nursery class. Every parent had the opportunity of participating in an adapted Portage scheme. All parents were given a file containing a checklist which covered all areas of development - i.e. muscular, cognitive, self-help, socialization and pre-reading. The tasks in the package were graded, and parents worked with their children for five or ten minutes each day, giving lots of praise for their children's achievements. The authors give examples of interesting entries from parents' diaries, which record details of their children's progress. An example of a nursery adapted Portage checklist used by one author for children aged three to five years and concerned with *cognitive development* contains the following items.

Towards: thinking, understanding and reasoning

1. Matches three colours.
2. Copies a circle.
3. Matches shapes.
4. Points to ten body parts when told.
5. Tells if object is heavy or light.
6. Repeats finger plays and rhymes with words and actions.
7. Counts to five.
8. Copies a series of V strokes joined VVV . . .
9. Names three colours on request.
10. Names three shapes □ △ ○.
11. Picks number of objects on request (one to five).
12. Copies square, triangle, circle.
13. Tells what's missing when one object is removed from a group of three.
14. Names eight colours.
15. Tells colours of named objects.
16. Draws a man (head, body, four limbs).
17. Counts ten objects.
18. Copies rectangle▭; oval⬭; and diamond ◇ on request.
19. Draws a man (head, body, limbs, eyes, nose, mouth, ears, hair).
20. Copies first name (e.g. Jane).
21. Can name rectangle, oval and diamond on request.
22. Can recognize numbers 1–10.
23. Can write own first name from memory. (pp. 42–3)

2. Brosnan, D. and Huggett, S. (1984) 'From checklists to curriculum – using Portage as a basis for curriculum development in a nursery school', in Dessent, T. (ed.) *What is Important about Portage*?. Windsor, NFER-Nelson, pp. 107–16.

The project described in this reading involved adapting the Portage materials so that they could be used as a starting-point for the development of a core curriculum in a nursery school setting. Before discussing details of the project, the authors attempt to set their work within the context of general changes that have been taking place in recent years in the field of special education. For example, they assert that over the last decade there has been an increasing dissatisfaction with global, general objectives in special education, not just because such diffuse 'general' objectives are difficult to evaluate in relation to 'successful' teaching, but also because the last ten years have witnessed the growth of 'accountability' in education – education is being asked to be increasingly accountable to its consumers. Thus, the 1981 Education Act's relabelling of the consumers of special education has meant that children are defined in terms of their *needs* rather than their *type*, and as a direct consequence teachers' responsibilities are directed towards working out ways of satisfying those needs and defining (in terms of special educational provision) exactly what it is they have to offer (p. 108).

Brosnan and Huggett describe a project involving some thirty to forty children, aged between three and five years, attending a nursery school which has catered for children who have been blind, deaf and physically handicapped and also for those who have various learning and behavioural difficulties. Because of a number of factors which precipitated the need for a major reorganization in the curriculum (for example a large increase in the number of severely handicapped children in the nursery, the appointment of a new speech therapist and a new psychologist) it was decided to use the Portage Guide to Early Education as a framework for curriculum development in the school. As a consequence, all children have individual programmes which are recorded either on activity charts or on other class charts. Each child has three short-term targets allocated for a week, which usually comprise one target from the 'cognitive' section of the Portage Guide, one from the 'motor' section where fine motor skills have been selected for teaching, and one from a 'language' item selected from the Derbyshire Language Scheme. Task analyses are performed on individual items to break them down into more negotiable steps. The authors illustrate a typical task analysis of a Portage item:

COG (Cognition) 34 – matches 3 colours

1. Present 1 yellow brick
   Give child 3 yellow + 3 red bricks
   Child builds all yellow bricks into the model
2. Present 1 red brick
   Give child 3 yellow and 3 red bricks
   Child builds all red bricks on to model
3. Present 1 blue brick
   Give child 3 blue + 3 yellow (or red) bricks
   Child builds all blue bricks on to model
4. Present 1 red and 1 yellow brick
   Adult gives child 3 red/3 yellow bricks randomly (one at a time) who places on appropriate tower
5. Repeat as 4 using blue and yellow bricks
6. Repeat as 4 using red and blue bricks
7. Present 1 red 1 yellow 1 blue brick
   Adult gives child 3 red 3 yellow 3 blue bricks randomly (one at a time) to place on appropriate tower (p. 111).

In a later section of the reading the authors discuss new developments in planning, which include (a) using a microcomputer to aid record keeping and curriculum development, (b) curriculum-related assessments for children to be considered for admission, (c) a Portage support service for day nurseries, and (d) the development of support services for parents teaching their children at home.

3. Russell, P. (1986) 'Parental involvement in the 1980s', in Cameron, R.J. (ed.) *Portage: Pre-Schoolers, Parents and Professionals*. Windsor, NFER-Nelson, chap. 10, pp. 142–58.

In this chapter Russell offers a very useful survey of the background to parental involvement, examining various government reports from Plowden to Warnock which have highlighted the need for collaboration between parents and professionals. She discusses the concept of 'partnership', commenting that 'in the commercial sense of the word, partnership implies "mutually profitable outcomes" ' (p. 143). The main thrust of Russell's contribution is directed to a comprehensive account of the development of the most widely known home-teaching programme - Portage, which she describes as 'an invaluable strategy for involving parents in not only directly teaching their children new skills, but in assessing which skills should be selected and how success could be achieved' (p. 146). The author examines the strength of Portage as a means of assessment followed by action, and considers in detail its role and use by parents with handicapped children. Of particular value is the author's summary of the research evidence which supports the use of this technique. Later sections of the chapter concern themselves with the use of Portage in a multicultural society and the implications of Portage for parental-professional partnership in school, day-care adult services.

REFERENCES

Aplin, G. and Pugh, G. (1983) *Perspectives on Pre-School Home Visiting*. London, National Children's Bureau.

Bronfenbrenner, U. (1974) *Is Early Intervention Effective?* A report on longitudinal evaluations of pre-school programmes, Vol. II (DHEW Publication No. OHO 75-25). Washington, DC, Dept. of Health, Education and Welfare.

Burden, R.L. (1980) 'Measuring the effects of stress on the mothers of handicapped infants: must depression always follow?'. *Child: Care, Health and Development*, **6**, 111-25.

Cunningham, C.C. and Sloper, P. (1978) *Helping your Handicapped Child*. London, Souvenir Press.

Davis, H. (1985) 'Developing the role of parent adviser in the child health services', in De'Ath, E. and Pugh, G. (eds) *Partnership Paper 3*. London, National Children's Bureau.

McCail, G. (1981) *Mother Start*. Edinburgh, Scottish Council for Research in Education.

Osborn, A. (1984) *The Social Life of Britain's Five Year Olds*. London, Routledge & Kegan Paul.

Pugh, G. and De'Ath, E. (1984) *The Needs of Parents*. London, Macmillan.

Sandow, S. (1984) 'The Portage project: ten years on', in Dessent, T. (ed.) *What is Important about Portage?*. Windsor, NFER-Nelson.

Sandow, S. and Clarke, A.D.B. (1978) 'Home intervention with parents of severely subnormal pre-school children: an interim report'. *Child: Care, Health and Development*, **4**, 29-39.

Shinman, S. (1981) *A Chance for Every Child*. London, Tavistock.

Smith, G. (ed.) (1975) *Educational Priority Vol. 4: The West Riding Project*. London, HMSO.

Tizard, B. and Hughes, M. (1984) *Young Children Learning*. London, Fontana.

Tizard, B., Mortimore, J. and Burchell, B. (1981) *Involving Parents in Nursery and Infant Schools*. London, Grant McIntyre.

Van der Eyken, W. (1982) *Homestart: A Four Year Evaluation*. Leicester Homestart Consultancy.

Wolfendale, S. (1985) 'Involving parents in assessment', in De'Ath, E. and Pugh, G. (eds) op. cit.

Reading 11

WHEN PARENTS BECOME PARTNERS

P. Widlake

The performance of children with special needs in mainstream schools can be dramatically increased when parents are drawn into the educational process. This has been demonstrated beyond all reasonable doubt. Moreover, when teachers and parents acknowledge their 'complementary expertise' and arrange to share it, the result can be an educational institution richer in experience, innovative in its day-to-day practice, more responsive to the pressures for change in a democratic society.

Members of the community who have not previously been involved in any kind of public work begin to demonstrate unsuspected abilities and a capacity for accepting responsibilities, including the administration of public funds. An empirical base for lifelong education is established. The raising of consciousness engendered produces irreversible effects and manifests itself in the more informed attitudes which so-called disadvantaged parents begin to display towards their children's education.

COMMUNITY SCHOOLS AND EDUCATIONAL STANDARDS

These assertions can be supported by evidence from my own findings. A survey was conducted of the reading and oral language achievements of primary age boys and girls in Coventry schools which were considered by the local authority's Community Education Project to have effective parental involvement programmes. The results have been widely reported (Widlake and Macleod, 1984; Topping and Wolfendale, 1985; Widlake, 1986) and those who are interested will find a full and detailed account in *Raising Standards* (Widlake and Macleod, 1984). The teaching I witnessed in these schools made a lasting impression on me. The

Widlake, P. (1987) 'When parents become partners'. *British Journal of Special Education*, **14**, 1, 27–9. Paul Widlake is a freelance educational consultant and writer. He is an honorary lecturer at the Centre for Educational Guidance and Special Needs, Department of Education, University of Manchester. Reprinted by permission of the author.

enthusiasm, ingenuity and professional skills which were being applied were well beyond the norms expected of primary school teachers.

However, other observers take a different view of schools which keep an open door for parents, which invite parents to take an active role in the classroom, which participate in broadcasts on the local radio station. These are the schools which follow the grain of the Plowden Report in their emphasis on imaginative methods, on finding out rather than being told, on seeking to meet individual needs, on encouraging creativity, on broadening the curriculum without losing sight of the virtues of 'neatness, accuracy, care and perseverance'. Critics claim this juxtaposition of achievements is impossible. But is it?

The overall Coventry reading means for these schools in disadvantaged areas were, in fact, equal or superior to those given in the test manual of the Hunter-Grundin Literacy Profiles for 'middle class' schools. (The profiles consist of five tests assessing attitudes to reading, reading for meaning, spelling, free writing and spoken language.)

The study in 1982–3 covered eight schools and nearly 1,000 pupils. It revealed high levels of achievement in oral and written language, and reading comprehension; 74 per cent of infant and 86 per cent of junior age children revealed positive attitudes towards reading. The spoken language tests on 116 infants, though they have attracted little attention compared with the statistics of reading scores, produced results which were enormously encouraging because, unlike the others, they could justifiably be related to the style of teaching. After all, great currency is given to the reports of distinguished authorities who have found that disadvantaged children display very poor levels of language, especially when required to perform under test conditions.

One of the schools where the testing took place had the most notorious catchment area in the city. Moreover, it was a particularly inauspicious time to be conducting research in schools, since industrial action was being taken by some teachers' unions. Yet 81 per cent of the children in this sample obtained high scores on confidence; more than 90 per cent were categorized as having 'intelligible speech' and more than half as possessing 'precise and carefully enunciated speech'. Eighty per cent scored well and 32 per cent very well on vocabulary, the measure which has almost universally been found to produce dismal results in this population. Something unusual was happening in these schools. It seems clear to me that infants' schools which keep an open door to adults can be expected to produce children who are confident in talking to adults, who speak clearly and develop their active vocabulary because they are encouraged to express themselves freely. As they move on through junior schools with a similar atmosphere, these qualities can be expected to reveal themselves in their free writing. Sure enough, samples collected from cohorts of seven-, eight- and nine-year-olds showed very high scores on legibility, fluency, accuracy and originality.

Just to round off this summary of 'encouraging results' (to borrow Hinson's (1978) neat title), I should like to mention that we conducted a follow-up study of the reading scores in three schools, which were asked to designate children according to the amount of parental support they were perceived as receiving. The schools varied considerably but in all three, in both the years tested, the more parental support the higher the reading scores.

Given these strong demonstrations of success, it is strange that there are few schools with the confidence to involve parents actively in educational decision-making. Explanations for this reluctance to follow the many examples of good practice which have now been recorded might be:

1. the complexity of the issues and society's tendency to use schools as dustbins, into which it dumps all its unsolvable problems;
2. the reluctance of professionals - teachers, social workers, health visitors and others - to recognize that their traditional roles may no longer be appropriate to the requirements of the late twentieth century;
3. the undifferentiated and stereotyped view of 'the parent' held by many professional teachers and the mirror image held by many parents about teachers, so that a high suspicion barrier has to be crossed before action is possible.

COMPLEMENTARY EXPERTISE

In my book *Reducing Educational Disadvantage* (1986), I have described how schools and other educational organizations of many different kinds have crossed this barrier. It seems easier and most common when the children are young and when the subject matter can be called 'reading'. One infants' school called their project 'Reading Together' and it had been in operation for a little over two years when observed in 1984. Before embarking on the project the school decided that each teacher should organize her own 'Reading Together' rather than adopt a uniform approach because:

1. they were trying something new, involving trial and error, and did not want to be restricted by too rigid a plan;
2. they could take advantage of a wide variety of approaches when dealing with problems and could draw on each other's experiences;

3. each of them had her own particular way of organizing reading in the classrooms and the project would need to fit in with that;
4. each had her own preferences for which group she wanted to start first and the number of children she wanted to involve;
5. no two classes were the same; there were classes of 'top' year children; some with 'top' year and some middle year children and some with all the children in the class being involved.

This variety was reflected in the arrangements for taking books home. One class took them away every night (with no adverse comment if the book was not read); another three times a week (if the child chose to); another allowed the child free choice. Children chose books from the same range that were read with the teachers. When the book was read at home, it was read again with the teacher *only* if the child wanted to.

All the staff were enthusiastic despite having to compromise their plans ('we couldn't always get the groups we wanted and had to settle for those who were prepared to get involved'); too much enthusiasm (some children wanted to be involved before the teacher was ready); teething troubles and failures (some parents were resistant but the staff were unwilling to leave them out).

This process may seem fairly straightforward to some teachers but many more prefer to keep parental interest within carefully defined boundaries. It was particularly useful, therefore, to be able to study two residential secondary schools which set great store on close co-operation with parents. Of course, it would have been easier had the schools not been miles out in the countryside, with few or no bus services, but the efforts made by the staff to overcome these limitations were impressive. A school for emotionally disturbed boys and girls aged nine to sixteen voluntarily accepted a heavier workload so that the post of home-school liaison worker could be created. An educational welfare officer (not a teacher) was appointed to this post indicating that more than lip service was paid to the need for closer co-operation between teachers and the other caring professions.

An inner-city school which appears to have broken through many of the traditional barriers to co-operative learning is Hazel Primary School and Community Centre in Leicester, opened in 1982 and awarded a Schools Curriculum Award in 1984. It was the first centre of its kind in the city and it provides for those living in the Tower and Walnut Street areas and the St Andrew's estate. Local residents were instrumental in obtaining the facilities and much of the work relies on the goodwill and enthusiasm of the local people. The headteacher is also warden of the centre; combining these two roles requires many varied skills. On one occasion I found her preparing lunch for the senior citizens club, assisted by three of her pupils (two boys and a girl). She talked about curriculum development while breaking eggs to make a sponge cake, mentioning the psychologist Jerome Bruner, the psycholinguist Gordon Wells and the television cook, Delia Smith. It was a virtuoso performance which impressed on me, as no doubt it had on the curriculum awarding panel, that this is both a very effective primary school and an unusual community centre, catering for the needs of a wide age and ability group, in a sensible and no-fuss manner. Courses offered by the community centre are determined by the needs of the community. At the time of my visit these were: wine-making, old time dancing, French, Indian and Caribbean cooking. More recently Fijian cooking has been featured.

These courses are available to unemployed people at a 75 per cent reduction in fees. Both the centre and the school issue brochures, describing their courses and curriculum, and a regular newsletter *The Walnut Grapevine* combines school and community news, using appropriate community languages. Most of the functions of the school brochures listed by Bastiani (1978) are to be found in these publications, including what he called the parental involvement model which 'encourages parents to become actively involved in the education of their children and the life and work of the school'.

The way that involving parents in the educational process can change lives is demonstrated more fully in *Reducing Educational Disadvantage* (Widlake, 1986), in sections on the Sutton Centre in Nottinghamshire, on home and school involvement in Salford and Leicester and on the Home Links Project in Liverpool. Here I shall refer to the neighbourhood centre which I observed in Hull. It was based on the McMillan nursery school and evolved slowly. In the first instance, parents were provided with the opportunity to talk, to be listened to and to share a problem. The school operated within a web of carefully fostered links with the social services, the health authority and the National Society for the Prevention of Cruelty to Children and with the neighbouring primary, junior high and senior high schools (whose older girls came in to play with the nursery children once a week). There was a library session at which the children, with a parent, were encouraged to take a book home, and where parents helped with the distribution of books. A newsletter went out once a month to inform parents about general activities. Staff and parents worked together on the school garden and made it a safe and attractive area with shrubs, trees and flowers. Informal contacts were promoted by creating a parents' room, where everyone was welcome without prior arrangement (every Coventry primary school had such a room incidentally). From these contacts, the idea of a neighbourhood centre was mooted by the parents themselves (mostly women, but a few men including one grandfather).

The neighbourhood centre was more strongly based because it grew slowly, in response to statements of need by parents at the McMillan nursery and by other adults in the local community. This evolutionary process enabled achievements at each stage to be consolidated and appeared to be more likely to achieve lasting results than provision based on the autocratic, paternalistic or response-to-pressure-group models.

In particular, *the neighbourhood centre was successful in identifying new community leaders*. Women who had not previously been involved in any kind of public work took active roles as chairperson, treasurer and secretary and demonstrated clearly that they were capable of accepting the responsibility of raising funds and administering them.

A necessary condition of the evolutionary model's success is that the *de jure* leader should be willing to hand over responsibility to the parent volunteers. There are few examples in British education of this process actually being carried to completion and the withdrawal of the centre leader to the status of co-opted committee member was a courageous and significant step. The indications were that those volunteer parents called on to accept responsibilities as officers were responding competently and enthusiastically.

There is great potential for parent education, as has been amply demonstrated in other projects (e.g. Palfreeman, 1984), and for more use of child development materials, such as the Open University courses, used with great success by the project organized by the Community Education Development Centre in Salford and Leicestershire. 'Family Matters' groups were led by a qualified teacher, who was also a single parent with four young children. The impact of this group on the women was observable in what they produced (written work; statistical summaries of a neighbourhood survey; drama and singing) and in their increased self-confidence and self-esteem - strongly manifested in the group's 'entertainments' at an open evening attended by the present writer. Interesting activities, based on neighbourhood needs, were flourishing. Impressive art work was on display. The pensioners' club and the parent–toddler club - both organized by volunteers - were attracting viable groups.

CONCLUSION

Several experiments have been reported and improved the educational opportunities of children through various forms of collaborative learning. Taken together, my observations suggest that a positive answer can be given to a question posed by Finch (1984): 'Can the recipients of education successfully resist its controlling features? Can they turn the situation to their own advantage?'

These questions can be interpreted as a call to professionals to seek new paths to collaborative learning. Though there are few examples of parents being able to grasp the possibilities, in Coventry, Liverpool, Hull, Bradford and elsewhere enough creative activity has been noted to indicate that communities can operate in and around the education system to produce more positive attitudes. It is clear that many dedicated professionals are working effectively, acquiring new skills (even learning community languages). Despite the bad press which schools often receive, many parents express great satisfaction and even fight to preserve a school which they feel is serving their children well (this happened in Blackburn, where Asian parents protested against the closure of a Church of England school).

That, however, is not the whole picture, or anything like it. Whatever definition of special educational needs we like to favour there is considerable mismatch with educational practice (Widlake, 1985). The system discriminates in favour of certain social classes, racial groups, geographical areas and types of ability or disability. Hundreds, thousands, of these community-oriented schools are required. Those who decide to take the path of collaborative learning can be confident that there is hard data beneath them.

TOPICS FOR DISCUSSION

1. Discuss the explanations which the author offers for his contention that 'it is strange that there are few schools with the confidence to involve parents actively in educational decision-making'.
2. '. . . my observations suggest that a positive answer can be given to a question posed by Finch (1984): "Can the recipients of education successfully resist its controlling features? Can they turn the situation to their own advantage?" ' Discuss.
3. 'Whatever definition of special educational needs we like to favour there is a considerable mismatch with educational practice. The system discriminates in favour of certain social classes, racial groups, geographical areas and types of ability or disability. Hundreds, thousands, of these community-oriented schools are required.' Discuss.

SUGGESTIONS FOR FURTHER READING

1. Topping, K.J. (1986) *Parents as Educators: Training Parents to Teach Their Children*. London, Croom Helm.

Topping writes that 'Parents, renouncing their bit part as peripheral irritants in the education system, have moved centre-stage. It has long been known that parental influence is considerably more profound than that of the school. Curiously, it is only in relatively recent years that the creative deployment of this positive force has begun to take place on a large scale' (p. 1).

This is a wide-ranging review, which critically analyses and evaluates over 600 international English-language research reports on the effectiveness of programmes of parental involvement and training. Topping discusses the evidence of the effects on children's progress of parental involvement in the activities of the school, looking particularly at the research to do with the impact of schemes of regular structured communication between home and school. Subsequent chapters consider programmes designed to train parents to accelerate the development of their children at home, beginning with 'ordinary' children. A large part of the book is concerned with reviewing projects targeted on children with various kinds of special educational needs - ranging from those whose special needs stem from widespread difficulty, for example social disadvantage or second language learning, to those children whose special needs are the result of more severe handicaps (behaviour problems, language dysfunction, developmental delay, physical and multiple handicap).

2. Dowling, E. (1985) 'Theoretical framework - a joint systems approach to educational problems with children', in Dowling, E. and Osborne, E. *The Family and the School: A Joint Systems Approach to Problems with Children*. London, Routledge & Kegan Paul, chap. 1, pp. 5-31.

Dowling considers how the two most influential systems in an individual's development (the family and the school) may be brought together as part of a therapeutic strategy to deal with problems in children. She examines the concepts of general systems theory as they apply to family and school functioning, specifying particularly the interaction between them when difficulties and problems of an educational nature occur in this dual context. The author discusses a systems way of thinking as referring to 'a view of individual behaviour which takes account of the context in which it occurs. Accordingly, the behaviour of one component of the system is seen as affecting, and being affected by , the behaviour of others' (p. 6).

Dowling describes the key concepts of general systems theory (context, circular causality, punctuation, equifinality, homeostasis, information and feedback). For example, in her discussion of 'information and feedback', the author stresses that families and schools are intimately interlinked over a long period of time during the family's development cycle. Thus, the two systems are closely interrelated in a dynamic two-way relationship, and this complex reciprocal influence determines how these two systems view one another. Dowling illustrates the 'cycles' perpetuated by the way families and schools perceive each other and what they expect of each other as in Figure 11.1.

The author comments that 'in this cyclical sequence it can easily be seen how a particular point in the circle can be in turn "cause" or "effect", depending where reality is *punctuated*. The definition of a school as *good* is highly dependent on the perceptions of the parents who in turn are constantly being influenced by the school's attitudes towards them, (p. 12).

In the last section of the reading Dowling considers common elements to family and school systems (hierarchical organization, rules and ethos). In discussing

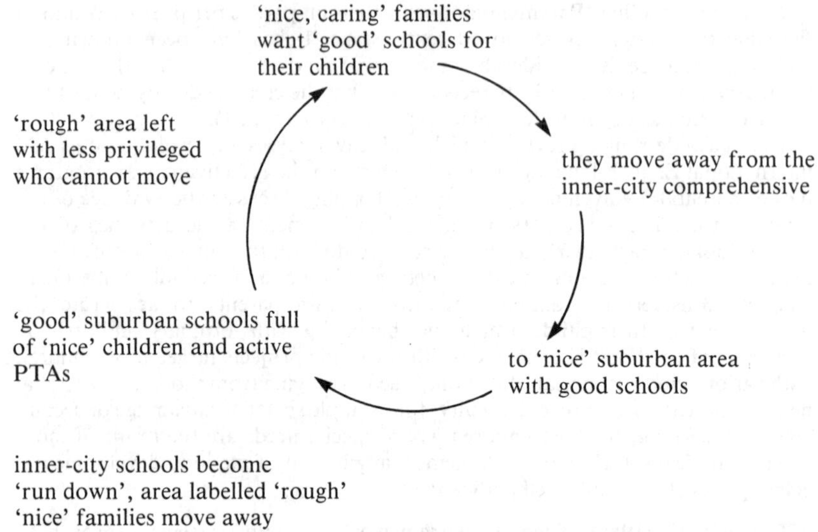

Figure 11.1 Dowling's (1985) family-school perception cycles (p. 11)

'strategies for intervention' the author affirms that when problems of an educational nature arise in children, families and schools perceive the problems in a number of ways. Typically, from the family's perspective, the problems are seen as having originated in the school, and parents implicitly or explicitly place responsibility with the school for the existence of the problem and its resolution, very often denying the idea of there being any problems at home. Conversely, the school staff attribute the origin and cause of the child's school problems as emanating from the family situation at home (for example separation, divorce, arrival of a new baby, move etc.). Thus, whatever the 'cause' of the problem there is often a mounting and polarized gulf between family and school (p. 15). However, both school and family are aware of the problem and are united in demanding that something must be done. Furthermore, the author writes, 'they are united in seeing the locus of problem in the child himself and notions such as "personality", "temperament" or "lack of ability" are suggested as reasons, permanent and irrevocable for the presenting problem' (p. 16). Usually, Dowling suggests, the *context* of the problem is played down and emphasis is directed on diagnosing and remedying the child's problem. Thus the differences between the family and the school tend to be minimized and not seriously investigated, the emphasis being placed 'on what the child *is* rather than what the child *does*' (p. 16). Because of this, the *interactional context* in which the problem behaviour occurs tends *not* to be investigated. The child is effectively 'labelled'. Dowling outlines the methodology of a joint systems approach which addresses such 'problems' in the dual context of family and school and focuses on the relationship between the two systems. She discusses the general framework for conceptualizing problems in this dual context, the various factors which affect the decision of how best to intervene, and the implications of this conceptual shift in terms of the development of alternative strategies.

3. Wolfendale, S. (1986) 'Involving parents in behaviour management: a whole school approach'. *Support for Learning*, **1**, 4, 32–8.

Wolfendale comments that although there has been considerable innovation and development work in the larger area of home-school links, for example in reading, there has been manifestly less work on emotional and behaviour problems and reported disruptive behaviour at home and/or in school even though the necessary techniques, skills and structures for involving parents directly in planning and evaluating behaviour change programmes *do* exist (p. 32). In this reading the author sketches the broader perspective of parental involvement and by examining the rationale and key concepts, provides the *context* in which involving parents in policy and practice of behaviour management is set. Wolfendale proposes a 'model' based on a school 'systems' approach which enables educators to formulate procedures for involving parents at a number of *levels*. With regard to special educational needs and parent involvement, the 'rationale' is based on a number of premises:

(a) that parents are experts on their own children;
(b) their skills complement professional skills;
(c) parents can impart vital information and make informed observations;
(d) parents have a right to be involved;
(e) parents should contribute to decision-making;
(f) parents can be highly effective teachers of their own children (p. 33).

As a corollary, devising 'strategies' for involving parents has a 'rationale' which is based on a number of assumptions:

(a) parents care about their children's welfare and well-being;
(b) parents want to bring about behaviour change, if it is in their child's best interests;
(c) parents want to co-operate;
(d) parents will respond to invitations to participate;
(e) parents can make a contribution (p. 34).

The *levels* proposed by Wolfendale, together with their overall aims, are as follows.

Level 1: *Current provision* Aim: to appraise existing provision and its bearing on and relevance to disruptive behaviour in school and/or reported at home.

Level 2: *The school system* Aim: to review the workings of the school system with a view to incorporating parents.

Level 3: *School-focused INSET* Aim: to identify professional skills required for working with parents and to provide INSET.

Level 4: *Direct work with parents and children* Aim: to examine critically how existing provision can be used and extended to involve parents and children in intervention approaches to disruptive behaviour.

In the last section of the reading, Wolfendale describes a number of intervention programmes which have been conducted in recent years which correspond to levels 3 and 4 cited above. Such approaches encompass both 'prevention' and 'treatment'.

REFERENCES

Bastiani, J. (1978) *Written Communication between Home and School*. School of Education, Nottingham University.

Finch, J. (1984) *Education as Social Policy*. London, Longman.

Hinson, M. (ed.) (1978) *Encouraging Results: Helping Children with Learning Difficulties in the Secondary School*. London, Macdonald Education.

Palfreeman, S. (1984) 'Valuing mothers'. *Journal of Community Medicine*, **1**, 4.

Topping, K. and Wolfendale, S. (1985) *Parental Involvement in Children's Reading*. London, Croom Helm.

Widlake, P. (1985) *How to Reach the Hard to Teach*. Milton Keynes, Open University Press.

Widlake, P. (1986) *Reducing Educational Disadvantage*. Milton Keynes, Open University Press.

Widlake, P. and Macleod, F. (1984) *Raising Standards*. Coventry, Community Education Development Centre.

INDEX